THE YOUNG LUKÁCS
and the Origins of Western Marxism

THE YOUNG LUKÁCS and the Origins of Western Marxism

ANDREW ARATO
and
PAUL BREINES

A Continuum Book
THE SEABURY PRESS • NEW YORK

1979
THE SEABURY PRESS
815 Second Avenue • New York, N.Y. 10017

Printed in the United States of America

Library of Congress Cataloging in Publication Data

Arato, Andrew.
The young Lukács and the origins of Western Maxism.
(A Continuum book)
Includes bibliographical references and index.
1. Lukács, György, 1885–1971. 2. Lukács, György, 1885–1971.
Geschichte und Klassenbewusstsein. 3. Communism.
I. Breines, Paul, 1941– joint author. II. Title.
HX260.5.A8L83155 335.4'092'4 78-31471 ISBN 0-8164-9359-6

To the memory of Georges Haupt

Contents

Preface

AT THE CENTER of this book stands another book: Georg Lukács's *History and Class Consciousness.* Upon its publication in Germany in 1923, it was recognized by critics and sympathizers alike as a major event in the history of both Marxist and bourgeois thought. More than fifty years later and nearly a decade since its author's death in 1971 at the age of eighty-six, an aura of charisma and controversy continues to surround it. The tensions and crises of which it was born still resonate through its pages: war and revolution, the collapse of old forms and the birth pangs of new ones, the calamitous close of the nineteenth century and the grim but hopeful beginnings of the twentieth. A groundbreaking manifesto of critical, humanistic Marxism, the book also provided a philosophy of the dogmatic and totalitarian Marxism it sought to avert. Against a backdrop of betrayal and compromise, here was an appeal to the critical role of intellectuals which simultaneously documented a leading intellectual's accommodation with a new house of power—the Soviet Union, for whose ideologues Lukács had been the heretic par excellence. And nothing less than a great and contradictory work was to have been expected from this man who, since the first years of the century, had pushed bourgeois thought and values to their outer limits in his quest for a redemptive and heroic alternative to what he deemed the suffocating rationality of bourgeois society. His conversion to Marxism and communism in 1919 was itself an occurrence of substantial magnitude, a surprise to such friends and admirers as Thomas Mann and Max Weber as well as to his new comrades. In dealing with Lukács, as one of his communist critics noted in a 1924 review of *History and Class Consciousness,* we are dealing with an innovator.

The present book attempts to accomplish three main tasks. Part One examines in depth the intellectual genesis of *History and Class Consciousness,* reconstructing the complex path Lukács traversed on his way to Marxism. Part Two undertakes a systematic analysis of the theoretical structure and dilemmas of the work itself. Part Three surveys the book's impact and destiny during the decade following its publication—that phase of the "Lukács-debate" which closed with the Nazi seizure of power. Part One is demanding, probing as it does philosophical and cultural terrain that will likely be unfamiliar to many readers with interest but little background in Lukács's original spiritual milieu. Part Two is the most dense segment of our work. Part Three is an historical narrative treating political and sociological themes with which some readers may find themselves more at home. Tackling Part Two after working through Parts One and Three would be an alternative way of proceeding.

Regarding the first and basic part of our title—*The Young Lukács*—we offer brief words of relief to some readers and disappointment to others: this is not psycho-biography. It is not even partial biography, but a study in what we consider the decisive phase of both Georg Lukács's thought and the permanent crisis of Marxism. We have borrowed this half of the title not from Erik Erikson's *Young Man Luther* but from the older Lukács's own studies, *The Young Hegel* (1948) and *The Young Marx* (1965). On the other hand, we have no interest in flatly rejecting psychoanalytically oriented studies of Lukács. We simply have not undertaken one. Lastly in this connection, it may be worth indicating that *History and Class Consciousness,* the crystallization point of what is increasingly commonly referred to as "the young Lukács," appeared when its author was thirty-eight years of age. Youth, in other words, can be a category of politics, philosophy and an historical moment, as well as one pertaining to the life-cycle of an individual. In our Conclusion we sketch some of the main contours of the older Lukács.

The second half of the title—*Western Marxism*—may be even less familiar to many readers. It received some currency in a 1955 essay with that title by Maurice Merleau-Ponty, in which he presented what remains perhaps the outstanding short commentary on *History and Class Consciousness*. The French Existentialist-turned-Marxist interpreted the book as the ovular text of a Marxism differing fundamentally from the ideology which by the mid-1920s was achieving dominance in the West: Soviet or Russian Marxism.[1] In employing the term *Western Marxism*, he was explicitly following the theme raised during the 1920s by both the Soviet critics of Lukács's book and the small band of its left-intellectual defenders in Europe. Since Merleau-Ponty's account, the term has been given wider usage, generally referring to a current of Marxian theorizing that began with Lukács and his contemporaries, Karl Korsch and Antonio Gramsci, extended through the work of Herbert Marcuse and other associates of the "Frankfurt School," influenced Merleau-Ponty, Jean-Paul Sartre, and other French "existential Marxists," and finally reached segments of the New Left in the 1960s.[2] Part Three of the present book is devoted to reconstructing the initial phase of this history; for the moment it may be enough to suggest its nuclear meaning: a self-critical, humanistic, Hegelian-dialectical Marxian theory at odds with the politically more powerful and internationally more influential Soviet Marxism.

Yet even for prefatory purposes this will not entirely do because the term *Western Marxism* should *not* be familiar. It *is* an odd term and it bespeaks an odd historical development. On the briefest reflection, for example, *Western Marxism* is a patent redundancy. Indeed, what could be more Western than Marxism? Or alternatively, where but in capitalism's Western heartland (Europe) was Marxism to have flourished in theory and practice? It is well-enough known, of course, that Marx himself was not unreceptive to the idea of anticapitalist revolution in precapitalist nations. Shortly before his death in 1883, he had looked with interest at such a prospect precisely where it occurred several decades later: Russia.

Nevertheless, a non-Western Marxism has dominated the history of Marxism in this century; to speak of *Western Marxism* is to speak of the overwhelming impact exerted upon Marxism itself by the Russian Revolution of 1917 and its subsequent development. Not only did a Marxist revolution take place where it was not supposed to, and a Marxist revolution *not* take place where it *was* supposed to (Europe, 1917–1923), but the Marxist ideology that resulted from this paradoxical set of circumstances—Soviet Marxism—came to prevail in the West as well as in Russia. *History and Class Consciousness* in particular and the story of the young Lukács more generally provide us with a unique mirror of this situation.

In the course of completing this work we have been fortunate in receiving a wide range of support, criticism, and inspiration. We have, for example, benefitted from a number of forerunners and peers in the area of studies of Lukács, among them: the late Lucien Goldmann, Paul Piccone, Iring Fetscher, Morris Watnick, Tito Perlini, Josef Gabel, Alberto Asor-Rosa, Rudi Dutschke, Jörg Kammler, Laura Boella, Peter Ludz, István Mészáros, Andrew Feenberg, Dick Howard, James Schmidt, and Russell Jacoby. In the early stages of our study, David Kettler's writings on the young Lukács were of special importance to us. More recently, Michael Löwy's work proved particularly helpful. As to studies of the young Lukács by the late George Lichtheim, Lucio Colletti, and Gareth Stedman-Jones, our own is in part a reply.

Nearly ten years ago each of us began separate correspondance with some of the associates of the "Budapest School" of social theory, a group of Lukács's former students and close friends. In fact, it was thanks to them that the two of us met in the first place. Since that time, we have had the honor not only of their assistance but of their friendship as well. Just as the associates of the Budapest School have had sharp disagreements among themselves, we have not always followed their suggestions and interpretations. Yet, in ways we probably cannot estimate, we are their students. To Mihály Vajda, Judit Háber, Ferenc Fehér, Agnes Heller, György Márkus, Maria Márkus, Sándor Radnoti, and Juli Kardos we extend our deepest gratitude. In Part One of this work, we have at several points relied heavily on recent writings by Fehér, Márkus, Heller, and Vajda. We also wish to thank Janos Kis and György Bence.

Discussions over the years with Paul Piccone, from whose own writings we have learned a great deal, have been of much value to us. Justus George Lawler of The Seabury Press made substantial improvements in the manuscript, firm yet supportive in his work as editor. We are, of course, fully responsible for the shortcomings that remain. Professor Rudolf Binion of Brandeis University was kind enough to read a segment of the work and provide us with a number of expert criticisms. Alice Arato gave us generous technical and moral support, patiently permitting us to interrupt her life. Steven Slaner of Wheaton College also assisted us in technical and editorial matters. Andrew Arato wishes to thank the National Endowment for the Humanities for its generous grant enabling him to complete his work on this project.

For vital support of intellectual and personal sorts, we want warmly and specially to thank the following: Jean Cohen, Dick Howard, Moishe Postone, Russell Jacoby, David Bathrick, Peter Weiler, Leonard Krieger, George L. Mosse, Liz Ewen, Stuart Ewen, and Wini Breines—whose sustained and supportive presence enabled her husband to complete his share of this work. If we are able to take pleasure in extending gratitude to those who have helped us directly and otherwise, we are saddened to speak of Georges Haupt, whose sudden death in 1978 removed from us and many others a wonderful scholar of socialism and an irreplaceable friend. We have dedicated the book to his memory.

PART 1

LUKÁCS'S "ROAD TO MARX"

CHAPTER

1

Revolutionary Without a Revolution

THE MAN WHO WOULD BECOME the greatest philosopher of Marxism since the death of Karl Marx and the most controversial communist intellectual in this century came from a family of great wealth.[1] Georg von Lukács, or György Lukács, was born on April 13, 1885, the second of four children of the director of Hungary's largest bank, the Budapest *Kreditanstalt*. His father had received the noble title in return for his role in the financial world of the Austro-Hungarian monarchy, and Lukács would retain the "von" in all German contexts until his entrance into the Communist Party of Hungary in 1918.[2] Well before he became a Marxist, he would be a trenchant critic of the cash nexus as the dominant social bond in the modern world. Born into an assimilated and settled Jewish family, his own life was to be singularly unsettled, characterized by a series of never quite complete assimilations into several cultures.

Lukács turned early to Germany as a spiritual refuge from the stifling atmosphere of official Hungarian culture and was welcomed by, among others, Georg Simmel, Max Weber, and Thomas Mann, as a most precocious interpreter of their intellectual heritage and situation. But they did not fail to recognize the essential meaning of his own work: the searching criticism of the internal tensions and antagonisms of German thought and art. When, in 1918, he looked to the international Communist movement as the sole concrete means of superseding the spiritual and material impoverishment of life in capitalist society, he quickly emerged and remained, for more than five decades, Communism's most critical apostle and its most obedient apostate.

Finally, both the von Lukács and the Lukács phases of his career were linked with travel between the great Central, Eastern, and Southern European cities. Florence, Berlin, and, above all, Heidelberg—where he was fully at home with some of the mavericks of German culture, Weber, Stefan George, Friedrich Gundolf—these were the focal points of geographic movement during the first phase. After 1918, Lukács's life continued to revolve around travel and association with select groups but of a radically different sort: the forced flight, exile, and periodic detention that constituted the underground existence of beleaguered revolutionaries. The main movements in this second phase were from Budapest to Vienna in 1919, where he was arrested and almost deported back to Hungary, which would have meant execution; from Berlin to Moscow in 1930, where, in spite of two arrests, he managed to survive the Stalinist show trials and executions; and later from Budapest to Bucharest, where he was held for a time under house arrest for his role in the abortive Hungarian Revolution of 1956.

The fact that travel, voluntary and forced, characterized Lukács's life is related to a decisive feature of his theoretical *oeuvre*. Attention has often been paid to the significance of Lukács's choice, throughout most of his career, of the essay rather than the systematic treatise as a medium of expression. All the major products of his pre-Marxian and early Marxian work are either collections of essays written over periods of several years or fragments of larger, projected works. These include: *The Soul and the Forms* (1910–11); *The Heidelberg Philosophy of Art* (1912–14); *The Theory of the Novel* (1916); *Aesthetics* (1916–17); and *History and Class Consciousness* (1923).

The essay and the fragment, in their brevity and incompleteness, remain true to the living reality of their objects. Incompatible with intellectual syntheses and resolutions of actual antagonisms, the essay and fragment are, in an antagonistic world, the dialectical forms of expression par excellence. They are also forms of expression peculiarly adequate to the traveler. They are, literally, all there is time for. More basically, they announce that one's thoughts remain en route, indicating that the destination may not be reachable by thought alone. *The Soul and the Forms,* first published in Hungary in 1910 and in Germany the following year, contains essays written in Budapest with an introductory piece—"On the Essence and Form of the Essay"—penned in Florence. The essays in *History and Class Consciousness* were written during the Hungarian Soviet Republic of 1919 and during the forced emigration in Vienna during the first years of the 1920s. They, not to mention Lukács's numerous uncollected essays between 1902 and 1933, are products of one who in mind and body is *in via.*[3]

According to his family's plan, Lukács was eventually to have pursued a business career, but he soon indicated a different choice. It is reported that as a youth he kept on his writing table a picture of an uncle who had renounced the workaday world for the Talmud and meditation on spiritual matters.[4] This story prefigures the basic impulse and the basic problem of Lukács's subsequent work until his adoption of Marxism and, in an altered form, of his Marxism as well: the conviction that the oppressive reality of the actual world advances with a logic and objectivity so ineluctable as to leave human subjectivity no alternative but flight into the ethereal realms of "pure" spirit. The image of the Talmudic scholar-uncle was not far behind when, for example, in 1910, in an assault on naturalism, Lukács upheld the "truth of *Mythos,* whose power is preserved through the ages in ancient legends and tales. The true poets of myth," he added, "simply sought the true meaning of their themes without concern for their pragmatic reality. They viewed the myths as holy and secret hieroglyphics and believed it their mission to decipher them."[5]

No matter how strong his kinship with the "poets of myth," among them Meister Eckhart and Dostoevski, the young Lukács was not one of them. Beginning with his earliest writings, Mythos, as well as the harmonious syntheses of the great philosophical systems and works of art, turn out to be for him no spiritual refuge at all, but restatements of the desire and need that generated them. Still within the framework of bourgeois idealist assumptions, the pre-Marxian Lukács recognized that the "truth of mythos" is true only because the world is false. Thus, in the years just before and during World War I, Lukács adopted as his own Novalis's definition of philosophy as "nostalgia, the impulse to be everywhere at home in the world."[6] Similarly, irony was for Lukács directly linked to the deepening fissures between man and world, thought and action, ethical values and their realization, which resulted from the progress of bourgeois society as the "negative mysticism of godless epochs."[7] And of Thomas Mann, whom Lukács deemed the greatest of modern ironists, he wrote in 1909 in a review of *Royal Highness:* "The deepest root [of Mann's irony] remains this feeling of dislocation from and yearning for the great natural vegetative community."[8]

These remarks raise the question of the fundamental intention of and the influences upon Lukács's thought. Too often his work is read almost exclusively in terms of the specific intellectual influences and the cultural factors that shaped it. This is a tempting and by no means useless procedure. For one thing the actual list of influences on Lukács—which we have intentionally not ordered chronologically—is extensive and rich: in addition to his Hungarian contemporaries, Ervin Szabó and Endre Ady, they include Marx, Tönnies, Thomas Mann, Bergson, Dilthey, Simmel, Weber, Husserl, Kierkegaard, Rickert, Windelband, Kant, Fichte, Hegel, Dostoevski, Sorel, Emil Lask, Ernst Bloch, and still others. On its face this list, whose very magnitude suggests the attempt at a major philosophical and sociological synthesis, is clearly weighted heavily toward German idealism, specifically toward "philosophy of life" and Heidelberg "neo-idealism." Moreover, a reading of Lukács's *History and Class Consciousness* reveals that its great achievements and its great dilemmas resulted from the preservation of "idealist" elements within the new Marxian framework. Further, focus on the cultural milieu of Lukács's pre-Marxian work also helps to show how deeply rooted it was in what he himself would later call "Romantic anticapitalist" tendencies, particularly within Central European thought at the turn of the century.[9] Thus, in its general aspects Lukács's early work was simply a part of a broader current of protest against the mechanized, positivistic, metropolitan *Gesellschaft,* or *Zivilisation,* in the name of *Gemeinschaft, Kultur,* idealism, authenticity, and *Seele.*

Unfortunately, in many studies of the genesis of Lukács's Marxism, an apparently historical approach turns out to be largely a reduction of Lukács's thought to one or several of its progenitors or to its general milieu. Thus, for example, it is argued that in order to understand Lukács's development, one must see that it emerged from the sociological theories of Simmel and Weber and from the philosophical views of Rickert and Windelband or from those of

Dilthey and Lask. Lukács himself, later the most active commentator on his own early work, fluctuated between this reductive approach and a rather static typology of the major strands in his work. Thus, he, too, often lacked a clear view of the unity of his early work.[10]

We shall attempt to view the whole matter of influences on Lukács's early work from the inside out, that is, from the standpoint of Lukács's own basic project, which was indeed situated within heterogeneous conceptual and disciplinary currents. Our guiding assumption is that in every case, but particularly in Lukács's, the problem of intellectual influences is misconceived if the main question is: From which previous thinker did this thinker derive that idea? The reason that Lukács's case is of special significance is that he was an especially original thinker. As one of his Bolshevik critics noted in a 1924 review of *History and Class Consciousness,* "Long before he became a Communist, Lukács had acquired a well-earned name as a philosopher in the German philosophical world; indeed, as a philosopher who goes his own way, thinks independently and does not merely regurgitate what the great thinkers of the past left behind."[11] What this ironically suggests is that rather than trying to make sense of Lukács by making sense of the influences on him, it might be worth trying to make sense of the influences by tracing what Rudas calls Lukács's "own way."[12] A further guide to such a hermeneutic of influences is offered by Lukács's own remark from 1910 on the possibility of a "science of art": there is a *Kunstwissenschaft,* he stated, but its specificity as a science is that it "shoots beyond the facts" to the artist's "vision which is there before the facts and which shapes them."[13]

Some essential signs of Lukács's "vision" have already been presented. Mann's "sense of dislocation from and longing for the great natural, vegetative community," for example, was Lukacs's own; he did not derive it from Mann's writings but from an experience of modern civilization similar to Mann's. Likewise, Lukács's experience of a "nostalgia, the impulse to be everywhere at home in the world," underlay his adoption of Novalis's definition of philosophy in these terms. The vision that shaped Lukács's sociological and formal analyses of art was, in short, the dream of the whole man, an ancient dream but one given an historically determinate form during Lukács's youth by the increasingly complete fragmentation of human experience and relations stemming from the onrushing mechanization and bureaucratization of society. The line between Lukács's early awareness of and protest against alienation and his subsequent turn to Marxism as the only real theoretical and practical critique is neither short nor straight. What is clear, however, is that when, as a political revolutionary, Lukács turned to Marxism, he read Marx not only as one who had dreamed the dream of the whole man: Lukács read Marx as the one thinker who had pointed the way toward its concrete, this-worldly realization. "It will be shown," the young Marx had written, "that the world has long possessed the dream of that which it must only become conscious of in order to possess in reality."[14] It was this basic vision, sketched roughly here, which among other things preceded and shaped the facts of the intellectual influences on Lukács's thinking.

Lukács began his public career early, with work in the two fields that would occupy his lifetime:art and revolution. In 1902, at the age of seventeen, he started regular publication of theater criticism in a Budapest cultural magazine.[15] In the same year, while at the university of Budapest, where he was a student of philosophy and aesthetics, Lukács joined the newly formed Revolutionary Students of Budapest. This little group which dissolved within a year and had no political impact, was organized by Ervin Szabó, who would soon emerge as the theoretical spokesman of Hungarian revolutionary syndicalism and as one of the dominant figures in Hungarian intellectual life in the years prior to 1918.[16] Although the revolutionary students group was only a passing moment in both Szabó's and Lukács's careers, it was nevertheless of some more general significance.

As a young socialist intellectual and admirer of Nietzsche, Szabó, during a visit to Vienna in 1897, came under the influence of émigré Russian revolutionary intellectuals. There, during secret, nighttime meetings, he was introduced to a revolutionary Marxism suffused with the ideas of Kropotkin and the subjectivist philosophy of Peter Lavrov. On his return to Hungary, Szabó wanted to create a new socialist elite of intellectuals who would function as militant revolutionary propagandists. The Revolutionary Students of Budapest was intended to be the organ for winning over the young intellectuals to the socialist cause.[17]

The little group dissolved quickly, partly because Szabó recognized its isolation and ineffectuality and partly because he became convinced it was based on erroneous principles. Under the impact of a wave of strike movements in Belgium, Holland, Russia, Sweden, and Spain in late 1902 and early 1903, he began to turn toward French and Italian syndicalist theory and to militant opposition to all elite theory and practice in the working class movement. Thus, on the one hand, he rejected the conspiratorialism he had previously absorbed from his Russian friends; on the other, while he entered the Social Democratic Party of Hungary, primarily as a means of carrying out cultural work among workers, he promptly emerged as a virtually one-man revolutionary syndicalist opposition.[18] Independently of Sorel in France, Szabó put the idea of the work place–oriented militant class struggle at the center of his Marxism, making this the basis of his unrelenting criticism of social democracy. He considered the latter an essentially bourgeois phenomenon whose parliamentarism prevented the proletariat from direct participation in the class struggle and which gave rise to a new bureaucratic elite based on intellectual and educational competence: the coming "dictatorship of parlor polemicists and journalists."[19]

From 1903 onward, Szabó, who would soon turn out the first Hungarian translations of Marx and Engels, carried on continuous criticism of both the Revisionist and Orthodox Marxists of the Second International who, he contended, were rapidly diluting the essentially revolutionary Marxian theory of class struggle. Among the themes of his critique were, first, that Marx and Engels were emphatically not philosophical materialists but revolutionary materialists. Second, Szabó argued that Marxian theory needed no expansion or deepening by the introduction of idealism and notions of individual freedom from without, since these were, in his view, already central components of Marxism, although evidently not the version presented by social democracy.[20]

Lukács did not follow Szabó into the Hungarian Social Democratic Party. His own relationship to Marxism and proletarian revolution would pass through several shifts and reversals before his final turn to communism in 1918–19. Indeed, the same can be said of his relation to the practical problems of social theory as a whole. Nevertheless, the two men remained members of the same small community of critically minded Hungarian intellectuals in which

Szabó, the most brilliant and perhaps the only real Marxian theorist in Hungary at the time, was the towering figure of the older generation and Lukács was the most precocious of its younger cultural critics. Certainly Lukács kept abreast of Szabó's work, and all evidence indicates that he was and would remain in basic agreement with Szabó's critique of social democracy if not entirely with his conception of Marxism as a whole.

Szabó's shift to proletarian cultural work which, in part, took institutional form in his role as founder and director of the Budapest city library, may well have helped inspire Lukács's own role as a co-founder of the Thalia Theater in 1903–4.[21] Along with Sandor Hevesi and several others, Lukács organized the Thalia, an itinerant troupe based in Budapest, whose aim, in addition to raising the standard of Hungarian national theater through performances of modern Western plays, was to bring significant drama to working class and provincial audiences. The Thalia project lasted somewhat longer than the Revolutionary Students of Budapest, although after several years of activity it was closed down by the city authorities when its studio was declared a fire hazard.

Lukács's youthful experiences with the revolutionary students group and the Thalia theater had an important impact on his thinking and plans. By 1905, if not earlier, he was fully convinced both of the oppressive backwardness of official Hungarian culture and also of the ultimate futility of the struggle against it.[22] It was in this context that he began to immerse himself in the study of German culture, specifically the traditions stemming from the period of classical German idealist philosophy and the art of the *Goethezeit*. The initial motive behind his turn to Germany (and to certain currents of French and Italian culture) was to find spiritual refuge from an unalterably reactionary and sclerotic Hungarian world. It is notable that this turn followed a uniquely unorthodox introduction to revolutionary Marxism.[23] But the impulses which propelled him did not disappear; they took on new forms: the more deeply he would immerse himself in German culture, the more severely he would demolish the possibilities of refuge it appeared to offer.

Thus it is that Lukács had begun his spiritual journey to Germany several years prior to his actual visits there between 1909 and 1914. In view of this very early preoccupation with German culture, it might seem a paradox that in 1906 he became an active contributor and associate of the two main journals of social, political, and cultural reform in Hungary. The paradox was real; nor was it Lukács's alone but, to a great extent, that of the whole Hungarian "second reform generation."[24] Much of the story is contained in the titles of the two journals, *Huszadik Század* (*Twentieth Century*) and *Nyugat* (*The West*).[25] To the group of technocratically oriented, reform socialist intellectuals of the Social Scientific Society (founded in 1900), which published *Huszadik Század* and whose leading figure was the political sociologist Oskar Jászi, Hungary needed above all to be brought into the twentieth century. They, like Lukács, looked westward, but they searched for models of economic and political modernization. Positivistic and evolutionist in its theoretical outlook, the Social Scientific Society bore numerous similarities to the English Fabians.[26] Such thinkers as Lukács and Szabó, who did not share the dominant standpoint of the *Huszadik Század* group, nevertheless regularly published in its journal, in part because it was one of the few available outlets and in part because the beleaguered intellectual opposition in Hungary was a unified community on numerous levels.[27]

Nyugat, which Lukács helped to found in 1908, likewise looked westward, initially to French Impressionism and late Impressionism. The journal's goal was the cultural and literary renewal and modernization of Hungary; its standard-bearer was the great poet Endre Ady. The majority of the essays Lukács published in *The Soul and the Forms* first appeared in *Nyugat* between 1908 and 1910. Of the "progressive cultural-intellectual movement" gathered around these two journals, its leading historian, Zoltan Horvath, has written that

> the same names always appeared; the movement remained confined to the same narrow group: the few intellectuals assembled around the radical sociologists and those who were the first confirmed disciples of Endre Ady. . . . They were the ones who composed the readership of *Huszadik Század* and *Nyugat,* and the radical daily, *Világ* [*The World*]. This handful of people, talking to and writing for one another, convinced themselves (and perhaps actually believed) that behind them stood a whole camp. They proceeded not only as if they were engaged in theoretical discussion with a real following, but actually exerting influence. In reality their own number and that of their audience was far too meager to have been a political force.[28]

Lukács himself, while sharing many of the hopes of the movement, did not share the illusions to which Horvath refers. In Ady's work, for example, Lukács glimpsed not only the supreme beacon of a new Hungarian poetry but also the passion and tragedy of the militant, democratic revolutionary in Hungary.[29] Yet the revolution appeared in Ady's verse only as that which it really was: a futile hope, a dream, a desire. Ady had written, "Forward Hungarian proletarian . . . . Rise, oh rise, holy red sun. . . ." And Lukács commented in 1909: Ady is the "poet of the Hungarian revolutionaries without a revolution. His audience is pathetically grotesque, consisting of men who feel there is no help other than revolution. They believe that everything that exists was never new or good . . . but bad; beyond correction, it must be destroyed to make room for new possibilities. There is need for a revolution, but it is impossible to hope, even in the distant future, of attempting one. There would be only leaders. . . ."[30] As Lukács recognized, Ady's situation and that of his "pathetically grotesque" audience was Lukács's own.

CHAPTER

2

In the "Iron Cage": *Kulturkritik* of Bourgeois Civilization

AS WE LOOK more closely at Lukács's early work, trying to reconstruct it from within, we need the reminder that a fully unified treatment of his development prior to 1919, when his first explicitly Marxist writings appeared, is nearly impossible. The ways in which he posed his problems, the methods and styles he employed, the very substance of his investigations and solutions all seem blatantly heterogeneous. And the price of his pluralism is more often than not a series of unreconciled contradictions.[1] His pre-Marxian *oeuvre* does, however, contain a significant measure of unity arising out of the central problem that dominated all his efforts: the crisis of modern culture and of subjectivity within it.[2] His interrogations of this massive problem in fact resulted in an original set of answers to the questions posed by the Heidelberg neo-Kantian theorists Max Weber, Wilhelm Dilthey, and Georg Simmel.[3] Yet here, too, an overly unified presentation would falsify both the richness and the intrinsic difficulties in Lukács's approaches.

In his earliest works (taking 1910 as a rough demarcation point) there are three *fundamental* approaches. First, in the *History of the Development of Modern Drama* (hereafter: *Dramahistory*),[4] which was written and rewritten between 1906 and 1909, and the essay, "Aesthetic Culture" (1910),[5] there is an historical-critical sociology of culture and cultural alienation. Within his sociology of culture, Lukács makes use of Marx seen through Simmel's eyes, but he also corrects Simmel by way of Marx. Second, in *The Soul and the Forms* (1907–10)[6] and the essay-dialogue, "On the Poverty of Spirit" (1911),[7] there is a series of critical-individual confrontations with the historical *results* of cultural alienation, results Lukács generally but not always interprets metaphysically. And, third, in the "Notes to the Theory of the History of Literature" (1910), there is a search for a comprehensive many-sided method appropriate to the study of literature as Absolute Spirit.[8]

These three dimensions are interrelated in Lukács's early work. As in Georg Simmel's, so in hiw own efforts, the development of modern Western culture stands as the historical ground of the dualism between what Lukács terms Life and Soul. Yet they are interrelated only ultimately; he initially follows the inner logic of his three diverse starting points without attempting to unify them in a consistent theoretical system. We need to examine the process in some detail.

To begin with, the importance of the *Dramahistory* in the development of Lukács's thought cannot be overemphasized—especially in view of the consistency with which so many commentaries have ignored it.[9] It contains, for example, the historical and sociological foundations of his formal investigations of past and contemporary art; indeed, it serves as a kind of historical sociology of his own philosophical aesthetics, delineating the social ground of the crisis of modern art that appears only symbolically or indirectly in his other writings of the period. In *The Soul and the Forms,* for example, Stefan George's verse is examined under the title "The Lyric Poetry of The New Loneliness," while Rudolf Kassner's essayistic *oeuvre* is seen as that of the "problematic man" whose desperate quest is to pass from "contingency to necessity." Similarly, Lukács views the dramatist Paul Ernst as an exemplar of the fact that, in the modern era, the true and great tragedian becomes the "poet of his own tragedy": the personality of the tragedian, like that of his own heroes, presses beyond the "veil of chaos" but is inevitably condemned to remain "an empty virtuosity of interiority."[10] The *Dramahistory* indicates the social sources and contents of the "new loneliness" and fragmented interiority of contemporary "problematic man."

Its introductory essay, dealing with the sociology of modern drama, is the embryo of the social and psychological analysis of the reified world that would later appear in revised, Marxian form in the decisive chapter of *History and Class Consciousness*. It is also evident that Lukács's initial understanding of reification and his view of the tasks of the sociology of culture were emphatically shaped by Georg Simmel, especially by his *Philosophy of Money* (1900). In itself, it is a point of mere factual interest that Lukács had closely studied and appropriated the main themes of Simmel's cultural sociology prior to his own visit to Berlin in 1909–10, where he attended Simmel's lectures and conferred with him in their private seminar. But there is more to this than chronology. For if, as Lukács himself and numerous other commentators have stressed, his early view of social theory generally and of Marx particularly was molded by Simmel, the introduction to the *Dramahistory* indicates that Lukács was at the same time using Marx to correct Simmel. Lukács was in fact, if not in conscious intention, revising both the attitude and content of Simmel's and Max Weber's sociologies of bourgeois culture and society in a problematic and incompletely Marxian direction.

His account of the sociology of modern drama is roughly as follows: modern drama is bourgeois drama, less a genuine realization of the perfected form of the drama than "an arm of the ideological class struggle of . . . the rising . . . bourgeoisie."[11] In his view only a declining class can experience and create genuine tragedy. Bourgeois drama, however, was the first in the history of the genre to arise out of "conscious class contradictions," the first "whose goal was to give expression to the modes of feeling and thinking of a class struggling for freedom and power, and to give expression to its relations to other classes."[12] The decisive experience of the emergent bourgeoisie was the French Revolution, which taught men that "there is history—as a form of life, not as a science—which means the recognition that everything, once it appears in the world, takes on an existence entirely independent of its creator and purpose, its harmfulness or usefulness, its goodness or badness. . . . We are speaking here of the category of 'being there' [*Bestehen*], naked existence as a force, a value, a decisively important category in the whole order of life."[13]

This new historical consciousness, Lukács notes later in the essay, was decisively reinforced in the capitalist transformation of the division of labor:

> From the standpoint of the individual, the essence of the modern division of labor is that it severs labor from the always irrational and

> thus qualitative capacities of the worker, and places it under objective, goal-oriented criteria which stand outside and have no relation to his personality. The main economic tendency of capitalism is this same objectification of production, its separation from the personality of the producers. Through the development of the capitalist economy, an objective abstraction, capital, becomes the real producer and capital has no organic connection even to those who happen to own it. Indeed, it is increasingly superfluous whether the owners are personalities at all (as in the case of joint stock companies).[14]

With the further development of the capitalist division of labor, "work takes on a specific, objective life over against the individual person, who is then forced to seek means of expressing himself elsewhere than in what he actually does."[15]

The links between Lukács's standpoint here and the theory of alienation developed by Marx in the "Economic and Philosophic Manuscripts" of 1844—a text not known to Lukács or anyone else until decades later—are striking. No less striking is the fact that, unlike Marx, Lukács does not recognize revolutionary possibilities in the process of the objectification/alienation of labor in capitalist society. There are, broadly speaking, two reasons for this. First, the actual state of the organized working class movement in Europe between 1908 and 1914 indicated its absorption into the ongoing extension of the logic of capitalist development rather than its revolt against it. And, second, the immediate basis for Lukács's standpoint was laid down by Simmel, who had used Hegel and Marx as the starting point of an interpretation of culture as an ultimately tragic process in which man is fated to lose himself in his own creations.[16] Lukács could neither accept Simmel's fatalism nor fully overcome it.

In the works of Hegel and Marx available to him, Simmel had rediscovered several important dimensions of the young Marx's theory of alienation: alienation from the created object, from other men in the horizontal sense, and from the human species.[17] But he neglected the crucial dimension, most significant for Marx's *Das Kapital:* alienation from other men in the hierarchical sense, the basis of the links between the concept of alienation and Marx's class analysis. Simmel sought to replace the historical materialist analysis of the specificity of cultural alienation with an historically unspecific, metaphysical analysis, and eventually succeeded in his later works. Lukács, however, attached himself to Simmel just where the latter was *closest* to Marx: that is, Lukács placed the problem of the modern division of labor at the center of the question of alienation. In addition, he deepened and historicized Simmel's analysis in two respects. First, he extended the scope of alienation to a realm Simmel had exempted from it—the realm of artistic creation. And, second, Lukács rediscovered a qualitative change in the structure of alienation in the historical emergence of bourgeois class rule and capitalism.

Simmel considered specialization and artistic creation antithetical. A work of art, he argued, is a closed unity and totality, expressing through its form the deepest internal experience of a single, unique subject. Lukács had little quarrel with this general definition; indeed, he extended it in his own later Heidelberg manuscripts on aesthetics. But whereas Simmel considered artistic creation a living and unproblematic antithesis to the alienation of labor, Lukács argued that cultural alienation had also invaded the world of art, threatening its autonomy and the very possibility of artistic creation.

The basic, if at this stage still implicit, difference between Lukács and Simmel, however, presented itself first in Lukács's introduction of the category of class struggle and, second, in his emphasis on the historically determinate character of what Simmel called the "tragedy of culture." For, if Simmel had appropriated certain elements of Marx's thought, he had in the end dehistoricized or ontologized them. He specifically insisted, for example, that "the 'fetishism' Marx assigned to economic commodities represents only a special case of this general fate of the contents of culture."[18] Faced with this "general fate" or "tragedy" of culture, all that is possible, as Simmel quite consistently concluded, is spiritual self-cultivation alongside resigned contemplation of the inevitable course of development. Lukács shared Simmel's view that, in the capitalist epoch, objective culture unfolds with an inescapable and deadly logic. And like Simmel, he could not formulate a theory of a concrete transformation of this logic, that is, a theory of social-cultural revolution. Nevertheless, his attitude was not one of resignation but rather of what might be thought of as "spiritual-ethical" combat.

To illuminate Lukács's tension-ridden position, we need to resume the account of his sociology of modern drama, tracing his analysis of the phenomena of alienation. Culture, for the early Lukács, ideally represented the unity of human life, the harmonious relation of subjective and objective or the adequate symbolic expression of the whole of life by whole human beings.[19] In his view, only "culture" could provide unity in a world characterized by egotistical, aggressive, unconscious human strivings, that is, unity in Hegel's *bürgerliche Gesellschaft* (civil or bourgeois society).[20]

Yet Lukács's analysis shows that what actually took place was quite the reverse. In this context, Lukács employed two concepts, "intellectualized culture" and "aesthetic culture," the latter being a special case of the former. The intellectualization of culture refers to the rationalization, quantification, atomization of all aspects of modern life. As in Max Weber's work, intellectualization or rationalization generalizes the logic of the modern physical sciences, extending them in various forms to other spheres of life.[21] In the process the symbols, myths, anthropomorphic qualities of culture, and the substantial elements of human relations are eliminated or, in Weber's term, "disenchanted."

The metropolis and urban life are the characteristic expressions of this development: the modern city cancels every aspect of what Lukács calls the social festival and likewise dilutes aesthetic sensibility by generating a compulsive search for ever more novel and "original" forms and styles.[22] The "rationalization" of economic and social life engulfs the mind, and the new world view, which Lukács terms "intellectualism," seeks to reduce everything to numbers and formulae, not only in the natural, but in the historical-social sciences as well. And intellectualism per se is alienation: its strongest tendency is to dissolve every human community, to separate people from one another and glorify their individual incomparability (that is, their loneliness and isolation).[23] Specifically, the modern sciences lose every link to the human personality; their methods simply mirror the objectified depersonalization of social life. Lukács contrasts this development with its predecessor, medieval science (such as alchemy and astrology), in which each element of knowledge was directly linked to a person (the "master") who personally passed on his secret to his students.[24] Similarly, in art the immediately sensuous mode of perception is replaced by the "mediately intellectual: the category of the qualitative is replaced by that of the quantitative, . . . The symbol is replaced by the definition, the analysis."[25]

As a consequence of the drama (and bourgeois art generally), there has developed a strictly bourgeois-class drama that is a cultural form of an economic minority (the rich) and, in contrast to medieval theater, finds itself severed from a qualitatively mass audience. The social isolation of bourgeois drama is likewise expressed in its features, which make its messages and themes opaque and incomprehensible to all but an intellectual audience. The deeper crisis of modern drama, however, is to be found in the overall process of objectification of life, the result of which is that life itself, as the material to be "worked over" by the dramatist or artist, is no longer dramatic "as it was in earlier times." Increasingly passive, bourgeois life lacks mythology, pathos, and genuine tragedy. As a result, the possibility of art itself is forced into a paradoxical situation.

What Lukács calls "aesthetic culture" initially presents itself as an alternative to intellectualism—as an aestheticization of life: in Simmel's terms, a cultivation of that inward spirituality that somehow escapes the tragedy of culture. But here Lukács is explicitly critical. For him the cultivation of interiority (*Innerlichkeit*) makes the aesthete a specialist of inner life, a passive, fragmented spectator of his own passing moods and fancies. The cultivation of interiority in fact severs him from any possible intersubjective unity of culture, just as specialization exerts the same toll on any area of modern life. More than this, however, the emergence of aesthetic culture threatens the very possibility of intersubjective unity. Aesthetic culture, Lukács wrote, has a peculiar unity which is the very absence of unity:

> it has a center: the completely peripheral nature of everything; it symbolizes something: that nothing is symbolic, nothing is more than what it seems to be at the moment of experiencing. . . . And this culture does have a dimension that surpasses the merely individual (it belongs to the essence of culture that it is the common treasure of men): that there is nothing that could rise beyond the merely individual. It implies a relation among men based on complete loneliness, on the absence of relatedness.[26]

Having become yet another specialist, the artist cloaks his specialty in ideologies of *"l'art pour l'art."*[27]

As Lukács depicts it, this completely bleak development has further results: the deactivization of the aesthete and any artist who accepts his creed; creativity and contact with the substantial materials for creation are lost.[28] Passive surrender to moods and sensations leads, in Lukács's argument, to the psychologistic dissolution of the ego, whose unity had rested on creation and self-creation.[29] Such egos can, in turn, create only an art of the surfaces, denying all depth and value—hedonistic, impressionist, formless "forms" of art.[30]

Lukács's purpose is to demonstrate that the most fundamental form of alienation, alienation from the species, can indeed invade that realm of artistic creation which for Hegel was one of the species' forms of symbolic self-reflection (that is, Absolute Spirit):

> there is something deeply professional in the effect of art today: writers write for writers, painters paint for painters (or at least for disappointed writers and painters). Because they hardly have anything to say, . . . only the expert can enjoy their products. . . . And since the (parallel) tendency of general cultural development, which utilizes men only at one point without touching their individuality, is to *weaken the human in man,* the dimly and weakly surviving spiritual needs cannot find contact with any art at all.[31]

Is art, then, possible at all within what Max Weber called the "iron cage" of the rationalized world? Lukács seeks to answer this question with his theory of drama, the definition of which is, in his account, purely aesthetic.[32] But for him, the aesthetic includes creator, the created, and the recipient. Drama's aim, accordingly, is mass effect attained by volitional and emotional (not intellectual) content and symbolic (not dialectical or logical) form. The particular contents of a drama must, therefore, symbolize *for an audience* a universal or typical fate. Thus, the drama can express even metaphysical events only in a sociological form. Moreover, in order to portray typical beings and fates in a vastly reduced temporal and spatial setting, the drama must concentrate on those aspects of human life that truly express the whole essence of a person—and for Lukács this can be only will, striving, action. But since no drama can depict the fate of only a single person, it must present the struggle and dialectic of *wills.*

Will, striving, action, struggle must, moreover, center around a life problem common to both author and audience;[33] there must be a common world view underlying the whole of the aesthetic experience.[34] And the final aspect of his definition: a perfect drama can only be tragedy. If struggle is to symbolize the whole of a person's life, it must be a relatively even struggle, but it must ultimately fail. Success relaxes dramatic tension and turns the struggle itself into something accidental in human existence.[35] For Lukács, life's deepest problems can be made conscious to great crowds with the help of immediate symbols only through tragedy. But when the feelings and valuations involved have *already* lost all solid foundation and have themselves become problematic, then the losing struggle of the typical symbolic person against his fate will appear too hopeless to be important at all.

Lukács's definition of the drama raised the issue of the (a priori) sociological conditions that make this most sociological (and intrinsically democratic) of all art forms possible. This issue, however, did *not* entail a reduction of drama to social and economic facts or tendencies. For Lukács took the word "possibility" very seriously indeed, meaning only necessary but not sufficient a priori conditions. Thus, sociology could reveal and explain only the framework of dramatic creation, but not creation itself.[36] Accordingly, the original issue raised two questions: When does a mass audience capable of being affected by drama exist? And, more important, what is the nature and what are the social preconditions of a common world view between the drama and the mass audience?[37] The first of these queries refers to the possibility of the unity of drama and theater, and only in the modern period has this become a serious problem. The second question raises the problem of ideology.

For Lukács, as we have indicated, the drama formalizes life symbolically as the dialectic of forces that destroy one another with ruthless energy. But a large social group can see life this way only when its habitual norms, values, symbols, myths, and feelings have themselves become internally problematic. A group can grasp its own life as portrayed in tragedy only when there is insoluble conflict among its different values: when the older values cannot compromise with those based on emergent conditions, when the ethical being can no longer consider life a central value.[38] When the highest values perish in actual life, the social group can take pleasure in the representation of noble death.[39] Thus, in order to respond to tragedy, the group itself must have undergone cultural decline. But the source of this decline must be an internal dialectic. Defeat and destruction at the hand of an external enemy (opposing class or nation), for example, can wipe away a culture, but it cannot create the internal tragedy of a group representing that culture.

In this connection, Lukács made it quite clear that he speaks of groups capable of dominating a whole culture, that is, classes, not groups in general:

> Every culture is dominated by a class, or rather by the economic and political relations of that class; the forms, tempos, and rhythms of its mode of life delimit the culture's forms of expression. When the basis of the class's domination of the culture becomes problematic, all this class's feelings, valuations, and thoughts, created in an unproblematic age, become problematic themselves. Indeed, the process of decline is expressed precisely in valuations becoming problematic.[40]

Again Lukács has not reduced values and valuations to social-economic developments or even to the history of culture as a whole. Concrete valuations remain functions of individual choice. Rather, he is arguing only that the possibility of the realization of values and of their compatibility with one another is decisively influenced by fundamental historical changes. One such change, the cultural decline of a class, is the *condition* of the possibility of that particular crisis in values and valuation that makes tragedy a plausible (even necessary) representation of life for that class. A rising class, then, can have no drama in the sense of true tragedy and in the sense of having a dramatic form purely its own, nor can a declining class that has lost *all* faith in its own values. The age of drama must still be a heroic age of a class in the process of decline. The key point, then, is that while the internal problems of the bourgeois class do yield the formal possibility of drama, the objective culture created by the bourgeoisie is increasingly impervious to expression in any symbolic form. And, as far as Lukács was concerned, it was too early in the present era to determine whether there were heroic individuals capable of reexpressing the whole of this cultural crisis in dramatic terms—and in his view *only* the whole is potentially dramatic material—or whether a new, rising class would sweep away the entire problem and with it (for a time at least) the possibility of tragedy.[41]

In examining Lukács's conception of bourgeois culture in somewhat greater detail, we need to separate for the moment his discussion of the crisis of bourgeois ideology and the emergence of the problematic individual from the problem of modern drama. Following Marx, Lukács stressed that the universal values and principles of the bourgeoisie—the fiction of the "universally human"—were only a projection of bourgeois goals, values, and feelings upon all of humanity. At least until the French Revolution, realizing the universality human in each individual was considered to be (in theory) merely a matter of Enlightenment.[42] But, Lukács argued:

> the bourgeois class [in its concrete actions] never could possess with metaphysical intensity [as in feudalism's relation to Christianity] the intuitive certainty and universal validity of its own mode of valuation. Or rather, to the extent that the bourgeoisie possessed this, it was only as philosophy, revolutionary demand, or desire.[43]

Following the French Revolution, the more perceptive could see that even these final traces of bourgeois illusions were gone. What Lukács called the "great experience, the new consciousness of history" had taught a vital lesson: that things and institutions, once created, take on a life of their own, more powerful and inertial than anyone had anticipated. Even moral and intellectual principles, once formulated, become independent of their formulators and have unintended consequences.[44] For Lukács, the French Revolution showed that history is objective spirit: to be precise—although this was not his own distinction—alienated objective spirit. And as objective spirit, history had shattered the abstract ideals of the revolutionary bourgeoisie. Its universal values and ethics became particularized, entering into conflict with other particularized values and ethics. To the extent, moreover, that members of the bourgeoisie (abstractly conceived) maintained the value of universality and the desire for a truly human community, the conflict of values had been internalized. In his account, the bourgeoisie's struggle against feudalism had indeed been for a more free, dynamic life. But this struggle, from the standpoint of the bourgeoisie's universal values, was hopeless from the outset. In this connection, the problem of individuality—the antinomy of individual and history—takes on special importance.[45]

As in Hegel and Marx, so in Lukács, "individualism as a problem of life" is a product of the modern bourgeois epoch. But for

Lukács, individuality as fact, universal value, and problem were all born simultaneously. The bourgeoisie's historic victory had indeed liberated individuals from the fetters of organic communities, serfdom, and guilds. But the same victory created around the liberated individuals a whole framework of less personal, more abstract, more complicated fetters.[46] Objective ties replaced personal ties. And while the new economic order created by the bourgeoisie implied boundless faith in the ability of unhampered individuals to create harmonious systems for satisfying needs, the actual result was the anarchy of production, the subjugation of the individual producers to impersonal forces.[47] The modern division of labor within the industrial system, moreover, further fragmented and depersonalized individuals, preventing their self-actualization as whole beings. And as individuals became more powerless on a cosmic scale, the realization and preservation of individuality emerged as the central life problem of bourgeois society.

Bourgeois drama, then, is not, strictly speaking, the drama of individualism but the drama of the crisis of individualism. In the corporative medieval world the "validation of personality" was not a problem of life and was thus not a central theme of medieval theater. The "new drama," in contrast, is the drama of individualism "with a force, intensity and exclusiveness" that were unknown previously because today "individualism and individual experience are conscious and problematic."[48] On the one hand, in bourgeois society the realization and preservation of the personality become the central life problem, with the desire to resolve this problem growing in intensity. On the other hand—and here is an absolute statement of the total determinism of the objective world—"those external conditions, which make this impossible from the outset, take on increasing power." As a result of this conflict "the mere maintenance of individual existence and its integrity moves to the center of the drama."[49]

As evidence for this exegesis, Lukács indicates that one of the "decisive antinomies of individualism" becomes a major theme of bourgeois drama and shapes its internal structural development: the validation of one personality becomes unthinkable without the oppression of the personality of another, whose own self-preservation in turn inevitably entails the annihilation of the first.[50] Thus, the confidant disappears from bourgeois drama—a symptom of the demise of the belief that one individual can understand or be understood by another. Similarly, dialogue is decisively altered in an increasingly impressionistic and intellectualistic direction as individuals progressively lose the ability to express their essential natures or the real motivations of their actions.[51] Compared with the heroes of premodern drama, the new heroes tend to be passive rather than active; things happen to them more than they themselves actually do things; their heroism is more often than not "the heroism of desperation and necessity, rather than that of audacious adventure."[52]

These tendencies in bourgeois drama, as well as in other art forms, are manifestations of the general tendency in bourgeois society toward the "thingification" (*Versachlichung*), homogenization, and quantification of life.[53] The theoretically extreme individualism of much of modern thought and art does not express a genuine progress in individuation but a growing uniformity in occupations, dress, transportation, education, and childhood experience. The "new life" liberates men from many former constraints (the church and religion, guilds, communities) and gives rise to the feeling that every bond among men, because it is no longer organic, is a fetter. At the same time, man is increasingly surrounded by a whole chain of more abstract and intricate bonds.[54] The entire state organization (the system of voting, bureaucracy, military organization) and every aspect of economic life (dominated by money and credit) reveal the same tendency: "depersonalization . . . the reduction of the qualitative to the quantitative" in every instance.[55]

Modern drama's situation is thus rendered virtually hopeless by the crisis of individuality. A truly great drama or dramatist might symbolically crystallize the tragedy of modern culture as a whole, but the audience for such presentation no longer exists. Dramatic *theater,* in Lukács's view, has been killed by mass entertainment.[56] Individuals in modern, bourgeois society can, moreoever, no longer comprehend symbolism, myth, dialogue, or true pathos (the basic elements of dramatic form) because their own empirical lives have been cleansed of these elements.

Toward the close of his introductory essay in the *Dramahistory,* Lukács takes up the question, What is to be done? The stylistic and technical problems of modern drama, he states, "reach beyond the circle of merely artistic-technical questions." The solution to these problems becomes a problem of life, a search for life's center which, in his view, had not been missing in prebourgeois epochs.[57] Yet Lukács would appear to have posed the problem of life in a manner that precludes resolution within the empirical world. The logic of objectification (which he identifies with alienation) and its specific bourgeois form—"thingification"—appears itself to be objective, its results inevitable: the facts and acts of individuality are increasingly suppressed; "the possibility of realizing the personality *in this sphere* is increasingly constricted." Yet, this is the only sphere in which the individual can be realized fully. Thus, as the "innermost life of the soul" in the bourgeois age is severed from the facts of the world and forced inward, becoming mere interiority, the subjective form of alienation par excellence is reached.[58]

We will soon consider Lukács's view of the possibilities of a solution to the crisis of culture (and drama) within the realm of artistic creation. The *Dramahistory,* however, offers the warning that any aesthetic resolution to problems with more general social roots is likely to be impossible. On the other hand, even if he had not yet posed the question of relations among aesthetics, ethics, and politics, Lukács did attempt to outline two possible directions toward a solution, one individualist, the other collectivist.[59]

The attempt is undertaken in a somewhat opaque and surprising passage in which Marx's name makes its first appearance in the *Dramahistory.* Almost in passing, Lukács suggests that "just as in its basic essentials Max Stirner's as well as Marx's whole philosophy sprang from a common source—Fichte—so every modern drama carries within itself this duality of its origins [the simultaneous emergence and cancellation of individuality], this dialectic of modern life."[60] This is a remarkable and revealing statement, unique in 1910. With it Lukács presents Fichte's thought, which had emphasized the identity of self-creation and world transformation, as having been divided into Stirner's focus on the self-creation of the unique individual and Marx's focus on the historical transformation of the external world. By placing Fichte at the source of the Marxian heritage, Lukács is reinserting the "subjective factor" into Marxism, from which the orthodox Marxists of the day had removed it. Marx, in this account, is not primarily the scientific interpreter of history's laws, but the radical revolutionary. At the same time, however, Lukács's statement discloses the tragedy of his own thought and situation: the antagonistic duality of the existing world is radically refused, but the foundation of this refusal is not and cannot be grounded in the world itself. It remains an ethical command, an "ought."

Much like Fichte, Lukács himself at this point remains suspended between Kant and Hegel, pushing beyond the one yet unable to advance toward the other. The implicit thrust of Lukács's sociology of culture presses beyond the Kantian separation of the (free) "thinking subject" and the (deterministic) world of objects by introducing the dimension of history and, within it, the idea that the subject can realize itself, and thus be truly free only in the objective world, only by finding itself in the objects of which it is the actual but estranged producer. On the other hand, Lukács continues to pose the whole problem in terms of an objective world that is totally alienated and thus fundamentally divorced from human subjectivity. As a result he can only pose a solution in pre-Hegelian terms of an ethical imperative which, so to speak, comes at the world from without. Hegel's critique of Kant and Fichte through the historical dialectic of subject-object is not yet Lukács's own.

In the comment on Marx cited above, Lukács does, of course, refer to the "dialectic of modern life," and his cultural theory at times seems under the sway of this concept. Yet in the last analysis the concept of life restricts him to an essentially abstract "philosophy of life" dialectic whose immediate sources are Simmel and Henri Bergson. The "philosophy of life" or "vitalist" dialectic amounts to an eternal conflict between the dynamic, creative flow of "Life" and the formalized static realm of mere "life" or survival.[61] As noted, Lukács had taken important steps toward historicizing such a dialectic, but he also retained certain of its abstract-naturalistic and undialectical elements. Above all, in his account, "Life" and subjectivity, on the one hand, and the objectified world, on the other, are ultimately viewed as absolute "others," not as dialectically linked components of an historical totality and movement.

The Marx-Stirner-Fichte nexus suggested by Lukács reveals another basic conflict in his thought during this early period: the problematic relationship between the individual and the collective, the "I" and the "We." The problem can be roughly stated as follows: the underlying values of Lukács's social and aesthetic thought are collectivist; in his view, true individuation and genuine culture are possible only in and through a conscious, coherent, and unified human community. The logic of development of bourgeois society, however, demolishes community, leaving in its wake a crippled, pseudo individualism and alienated fragments of culture. Nevertheless, it is only from within this specific historical world that the bearer of a new culture and a truly creative individualism can emerge; moreover, Lukács's perspective implies that the bearer, or subject, of cultural renewal must itself be a collective, universal "We" subject. Yet Lukács did not, and probably could not, say much about such a "We" subject and thus concerned himself instead largely with certain unique "I" subjects, great artists and thinkers whose lives and works pointed beyond the prevailing quagmire of alienation. It appears, then, that in his own life and work, alternatives to the crisis of culture were posed in individualistic, even anticollectivist terms.

However, this was not entirely the case. He in fact believed that the source of a renewal of culture and life could have been the proletariat, just as the theory of this renewal could be or could have been Marx's. Yet his linking of Stirner and Marx, collapsing their philosophical origins into Fichte, had its corollary in his own conception of a proletarian-revolutionary alternative to bourgeois culture: this conception remains restricted to an abstract utopia or even a "might have been," while the only seeds of a world beyond alienation are embodied in a select number of uniquely sensitive individual poets and philosophers. This is simply another way of saying that Lukács's individualism is not based on egotistical principles but is, rather, a holding action in the service of an invisible yet absolutely necessary reconciliation of individual and community.

But the question arises: Lukács and a search for community; Lukács and socialist revolution; Lukács and Marx—in 1910? These pairings conflict with the predominant image of Lukács prior to 1918 as one so deeply immersed in aesthetic-cultural thought and so elitist in his social outlook that the very idea of socialist revolution and its related phenomena were entirely foreign to his thinking. This image is both more and less accurate than is generally thought, and several things need to be said about it. The first is that the same Lukács who was immersed in aesthetic-cultural speculation and whose social outlook contained clearly elitist elements nevertheless also believed, in a fervent if unusual manner, in socialist revolution. The second is that these two apparently antagonistic poles of his thought had a common source and were, no matter how problematically, inextricably bound together. As we hope will be indicated in the ensuing discussion, Lukács had the disturbing habit of sometimes presenting the sharpest expressions of collectivist, anti-individualist and anticapitalist values during the very moments of his early work, when he was, so to speak, the most aesthetic, individualistic and "unsociological."

One of the few places in this period in which Lukács links together these two dimensions of his thinking is in the 1910 essay, "Aesthetic Culture," which can be viewed as an addendum to the *Dramahistory*. In the 1910 essay, as we have noted, Lukács condemns "aesthetic culture" as an alienating pursuit of interiority. As an alternative in this connection he makes a striking assertion: "the only hope could have been in the proletariat, in socialism; the hope that the barbarians come and with rough hands tear apart all overrefinement; the hope that the revolutionary spirit which unmasked every ideology and saw everywhere the real moving forces could have seen and felt clearly here, too, sweeping away everything peripheral, returning to the essential."[62] It hardly needs adding that no less remarkable than the vision itself is the tense in which it is presented.

This vision, moreover, is consistent with the major argument of the *Dramahistory:* if the culture of the "tragedy of culture" was created by the class domination of the bourgeoisie, then a new and different culture could be based on the victory of another class, even as that class—"proletariat . . . barbarians"—is immediately opposed to all higher culture. In connection with this specific theme of relations between class and culture, Lukács in the *Dramahistory* introduces two important perspectives on Marx which, if we keep in mind his view of Marx as Fichtean, suggest something of the complexity and richness of his early understanding of his later master. First, Marxism as a theory of history, according to Lukács, tends to "deemphasize the significance of merely individual wills, thoughts, feelings, deriving them from deeper, more objective sources."[63] Precisely this aspect of Marxism, he claims, places it in opposition to all superficial cultivations of surfaces, of the moods and feelings of alienated egos. In this respect, Marxism implies a world view that cannot be expressed in drama, where a self-contained dialectic of individual wills must be symbolically represented. On the other hand, "the wonderful dialectic of Marxism" moves only on the level of the total society; the tragedies of individuals appear to be only temporary, transitory.

The other conception of Marxism in the *Dramahistory* is especially pertinent to the possibilities, as Lukács conceives them, of a revolutionary creation of a new culture:

> The system of socialism and its world view, Marxism, is a synthesis. It is the most cruel and strict synthesis since medieval Catholicism. To express it, when the time comes to express it artistically, only that form will be adequate which is strictly comparable to Catholicism's true art (Giotto and Dante in the first place).[64]

Marxism is, thus, a great theoretical synthesis of world-historical importance, although in Lukács's view most socialists are sensitive only to its social and political aspects and, consequently, unable to contribute (as yet) to its cultural dimension. Throughout Lukács's judgments in the *Dramahistory* and "Aesthetic Culture," there is an implicit yet clear differentiation between the power of Marx's original synthesis, on the one hand, and the realities of the Marxist movement in his own time, on the other.

Nevertheless, prior to 1917 Lukács did not see Marxism in any form as an alternative solution to the crisis of culture, even as he continued to regard Marx's work as entailing a most important sociological method. Instead he proposed a solution of his own, repeated in several contexts. While in retrospect it can be seen as a problematic restatement of the problem itself, it was equally—as we have said—a kind of holding action based on hope in an as yet indiscernible alternative.

It is not surprising that in "Aesthetic Culture" Lukács termed the "escape to socialism" an internal débâcle.[65] What he had in mind was the moral surrender by individuals to the deterministic forces of history. The consequences of this interpretation of socialism are clear and intriguing. For the moment Lukács did not dispute the all-pervasive character of the iron cage: "The external situation is given," he wrote. "There is no genius who could shake its iron necessity. There is no individual, internal culture that could create a social and external one."[66] Nevertheless, "this recognition of determinism" implies fatalism only for the weak, for those "who cannot bear their tragic predestination to be alone," for those who surrender their highest values to quiet and security.

There was, for Lukács, another possibility: that of a new man, a new individual, a hero of internal life who could successfully face (though not alter) the iron necessities of the given reality.[67] He was not, in other words, willing to surrender the value or the ethical imperative of a free and communal individual. Yet it is hard to see how we are to understand a community that lacks an intersubjective medium of objective spirit. The postulate on which his solution to the tragedy of culture rests, then, flows from this paradoxical circumstance: "anything that is truly individual, deep into the depths of the soul, transcends mere individuality."[68] The dilemma, however, has returned: How can we distinguish between this deeper individuality and the alienated individuality of the bourgeois epoch? For Lukács, only the artistic formation of the soul supplies the distinction, although his critique of aesthetic culture—the specialized cult of interiority and the aestheticization of life—makes this position highly precarious. In response to his own objection, Lukács postulated a distinction between an aestheticization of life based on superficial criteria (impression, mood, technique) and implying passivity and, alternatively, an aestheticization of life according to the primary criterion of art—form—implying active creation.

What he did here was to postulate the possibility of a *direct* route to the self-formation of the soul, one that would bypass mediation by the external world of objective culture. It is hardly surprising that one of his central references in this context is to Meister Eckhart. But Lukács's purpose was not to demonstrate the possibility of unity with and dissolution in the divine. He wanted to show, rather, that a consistent self-formation or self-transformation that reduces everything inessential (social and psychological) in the life of an individual is capable of transforming individual life into a *purely symbolic life*. Presumably, such a life would symbolize (without being tragic itself) precisely what is so difficult to capture in modern tragedy: the tragedy of modern culture and individuality. And while this act of self-transformation is an individual act of a new type of illusionless human hero, if it is successful, the result—the formed life—will coincide with the acts and lives of other individuals of the same type. Thus, he paradoxically held out the promise of community on the horizon of the true depths of loneliness.[67] Hoping against hope itself, Lukács sought to probe this promise in the essays collected in *The Soul and the Forms*.

CHAPTER

3

The Problematic Individual: Essayistic Philosophy

TAKING LUKÁCS's early (pre-Marxist) *oeuvre* as a whole, its most stunning feature is the relentlessness with which he disclosed the contradictions of every path he pursued toward transcendence of the alienated world. His essay collection, *The Soul and the Forms* (Hungarian, 1910; expanded German version, 1911), displays this most vividly. This study of the tragic version or sensibility, when published in Germany, promptly established its author as an emerging influence in the world of letters.[1] Written between 1907 and 1910, the essays treat nine of the writers with whom Lukács appears to have felt the strongest kinship and whose works he considered signposts of the crisis of modern art and "soul": Rudolph Kassner, Søren Kierkegaard, Novalis, Theodor Storm, Stefan George, Charles-Louis Philippe, Richard Beer-Hoffman, Laurence Sterne, and Paul Ernst. His otherwise self-contained essays are united by an absent center: the unalienated individual, community, necessity. "To move from contingency to necessity," Lukács states in the essay on Kassner, with whose Platonism he was in deep solidarity, "is the way sought by every problematic man; where everything becomes necessary and expresses the essence of man . . . ; where everything becomes symbolic and, as in music, is only what it means and means only what it is."[2]

This is Lukács's way as well. The volume represents both his self-reflection and his self-transcendence. We now know, thanks to the recent availability of his diary and correspondance from this period and Agnes Heller's commentary on them, that many of his essays are in part autobiographical.[3] The volume's introductory piece, "On the Essence and Form of the Essay," is the essayist's reflection on his chosen form, but it, too, is anything but a final statement. In fact, there is a significant if muted shift between the original Hungarian and subsequent German version, with the first (1910) arguing for the essay as a unique art form, as philosophical poetry, and the second version (1911) stressing the essay as a forerunner of a systematic aesthetics. Evidently, Lukács was on the verge of a fundamental personal and intellectual decision: to dedicate his life to a work which would henceforth enter the terrain of philosophy.

The *Soul and the Forms*'s great achievement, as Lucien Goldmann was the first to argue, is that it made the tragic sensibility—the "metaphysics of tragedy"—conscious of itself as a style of art and life. Yet this achievement only heightened the tragedy of the tragic vision: it now knows itself *not* to be the *answer* to the question, How can the essentially human be brought to life? but its *restatement*. For Lukács the greatness of the writers he discussed was that their art symbolically expressed the tragic vision as the only possible philosophy of life in a world without a life center (*Lebenszentrum*), where all is chaos, transience, alienation. They knew what he had come to know: that the "way sought by every problematic man" is only a way sought, not found. As a philosophy of life, then, the tragic vision is positive only in its negativity; only as the announcement that the essentially human has not been brought to life; only as the promise of fulfillment, not the fulfillment of the promise.

Thus far we have seen two contradictory moments within Lukács's theory of culture. On the one hand, cultural alienation, typified by "aesthetic culture," tends toward the destruction of form and thus the reduction of all life to everyday life, all subjectivity to the "empirical ego." On the other hand, form still exists, at least in art. The first question that arises, then, is whether and how artistic form can survive in the face of cultural alienation. The second question is whether or not artistic form can play a role in the abolition of cultural alienation, in the creation of a new culture. As we will see, Lukács's two Heidelberg aesthetics would attempt to tackle the first question. But from the standpoint of his overall philosophical development, the major question of *The Soul and the Forms* seems to be more important: Can life itself be formed? Only after he had answered this question negatively would that of art's role in the overcoming of alienation become (temporarily) predominant.

To the central question—Can life itself be formed?—Lukács's essay on Novalis (1907) proposes the boldest response: the formation of alienated everyday life into a new culture by a new community. The leading German Romantics (The Jena Circle and Novalis) had sought a new world in which the great man, the poet, "has a home." With his *Wilhelm Meister* Goethe discovered this new world in the presently existing world and by this discovery, according to Lukács, parted company with the Romantics. Significantly, he endorses Novalis's view of Goethe's famous novel as a "*Candide* directed against poetry."[4] Goethe, that is, had forsaken the essence of Romanticism, its "panpoetism," which Lukács defines as follows: "To become God, to be a man, to form oneself"; these, Schlegel had written, "are expressions which mean the same thing."[5] This, Lukács notes, is the "ancient dream of a golden age." Yet the Romantics grasped that it is not a lost refuge of past eras which occasionally haunts contemporary man in ancient legends and tales; they understood it as "the goal whose realization is every man's life-responsibility."[6] Panpoetism was originally an active program of turning empirical life into poetry, into utopia.

Unlike the Romantics, Lukács sees the realization of the "golden age" only in terms of an ethical imperative, not as a concrete and determinate historical possibility. In this connection it is important to note his distinction between tragedy and failure. Romanticism's tragedy was to have culminated in a "poetization of destiny, not its overcoming"; the inward route taken by the Romantics could lead only to an "organic fusion of all givens," that is, only to a "beautiful harmony created out of pictures of things, but not a mastering of things." Yet, Lukács adds, the inward way was the "*only* possibility open to their quest for a great synthesis. . . ."[7] The failure of Romanticism, discovered by Goethe and ultimately, according to Lukács, by the whole "school" with the sole exception of Novalis, lay in its false transcendence or betrayal of its destiny by finally identifying the unified, organic world of poetry with the actual world. As a result the "immense tension between poetry and life" was lost to the Romantics.[8] The capacity to remain suspended within that tension *is* the tragic sensibility. And, as Lukács fully realized, the real tragedy of Romanticism reappears in his own account of it. *The Soul and the Forms* is its meta-tragedy.

Lukács does indicate, however, that the failure of Romanticism as well as its tragedy arose from a sound impulse: that of unifying theory and practice. In his view Romanticism as an "art of life" (*Lebenskunst*) was "poetry become action" (*eine zur Tat gewordene Poesie*); the imperatives of life were drawn from the "innermost and deepest laws of poetic art."[9] Lukács's conception of action here is essentially individualistic and aesthetic, referring to the unity of the works and life of the poet or, more generally, the creative genius. At the same time, however, he implies but does not develop the idea that there is more: the egoism of the Romantics, he states, had "a strong social color." They hoped that the "fullest unfolding of personality would ultimately bring men closer," and they themselves sought salvation from "loneliness and chaos" by attempting to found their own new communities.[10]

Yet panpoetism could not accomplish the active transformation of life; the Romantics could neither avoid nor overcome "aesthetic culture." Unwilling to sacrifice or judge any aspect of their immediate experience—the struggle for form—the Romantic philosophers of life had to sacrifice order and the possibility of action. Only Novalis succeeded in transforming his life into poetry, but instead of generating new intersubjective cultural forms, his "life poem," in Lukács's view, yielded only a beautiful death.[11]

Death as a means of creating form links the essay on Novalis with that on Kierkegaard, where the question of form's relation to life is posed still more starkly.[12] Kierkegaard, as Lukács viewed him, had no illusions about either the communal creation of a new culture or about the rational (dialectical) transition to form within the world of everyday life. From Kierkegaard's standpoint, ethics (the realm of community) is a relatively impoverished stage or form of life open to the confusion of heterogeneous psychic motivations. It is to be transcended only through an irrational leap.[13] Having dispensed with the illusions and flatness of the Romantics' world, Kierkegaard grasped the essence of formation in a Spartan, nonutopian manner. That is, he sought to create only a single form as a bridge to his own authentic life and to a single other being, his deliberately abandoned love, Regine Olsen. This form was his whole life molded and frozen into a gesture incorporating love, abandonment, higher love, and, finally, death. But the whole of everyday life once again resisted formation, even though with Kierkegaard this formation consisted of bold choices and leaps instead of passive poetization.[14]

As Lukács shows, in a strenuously dialectical fashion, Kierkegaard, having rejected the conventional ethic of marriage as a form that would have destroyed his creative sadness and as a convention that would have rendered impossible true understanding with his beloved, then created a form that Regine Olsen—the one "other" who had to be able to understand the form in order to make it a form—could "understand" only peripherally.[15] Lukács found lucidity and courage in Kierkegaard, who is the real hero of *The Soul and the Forms*. Not surprisingly, he is a true tragic hero.[16] By his own admission, Lukács notes, Kierkegaard "struggles in vain" to "live what cannot be lived": a life that is absolute—in Kierkegaard's case, an individual life in absolute relation to God.[17] For Lukács, there are several elements of Kierkegaard's achievement: first, his insistence that the life of an individual has meaning only in the attempt to be absolute, "not merely relative." Second, Kierkegaard's quest for an absolute life was undertaken *absolutely;* that is, all possibilities were subjected to a radical clarity, and all choices were made on the basis of a decisive "either–or" rather than on the basis of an "as well as." And, third, Lukács emphatically affirms both Kierkegaard's conception of truth as subjectivity—as a passionately inward grasping of that which is objectively uncertain—and his opposition to all "rational systems of thought" which achieve an intellectual unity only by soaring beyond the concrete, living individual.[18]

Early in his essay Lukács summarizes Kierkegaard's "stages on life's way," the aesthetic, the ethical, and the religious which, however, are not stages in the rationalist sense, since for Kierkegaard they are separated from each other by an "unbridgeable gap." The only link between them, Lukács notes, is the "miracle, the leap, the metamorphosis of the whole of a man's essence."[19] What interests Lukács is the concept of the leap; he appears to feel the closest bond with the single-mindedness with which Kierkegaard took his leap, rather than with the particular leap of faith in God. Kierkegaard saw the crossroads, says Lukács, and followed the road he had chosen to its end. In an alienated world whose inevitable cultural and individual results are in the direction of overrefinement, intellectuality, and passivity, Kierkegaard sought to *live* absolutely the impossible pursuit of the absolute.

Lukács's conclusion to the Kierkegaard essay is characteristic of the conclusion to each of the essays in *The Soul and the Forms* and signifies the conclusion and situation of the book as a whole. On the one hand, Lukács refuses to accept the point to which Kierkegaard carried his life and thought as *the* end of the road. It is clear that with Kierkegaard, as well as with the others examined in the essays, Lukács is not dealing with culminating points to be fondled in the hope of deriving some spiritual comfort but rather with orientation points to be surpassed. He does not ignore the fact that the bad reality of a fragmented and objectified existence remains bad and real. On the other hand, Lukács offers and can offer no more than vague, even opaque, calls for other possibilities and new beginnings.

Kierkegaard, Lukács concludes, struggled against the Christianity of his time and "was in the midst of the most furious battles, with nothing to seek in life outside of his struggle . . . when death overtook him. . . . He collapsed on the street and as they brought him to the hospital he said he wanted to die because the cause he represented had called for his life. . . . And he died."[20] Interestingly, however, Lukács does not accept Kierkegaard's interpretation of his own death. The questions remain open, Lukács argues, as to "where the route, which suddenly breaks off with [Kierkegaard's] tombstone, would have led? Where was he going when (according to his own account) he *had* to meet death?" For Lukács the "inner necessity" of Kierkegaard's death is "only one possible explanation among a great many," and if other explanations are possible, one "cannot take the end of his own journey as an end . . . [but] . . . must in spirit follow its further twists and turns."[21] Kierkegaard's own soul could not be contained by his gesture. His life could not be subsumed under a single form; his relation to his own life gesture remained profoundly ambiguous. In the end, the ambiguity of his whole life and death shattered the gesture he had created through great struggle and self-sacrifice.

Kierkegaard's goal and that of the Romantics constitute opposite poles of Lukács's early essayistic philosophy. The self-realization and self-formation of an authentic, illusionless, ruthlessly honest, struggling, ascetic hero stands at one end. The creation of a new and rich objective culture with art (an "art that can be learned") at its center stands at the other. Yet these poles are complementary. Moreover, they share a common characteristic: in both, the resistance of empirical, everyday life shatters the project of formation. The four essays composing the bulk of *The Soul and the Forms*—those on Storm, Beer-Hoffman, Philippe and George—and to a lesser extent the last two essays on Sterne and Ernst, attempt both a partial synthesis of the two poles and an overcoming (or bypassing) of the problem of the recalcitrance of everyday life. But the price paid in these instances seems to be the loss of any connection to everyday life. The important essay, "*Bürgerlichkeit* and *l'art pour l'art:* Theodor Storm," displays this separation from the everyday empirical world at its sharpest, revealing it to be the result of the historical development Lukács had analyzed in the *Dramahistory*.

The essay on Storm is the historical center of *The Soul and the Forms*. According to Lukács, the title, "Bourgeoisness and Art for Art's Sake," expresses a paradox: that of an age in which bourgeois society seems increasingly antithetical to art and culture, while art for its own sake means increasing distance from the everyday life of the bourgeois. But the paradox itself results from the historical development of bourgeois society. In the bourgeoisie's heroic age, everyday pursuits and honest calling (including honest craftsmanship) complemented one another. In the age of dissolution, however, duty in one's calling, having lost its roots and justification in communal life, can only be an end in itself.

In his analysis of the historical change in the function of the *ascetic ethics* of duty in one's calling, Lukács's relation to Max Weber's thesis on Protestantism and capitalism emerges. For Max Weber, the work ethic, and its corresponding rational, ascetic organization of daily life, is a necessary if not sufficient condition of modern capitalism. In Weber's account, the work ethic, which assisted in destroying traditional communities and legitimations, could have established itself only by penetrating, through the medium of religious world views, the daily lives of whole communities of people.[22] Once established and externalized in a vast system of "mechanical petrification," the "spirit of capitalism" is spontaneously reproduced in individuals' consciousnesses *without* the support of organic communities or religious ideologies. Calling (*Beruf*), in other words, becomes an internally hollow, meaningless end in itself.[23]

Lukács examines only one special type of calling, that of artist and craftsman, but his reconstruction of it is analogous to Weber's. In the essay on Theodor Storm, he presupposes the historical process through which the intrinsic relations within a cultural community—a common (work) ethic, an artist, and works of art—have been severed. In the new context, the forms (ethics and works of art) have been separated from life; formal bourgeois ethics—*Bürgerlichkeit* in Lukács's view—have become mere tasks.[24] For representatives of the older bourgeoisie, the immediate self-evidence of formal ethics in everyday life had defined the whole of existence, with Immanuel Kant's categorical imperative being, in Lukács's view, the highest expression of this definition. The rule of ethics in life had entailed the rule of order over mood, constancy over moment, surrender of self over egocentric behavior, and community over isolation.[25] It had permitted a channeling of energies into useful labor (*Arbeit*) and works (*Werke*) and had united specialists in the division of labor, among them artists, in common work for a single community. Finally, the same ethic of work had given meaning and order to everyday life, thereby enabling the "holy everydays" to become adequate materials—intrinsically communicable, already formed materials—for artistic creation. The result, in Lukács's interpretation, was the poetry of the subtle richness and ethical constancy of daily bourgeois life.[26]

But by the nineteenth century, the social bases of *Bürgerlichkeit*, a bourgeoisie in town communities, existed, as far as Lukács was concerned, only in some isolated pockets of European civilization. Nevertheless, as for Max Weber, so for Lukács: the pure form of *Bürgerlichkeit*—the ascetic ethics of calling and duty—had survived beyond this limit in space and time. Yet, for Lukács, who is speaking of artists, this survival of asceticism is a problematic phenomenon. Life for the artist or aesthete has become the virtual opposite of being bourgeois in the traditional sense: "glitter and estrangement from relations, the drunken and orgiastic dance of the soul in the constantly changing groves of moods."[27] In this situation, renouncing life for the sake of works of art, that is, asceticism or being bourgeois, becomes for the artist a form of slavery and forced labor, a mask hiding the pains of renunciation. *Bürgerlichkeit* has survived, but it now stands in a highly antagonistic relation to life.

Thus transformed into an end in itself, ascetic renunciation remains the only possible means to the genuine creation of works. But this question then arises: For whom are the works intended when a receptive community no longer exists and when everyday life has become formless? Here Lukács's response differs from Weber's. Even art for art's sake—the work as the sole meaning of life—preserves the abstract hope, nothing more, of a new culture, of new communities of the hypothetical future.[28] Thus, perhaps unexpectedly from our standpoint, the bourgeois ethic of duty, sacrifice of life's richness for the sake of works, provides Lukács with a more feasible path to the attainment of form in life than the paths of either Kierkegaard or the Romantics. After Theodor Storm, however, this potential solution involves sharp separation from the everyday lives of individuals. The ethics of *Bürgerlichkeit* no longer permit a synthesis of the desire to form life through a cultural community and the desire to form an authentic individuality.

Thus, in Lukács's essays on Stefan George, Charles-Louis Philippe, and Richard Beer-Hoffman, emphasis is placed on the self-formation of individuals through the ascetic struggle for the attainment of artistic form. Very little is said of the utopian, symbolic community of authentic individuals. In addition, the self-formation of individual life cannot transcend or abolish the dualism of life and form, life and soul (genuine, creative life). This is one of the conclusions of *The Soul and the Forms* and is amplified in the last two essays in the volume.

"Richness, Chaos and Form: A Dialogue on Laurence Sterne" (1909) offers the sharpest presentation of the philosophical problem of the dualism of soul and form as a life problem. The dialogue, reminiscent of Thomas Mann's *Tonio Kröger,* enables Lukács to disclose the intrinsic human difficulties of his position. Through his two speakers, he unfolds a confrontation between Kant and "philosophy of life" (*Lebensphilosophie*), that is, respectively, the point of view of forms (an ascetic, ethics-oriented rationalism) and the point of view of life (a hedonistic, intuitionist irrationalism). Significantly, Lukács represents both positions with equal vigor and ability. *Lebensphilosophie* affirms the irrational richness of life that transcends all conceptualization, valuation, and absolutes, insisting on the unlimited nature of passive, receptive subjectivity for which "a communicable life would be empty."[29] The attack on *Lebensphilosophie* affirms choice, valuation, absolutes, and the transcendence of isolated subjectivity through communicable, intersubjective forms. The disorderly and chaotic richness of immediate experience is criticized from the standpoint of a rationally structured and ordered totality.[30] In the end, Lukács tends to subsume *Lebensphilosophie* within his special brand of Kantianism, foreshadowing his subsequent emphasis on objective, intersubjective forms against all solipsism.[31]

The concluding essay, "Metaphysics of Tragedy: Paul Ernst," written in 1911 and included only in the German edition of *The Soul and the Forms,* represents a further step in this direction. Proposing both the possibility of a new tragic genre embodied in Ernst's works and the fundamental tragedy of human existence, the essay again places at the center the deep dualism between present life and authentic life. Present life, the realm of facts, is without meaning or value: "nature and fate were never as soulless as today."[32] On the other hand, the true heights of authentic life, where value creates its own reality, where "intellectual intuition" reigns, is a realm in which no one can in fact live.[33]

Thus, both the meaning and paradox of tragedy lie in the attempt to answer the question, "How can the essential be brought to life? How can it be truly realized as the only reality in its sensuous immediacy?"[34] If we cannot live on the heights of essential life within empirical life, can we transform the heights of existence into everyday reality?[35] Tragedy, then, lies in the striving for this possibility and the recognition of its empirical impossibility. Paul Ernst had written: "Only when we have become utterly Godless will we again have tragedy."[36] This passage allows Lukács to move from the tragedy of existence to tragic genre, and his discussion of the latter deepens his philosophical problem but also introduces a utopian dimension. As we will see shortly, though, it was, as always with the early Lukács, a consciously problematic utopia.

For Lukács, tragic drama raises the experience of great moments, of authentic life, to a systematic whole, with the participant in real tragedy attaining genuine experience of the self.[37] Such authenticity requires struggle, a stretching of the empirical self to a point at which it transcends itself and becomes a symbol of fate.[38] But this symbolic self-transcendence is also a movement toward other symbolic individuals; a true tragedy is a dialogue of naked souls and fates, stripped of everything inessential and merely empirical.[39] While Lukács would soon push this conception further toward the utopia it implies, it is notable that he does not do so in "Metaphysics of Tragedy."[40] There the Kantian dualism of fact and value remains central. This is because, as in several of the essays in *The Soul and the Forms,* death and brave recognition of death are internal limits and preconditions of true form. Only by recognizing death as the limit of existence can one attain authentic self-consciousness.[41] In addition, in an age in which the material of life has become meaningless, even the tragic genre cannot shape the components of everyday life and history; tragedy, in other words, becomes entirely formalistic. The tragic form can create or re-create an intelligible world, the realm of values; it can yield a pure ethics of human conduct. But the "validity and power of ethics are independent of their realization." The road between life and form is thus blocked in both directions. Instead of a utopia, the "Metaphysics of Tragedy" can be once again only its own "metatragedy." A true tragedy can finally represent only the (metaphysical) tragedy of culture.[42]

The concluding essay in *The Soul and the Forms,* then, ends in renunciation, although not of the tragic art form. Yet two of the book's themes point beyond renunciation. The first of these is its implicitly utopian moment. The other is a basic ambiguity in its understanding of ethics. For in the "Metaphysics of Tragedy" it seems that Lukács abandons a Fichtean, activistic ethics that demands the realization of the essential in favor of a formalistic, neo-Kantian ethics. But still there is no question of a final position. Indeed, the battle between the two ethics within Lukács's thought, as well as the problem of utopia, reemerges in his important essay "On the Poverty of Spirit," also published in 1911.[43] In this extraordinary piece, for which Lukács again adopts the dialogue form, he confronts the conceptual apparatus of *The Soul and the Forms* with a tragic event in his own life, the suicide of his beloved, Irma Seidler.

The dialogue form of "On the Poverty of Spirit" expresses exactly what is now known of the events in Lukács's life at that time. He felt that, had he been a different person, he might have been able to prevent the death. We have noted the importance of death in his early thought—death as a limit, as a dimension of form and formation. He had written in 1908:

> Someone died. And for the one left behind, the eternal distance, the unbridgeable space between beings, petrifies in the form of a question forever unanswered. . . . And the break—if it was not a conscious break, a farewell which tears out every fiber of the past from living life to tie them together in a close, finished existence rigidified into a creation of art—every break cuts off forever not only the future, but the whole past as well. . . . In death, in the death of the other, the great problem of the life of an individual among individuals is expressed, . . . the possible meaning of one person in the life of another.[44]

Following Irma Seidler's suicide in 1910, Lukács pursued these themes of two years before, undertaking to reexamine and perhaps "cut off forever" his past in order to face openly "the possible meaning of one person in the life of another." Yet he was equally consistent in examining and reevaluating the conceptual apparatus of life—form—or genuine life in a "thought experiment" situated within the frame of his own life.[45]

The essays in *The Soul and the Forms* possess an autobiographical dimension, although in all of them the life of the essayist himself remains rather carefully hidden, with the concepts, often repeated, seemingly gaining a formal independence. In "On the Poverty of Spirit," however, the concepts are brought into dynamic tension with the life that most closely approximated his own. At this point, the terms of *The Soul and the Forms* became inadequate. Of the two suicides in "On the Poverty of Spirit," the second, that of the hero, is entirely fictional. A "beautiful death" could have made Lukács's essayistic philosophy complete. But, after seriously considering taking his own life, Lukács chose to live and to attempt to destroy his old form.[46] "On the Poverty of Spirit" is the personal and intellectual documentation of this transition.

The two characters are a man and woman, the first clearly standing for Lukács in the immediate sense, although he must be distinguished from the author of the dialogue, who also speaks through the figure of the woman. While the latter is the sister of the woman who committed suicide in the dialogue, she appears to represent

Irma Seidler. The man presents Lukács's own philosophical concepts in a particularly rigid manner. Dividing existence into the three levels of everyday life, of forms, and of authentic life (termed "goodness"), he assigns each level its own ethic and human types. "You are trying to resurrect the castes on a metaphysical foundation," the woman reproaches him.[47] Frequently, her intellectual position is severely shaken, although she also scores her points on occasion. It is clear that only the man possesses a theoretical system. Yet her objections force him toward an increasingly precarious position. Finally, the system and the life tied to it collapse.

Intellectually, the dialogue *"Von der Armut am Geiste"* consists of three basic parts or stages: a critique of ethics and an elaboration of "goodness," in the quest for which the "spiritual poverty" of the works is the preparatory phase. Ethics or the ethical life, whose prototype for Lukács is Kantian ethics, is sharply rejected as a form of alienation, the ultimate function of which is to entrench man's separation from his authentic self and from real communion with others.[48] In this critique and in the presentation of "goodness" as authentic existence not only beyond alienation but beyond rational thought as such, the aristocratic elements of Lukács's standpoint receive their most extreme expression. The central passage of his critique of ethics is worth citing at some length:

> It is a question of Life: one can live without Life [*man kann ohne Leben leben*], but this must be done consciously and with clarity. Certainly most men live without Life and are unaware of it. Their lives are merely social . . . they can do with responsibilities and fulfilling them. Indeed, for them the fulfillment of responsibilities is the only possible means of enhancing their lives. For every ethics is formal, a postulate, a form; and the more complete a form is, the more it takes on a life of its own and the further it is from every immediacy. Ethics is a bridge that separates; a bridge across which we traipse back and forth, always reaching only ourselves but never meeting one another. These men can never get beyond themselves for their contact with others is at best a psychological interpretation, while the force of responsibility gives their lives a firm and secure, if shallow, form.[49]

This sharp critique of the surface of alienation is combined with, even based upon, an elitist-aristocratic disdain for "most men," those who somnambulistically proceed with the business of alienated existence. Lukács similarly implies that only a small circle of uniquely gifted and creative individuals is capable of awakening from and transcending this state. Yet the intellectually elitist character of Lukács's attitude toward "most men," who are condemned to live according to the alienated formalism of ethics and thus to live "without life," has another side.[50] For the real object of his imperiousness is not the great majority of men in society as a whole but, more specifically, bourgeois man. Of course, Lukács says "most men" and is at this time far from suggesting sharp distinctions between bourgeoisie and proletariat in the context of the possibilities of a life beyond alienation. Nevertheless, as noted in his remarks on Theodor Storm, for example, the primacy of ethics in life is, for Lukács, the paradigm of bourgeois life. Moreover, as his critique of ethics makes clear, the self-consciousness attained by bourgeois man, based as it is on formal ethics, is a false-consciousness: from the standpoint of bourgeois man the essential and authentic life remains inaccessible to thought and experience.

From the standpoint of the male protagonist in the dialogue, then, formal ethics has become "one of the powers of alienation."[51] The ethics of everyday life is indeed "formal ethics," that is, keeping one's hands clean in a world of sin and cruelty. The dialogue's hero conspicuously did his duties, keeping his hands quite clean and thereby estranging himself from the woman who desperately needed his help. Formal ethics may be the only way for the ordinary individual to become "social," to rise beyond the raw immediacy of everyday life. Yet from the standpoint of something concrete, even a concrete work of art, the ethic of duty *is* a hopelessly empty form, inadequate as a basis of understanding and action.

Following several weak counterobjections by the woman defending duty, the hero of the dialogue "leaps" to a different ethic, that of work, of the creative form, a robust Fichtean ethic of transforming life. At this point, the relation between virtue and sin is reversed. In everyday life, virtuous behavior implies, from a higher point of view, sin. In the realm of forms, cruelty and sin, sacrifice and self-sacrifice, lead to works representing the possibility of "goodness." This possibility presupposes yet another "leap": the leap of "grace." Once again, dialectical transitions are excluded in the manner of Kierkegaard. The creation of works empties the creator, making him "spiritually poor," and thus fashioning him into a vessel capable of receiving the grace of goodness that will turn the inhumanity of formation into a higher humanity.[52] Spiritual poverty is no guarantee of the gift of goodness. But spiritual poverty—freedom from all psychic determinations, "the sacrifice of self for the realization of the work"—needs no such guarantees.

"Goodness" is the mode of "true consciousness" in Lukács's dialogue and as such is a departure from necessity and determination into the realm of freedom. Once again, however, he indicates that freedom and true self-realization are possible only in a unique suspension outside or above the realm of necessity. When "goodness" appears in us, the protagonist announces, "paradise has become reality and the deity has awakened within us."[53] The "good" soul is emptied of every psychological content and lies beyond all causality; its actions, moreover, are undertaken without a view to their results "for the results fall in the *external world of mechanical forces which operate independently of us*."[54] Destiny writes its "absurd commands" on the "pure white sheet" of the "good" soul, and these commands are "blindly, rashly and cruelly" carried out.[55] The ordinary life lies on this side of the forms, while "goodness" or "living Life" (*lebendiges Leben*) lies beyond; as a "state of grace," it possesses the right to violate the ethical forms and norms.[56]

The models of the "good man" are Dostoevski's Sonia, Prince Mishkin, and Alexei Karamazov whose actions, while "hopelessly confused and without positive results," are carried out in a realm beyond tragedy, pure ethics, and beyond even the cosmic.[57] They are, then, acts of redemption. And, although one cannot will himself to be "good," there are a select few who can take steps to prepare themselves for "goodness." The ordinary and "unclear man" is never "impoverished in spirit." The task of those few who are, however, is to begin to free themselves from their own psychological determinations in order to give themselves over to their own "deeper meta-physical and meta-psychic necessity."[58]

Accompanying Lukács's constant assertions of the purposelessness and miraculous character of "goodness" are indications of a notably different type. If ethics is man's first step out of the chaos of ordinary life, Lukács states, it is also a "departure from himself, from his empirical state, while goodness is a return to authentic life, man's true return home."[59] "Good men" are "gnostics of action";

with them knowledge becomes action; their thought departs "from merely discursive knowledge; *their perception of men has become an intellectual intuition.*" And, perhaps most decisively in this context, "goodness" is a "totally illuminating knowledge of men, *a knowledge in which subject and object converge*"; the "good man" no longer interprets the soul of another but "reads it as he reads his own—*he has become the other.*"[60] And, finally, "the Sermon on the Mount promises bliss, but for Fichte [and for Lukács] that means life itself: blissful life."[61]

Articulated in mystical-messianic terms, the concept of "goodness" in "On the Poverty of Spirit" is nevertheless an image, highly abstract, of a this-wordly, social utopia. "Good men" are agents, not of a pure or transcendental subjectivity or of an absolute relation to God, but of a pure intersubjectivity. Lukács's "gnostics of action" have as their object a total abolition of man's estrangement from himself and others; they are the spiritual Luddites of the alienated world who are out to wreck the "bridge [ethics] that separates." Obviously and inevitably, Lukács's standpoint carries these implicitly social-revolutionary insights into a cosmic realm far beyond all concrete social and historical problems and possibilities. But it should also be clear that, while hardly inevitable, a "leap" from this particular cosmic realm to the camp of Communist revolution is at least imaginable, given the promise of such a revolution to break radically with the existing world of alienation.

Nevertheless, the contradictions—and dangers—of the utopia of goodness are not to be denied. As it aims at full intersubjectivity, that is, community, goodness does not concern itself with results in the objective world. And how could it be otherwise if forms, objectifications, externalized symbols, and meanings are bridges of alienation, bridges that separate? Here Lukács is forced back to a position that for the moment hardly seems to differ from Simmel's metaphysics of life, his codification of the insuperability of the "tragedy of culture." Of course, the utopian postulate of goodness remains, but in the absence of objective mediations, it can be either an explicitly mystical alternative or an extreme version of the Kantian antinomy of purely subjective freedom and fully deterministic objectivity. As the woman in the dialogue charges, the utopia of goodness, in spite of the cruel road leading to it, has a tendency to degenerate into something utterly empty and bloodless. From the standpoint of everyday life, moreover, it tends to degenerate into precisely that abstract Kantian ethical postulate that Lukács had sought to surpass by an ingenious combination of the ethics of Fichte, Dostoevski, and Kierkegaard. The hero's suicide represents, on the one hand, the ultimate impossibility of his position and, on the other, the successful transformation of his life into a work, a form. Having rejected everyday life, unable to achieve the level of goodness, defining his own level as that of self-alienation, he had nowhere to go. His form is defined, as was that of Novalis, in the end by two deaths.

"On the Poverty of Spirit" stood at the close of Lukács's essayistic philosophy. Several partially distinct paths led out of its internal difficulties. First, there was a possibility of a new synthetic method capable of uniting or at least containing all the diverse perspectives which, in Lukács's view, were required to investigate a world divided into fact and value, is and ought, life and form. Such a solution was rooted in the conceptual structure of the essayistic philosophy. While it initially had points of contact with the "philosophy of life," Lukács would soon carry it toward more traditional concepts of German classical philosophy. This shift, as will be seen, was conditioned by the other attempts at a solution, especially Lukács's struggle toward a systematic philosophy, of which only large parts of an aesthetics were ever written.

From the outset, Lukács's aesthetics sought to resolve one of the basic problems of the essayistic philosophy: the problem of form and communication. He sought to work this out by way of a theory of objectifications. But even grounding the possibility of art works as objectifications could not yield a theory pointing at the creation of a new culture which would transcend cultural alienation. Yet precisely this remained an essential, perhaps *the* essential, project for Lukács: to form life, to make it essential, to overcome the separations indicated in both the theory of the "tragedy of culture" and the Kantian "two worlds" (empirical and ideal). This central goal would be incorporated in Lukács's effort to ground the possibility of a new culture first in a philosophy of history that still drew its utopia from Dostoevski and its activism from Fichte. Lukács would then take a step that entailed both a radical turn and a fully consistent extension of his previous labors: a turn toward an ethical-idealist conception of revolutionary politics.

CHAPTER

4

Between Heidelberg and Marx

THE MAN WHO PERSUADED Lukács to come to Heidelberg was the greatest admirer of Marx in the German world of neo-idealist letters: Ernst Bloch. In Lukács's own testimony Bloch convinced him of two things: that philosophy in the classical sense of German idealism was still possible and that in Heidelberg Lukács would find, after rejection and only half-understanding in Budapest, a receptive and stimulating intellectual milieu.[1] And, indeed, among the earliest admirers of Lukács's work was to be Max Weber. In her biography of her husband Marianne Weber refers to the deep impact exerted on him by the "profoundly artistic essay of his friend [Lukács] on the spiritually impoverished, in which the right to violate ethical norms is accorded to the redemptive force of creative love."[2] In late 1912, Lukács had arrived in Heidelberg, where he became a part of the discussion circle that met Sundays at Weber's house and a regular contributor to the influential *Archiv für Sozialwissenschaft und Sozialpolitik,* of which Weber was an editor.

Regularly present in the discussions of the Weber circle in addition to the Webers, Bloch, and Lukács were Friedrich Gundolf, the disciple of the poet Stefan George; Paul Honigsheim, the sociologist who has left several valuable recollections of the group; Karl Jaspers; and numerous Russian mystics and nihilists who had come to Heidelberg University in part because it was a center of idealist criticism of materialism and positivism and, in part, because the matriculation and habilitation requirements for foreigners were less rigid there than at other German universities. Among the visitors to the discussions were the leading "Heidelberg neo-Kantians," Wilhelm Windelband and Heinrich Rickert, whose lectures Lukács attended, and Emil Lask, their most accomplished student, with whom Lukács was closely associated. Stefan George himself made occasional appearances. Lukács's work from 1912 through the early years of World War I must in part be viewed in its relation to the Weber circle.[3]

Weber himself was the dominant figure. Only a few of the participants, Marianne Weber has indicated, such as Gundolf and Lukács, possessed both the intelligence and mastery of expression sufficient to make themselves independent focal points of discussion.[4] The ideal for which Lukács was spokesman, in conjunction with Bloch and some of the Russians present, was that of Slavic culture and mystical thought as an alternative to the "worldly asceticism" and "goal-oriented action" of the bourgeois West. He propounded a vision of a "life in the spirit of Dostoevski" and, as numerous commentators have indicated, was instrumental in interesting Weber in the "Russian spirit" as a consistent and meaningful rejection of the "spirit of capitalism" about which Weber, since 1910, had begun to feel increasingly ambivalent.[5] Weber's essay, "Religious Rejections of the World and their Directions" (1915), was clearly inspired by his exchange with Lukács.

In his accounts of the Weber circle Paul Honigsheim has left an informative picture of Lukács in the 1912–14 years. He was, Honigsheim writes, "very much opposed to the bourgeoisie, liberalism, the constitutional state, parliamentarism, revisionistic socialism, the Enlightenment, relativism and individualism."[6] And Honigsheim recalls accompanying Lukács to a meeting of the Social Democratic Party in Baden where Ludwig Frank, a leading party spokesman and trade unionist, attacked a government agency for acts in violation of the constitution: Lukács "referred to this a number of times that evening. As we left the meeting hall, he shook his head excitedly and said in a rage, 'a socialist who wants to defend the constitution!' "[7] Equally characteristic of Lukács's attitude at this time was, on the one hand, his constant insistence that culture can exist only on the foundations of community and, on the other, remarks such as the following, attributed to him by Honigsheim: "All this individualism is just humbug; Stefan George is allowed to be a personality, but a policeman and coachman are not."[8]

In this connection it should be noted again that while fully utopian and aristocratic, Lukács's conception of socialism in these years was consistently self-critical and more realistic than it first appears. His reference in 1909 to Endre Ady and implicitly to himself as "revolutionaries without a revolution" may be recalled. And in the context of the Weber circle, where questions of Marxism and the working class movement were regularly debated, the utter disgust with which Lukács and his neo-Romantic, mystical-socialist friends viewed the "unheroic" and bureaucratic practice and the mechanically materialist theory of social democracy was not wholly unfounded.

In addition—and once again it is surprising to realize this—Lukács, no matter how abstractly, continued to return to the theme that the proletariat would be the concrete social agency of the renewal of culture and life. In a review essay of 1914 dealing with methodological questions of cultural sociology, he voiced his hope that the "economic organicism and synthesis of the workers' world would lead to a new rule of the general over the personal, of community over freedom in isolation . . . to a new universality" beyond the fragmented rationalism and individualism of the bourgeois world. Yet, he immediately added, as long as positive content could not be given to this universality, it was "not knowledge but a mere hope," and the two should not be confused.[9]

In particular, Lukács rejected Romantic notions of the proletariat which otherwise might have seemed to follow from his own standpoint. What appears to some to be the present universality of the working class in contrast to the bourgeoisie, he argued, is in fact an "abstract and culturally neutral universality" which results from the "historically conditioned and, even within contemporary culture, perhaps only momentary spiritual primitiveness of the worker."[10] That is—and here Lukács had in mind the actual situation of the German working class as organized in the Social Democratic Party and the trade unions—it is "entirely possible that the cultural advancement of the workers' world will also lead, within that world, to individualism, to class-free differentiations, and to the emergence of spiritual autocracies which are no less disoriented and overrefined than their bourgeois counterparts and which stand over and against the remaining obtuse and indifferent masses of the workers."[11]

In this assessment Lukács gave more than embryonic expression to a central theme of his Marxism of the early 1920s, namely, that the reified bourgeois world reproduces itself within the proletariat and thereby blunts the possibility of proletarian class consciousness and proletarian action. However, while no concrete alternatives to the cultural bourgeoisification of the proletariat appear to exist, Lukács held open at least the abstract possibility of another course and rejected the view, widespread among intellectuals in his circles, that the proletarian character or "psyche" is inherently opposed to genuine culture.[12] From a theoretical standpoint, he asserted, it would be the task of the sociology of culture to show that "none of the organizational forms created by the workers' world are obstacles to the reception and support of a new and today nonexistent culture."[13]

It would be hopelessly anachronistic to suggest that had Lukács only studied Marx more carefully, he would have been able to elaborate a more coherent conception of the relationship between cultural renewal and proletarian revolution. Lukács did, however, occupy himself with Marx during the Heidelberg years, but his whole understanding of Marx was rendered partial and fragmentary by the same factors that determined the extreme and "tragic" utopianism of his vision of the new man and the new culture.

Marx's name appears for a second time in Lukács's pre-1919 writings in his 1915 review of Benedetto Croce's *Theory and History of Historiography* (1912–13; German translation, 1915).[14] The context, briefly, is the debate over "historicism" and Lukács's attempt to suggest a way out of the pitfalls of relativism and dogmatic metaphysics. These two erroneous conclusions to the problem of the historical character of human values derive, according to Lukács, from a common failure to clearly distinguish between absolute and objective spirit—a distinction which Lukács adopts from Hegel. The dimensions of absolute spirit—art, religion, and philosophy—have histories, he argues, but are themselves not products of historical development. The "historicity" of the "in itself timeless absolute spirit" and the question of how it is possible for its dimensions to have histories at all, Lukács adds, are issues which the leading theorists of history have overlooked.

But, he insists, these issues are entirely separate from those regarding the historical character of objective spirit (family, society, state), since the latter is a product of historical development. In this context, Lukács attacks Croce for hypostatizing the empirical methods of historical sciences into a metaphysical philosophy of history. Against Croce he upholds Heinrich Rickert's distinction between the inevitably relative, time-bound concepts of the historian and the absolute, trans-historical value system of the philosopher. On the other hand, Lukács contends that in their theoretical accounts of history as a science—that is, in their understanding of objective spirit—both Croce and Rickert fail to really overcome the problem of relativism because they are not sufficiently relativistic; specifically, they are not sufficiently sociological.[15] This is where Marx enters.

Sociology, Lukács argued, has the tendency to reveal the concrete social roots and content of specific concepts and values and in so doing "preserves their relative objectivity and validity from subjective irrationality as well as from a false, dogmatically metaphysical, transcending rationalism."[16] Had Croce, Rickert, and others occupied themselves more seriously with Marx, they might have found the means to give concrete, historical foundation to their otherwise entirely abstract claims for the relative objectivity of certain ideas and values. For, Lukács asserts, the fact that

> historical materialism, the most important sociological method to date, has almost always become a metaphysical philosophy of history ought not allow us to neglect the epoch-making value of the method on which it is founded. What Marx calls the problem of ideology contains—when cleansed of its metaphysical concept-formation and made methodologically pure—the way to a solution of the issue . . . raised here: it shows that the . . . concepts of the sciences of objective spirit are necessarily filled with concrete content. . . . [It shows that] everything which does not actually derive from the absolute is a product of social conditions. . . .[17]

This thesis illuminates a great deal about the relationship between Lukács's pre-Marxian and Marxian work. It indicates, first of all, one of the central paradoxes in the whole of his pre-Marxian thought: namely, that where Lukács is, so to speak, most Marxist—as, for example, in the remark cited above or in *Dramahistory*—he is furthest from grasping Marxism as a theory of revolution. On the other hand, where he is least Marxist—as in *The Soul and the Forms* or "On the Poverty of Spirit"—he appears to be straining toward a position far more revolutionary. Reduced to a formula, Lukács's thought as an essayistic, philosophical critic of alienation could be described as activist, even implicitly revolutionary, although it stands explicitly and completely outside the realm of social action, while as a quasi-Marxist sociologist of bourgeois culture and social life, his thought tends to be relatively resigned, detached, "scientific." Within this scheme, however, it is important to note not only that neither side of Lukács's early thought is "complete" in terms of a possible future critical theory of bourgeois society, but also that these two sides cannot be completed simply by being placed together in a "new synthesis." Rather, to reach his revolutionary standpoint of 1919, Lukács had to rework and transform both sides of his pre-Marxian thought in order to articulate, on the one hand, the objective-historical context of the earlier, subjective-activist side and, on the other hand, the subjective-activist project missing from the earlier, sociological side.

More specifically, Lukács's argument in his review of Croce anticipates two famous theses he would present in 1919 as a Marxist. First, he defines the essence of Marxism not in any of its particular results or predictions, but in its method. Of course, this is, in part, a formal anticipation, since in 1915 Lukács was clearly unaware of what he would discover three years later as the essence of the Marxian method: the revolutionary subject-object dialectic. Yet Lukács's conception of the Marxian method in the Croce review suggests also somewhat more than a merely formal anticipation of his subsequent standpoint, since Marx's critique of ideology would be for him a central component of the revolutionary subject-object dialectic.

Perhaps an even more interesting anticipation of Lukács's view of Marxism in the review of Croce is the distinction he draws between the Marxian method and the Marxian "metaphysical philosophy of history." At first glance, this distinction entails the revisionist separation of science and revolution—that is, the derevolutionization of Marxian theory—whose most trenchant philosophical critic after 1919 would be Lukács himself. And there is no question but that his reading of Marx in 1915 is nonrevolutionary. Yet, when viewed within the context of Marxian thought at that time, Lukács's position is actually somewhat more complex. First, it obviously cannot be assumed that, in rejecting Marxism's "metaphysical philosophy of history," Lukács was rejecting the

Marxian theory of history and revolution which he and others would discover in the years following 1917. That theory simply did not exist for Lukács—nor for others—and its very possibility was, in 1915, beyond the immediate horizon of his thought.

On the other hand, what Lukács was then opposing from a non-revolutionary, yet critical, standpoint was the "metaphysical" Marxism of the Second International, specifically that of Kautsky and Plekhanov.[18] The real object of his criticism at this point, as it would be in 1919–22, was a Marxism that had become a deterministic, evolutionary, materialist philosophy which was itself not revolutionary. Even more, in his desire to use Marxist sociology, he wanted, above all, to avoid the reduction to sociology, the sociologization of the realms of the absolute spirit. Far more was at stake than is at first apparent—in fact nothing less than Lukács's fundamental theoretical project: the unity within the heterogeneity of his early development.

It is quite remarkable how the same criticism of historical materialism (and of Marx) appears and reappears in Lukács's works from 1910 to 1922: in 1910 in a Hungarian essay on the method of literary history that he called in a letter a self-conscious confrontation with historical materialism;[19] in his *Heidelberg Philosophy of Art* of 1912;[20] in the Croce review; in an obituary article on Simmel in 1918;[21] and in one of his first and finest articles as a Marxist, "The Change of Function of Historical Materialism" (July 1919), that was reproduced in an altered form in *History and Class Consciousness* (1923). The point is repeatedly made that historical materialism as a sociology of culture is an epoch-making method for the study of ideologies (objective spirit), that it has important uses for the study of the *sociological* conditions of the possibility and realizability of works of art ("absolute spirit"), but that it degenerates into an unacceptable, metaphysical philosophy of history as soon as one attempts to use it to derive, reduce, or functionalize either the great forms of art or the creative process itself.

The method, even at its best, has therefore only a negative role to play concerning the young Lukács's two major questions: (1) Can life itself be formed; how is this (culture) possible? (2) Works of art exist; how are they possible? Instead of providing answers, sociologism or economic reductionism does away with the questions themselves by eliminating precisely the autonomous element that makes art, art and culture, culture. Even the negative role of the sociology of culture, which could indeed yield the answer that neither art nor culture is sociologically possible in some epochs, presupposes an a priori determination of the concepts of art and culture. The determination of the a priori conditions of the possibility of art was the task of the two unfinished, fragmentary "systematic" projects of the Heidelberg period: the *Philosophy of Art* (1912–14) and the *Aesthetics* (1916–17). While these works also touch upon the concept of culture that was ultimately both more important and more precarious for Lukács, the determination of its theoretical conditions of possibility was left to a projected work on the philosophy of history, the greatest surviving part of which was the *Theory of the Novel* (1914–15).

The watershed between these works was the world war. It was to produce a turning away from aesthetics and was to allow a temporary return only in terms of a framework that at all costs prohibited an aestheticization of life, that is, any kind of "resolution" of the antinomies of everyday life in artistic utopias. To be sure, the *Philosophy of Art* of the prewar years already sharply distinguished between everyday life (here called *Erlebniswirklichkeit,* "world of experience") and the "utopian reality" of art. The "world of experience" is fragmented, solipsistic ("a prison of individuality"), without communication and community, without the guidance of norms and meanings; it is full with unrealized longings, unfulfilled wishes and desires. The "world of experience" is the mere empirical, ordinary life of *The Soul and the Forms;* it is the experiential reality of "alienation," the "tragedy of culture," the "iron cage."[22] It is "philosophy of life" without the hope of intuitive understanding.

In the *Philosophy of Art,* the concept of *Erlebniswirklichkeit* treats alienation in the manner of Simmel, as an ontological given.[23] Thus, the amazing conclusion and answer to Lukács's first key question (amazing given Lukács's sociology of culture) is that culture is ontologically impossible. But the first question is eliminated only to pose a second: "Works of art exist. How are they possible?"[24] Works of art express a utopian reality. We quote a striking statement of this from the unpublished 1913 "Lecture on Painting," theoretically under the aegis of the *Philosophy of Art:* "The work means that there is a world completely harmonious, closed in itself, a totality of happiness. This world is a kind of utopia wherein everything corresponds to a reality we long for and desire. . . ."[25] The utopian reality of the art work, according to the *Philosophy of Art,* embodies the highest possible closeness of creative subject and created object without abolishing their distinction.[26] It recognizes, abolishes, and redeems in new meaning a determined element of non-sense in the world.[27] It is a harmonious totality that excludes disharmony and fragmentation; it unites being in time (historicity) and timeless eternal form. In short, the work of art is the created utopia of nonalienation, in every way opposed to the ontological alienation of experiential reality.

Yet perhaps it is not opposed in *every* way. To continue the quotation from the "Lecture on Painting": "Every art corresponds to some kind of need, some kind of deep suffering of humanity, this human suffering being brought out by objectivity, by a world that is not empirically adequate either to itself ["its concept"] or to us, a world to which another can be juxtaposed, one that is adequate to itself with respect to precisely these needs."[28] In other words, the utopian reality of art is the utopia of empirical reality itself; it is *its* utopian reality.[29] In a sense, then, experiential reality contains some of the elements of utopia but in a confused, fragmented, still meaningless way.[30] The crystallization of the artistic utopia, though always presented in a Kierkegaardian and anti-Hegelian fashion as a leap, is nonetheless also activated by empirical need, suffering, longing, desire and is in this sense a "continuation of concrete joys and suffering caused by concrete reality."[31] Finally, the realization of a genuine form of art always fulfills, overcomes, and redeems the distance between reality and its utopia.[32]

To avoid misunderstanding, two points must be raised immediately. The work of art does not reestablish the absent communication of everyday life, but only raises what Lukács considered the necessary empirical misunderstanding of everyday life to a normative, constitutive misunderstanding inherent in all reception of art.[33] But it is also undeniable that the misunderstanding inherent in art involves a transmission of emotional-experiential intensity and the normative posture itself. Even misunderstanding presupposes something in common (carried by the work object, of course) to misunderstand.[34] Nevertheless, the consequence is still clear: art lacks the power to promote the solidarity and community of all individuals.[35]

The second point is just as crucial. The artistic utopia does not in any way redeem the empirical person of either creator or receptor. The tragedy and the alienation of the artist, to whom his own work must become a foreign, alienated entity, is a constituent condition of art: "My works are nearer heaven but I sit here."[36] Lukács quotes Browning, after saying that artists necessarily experience the "eternal human condition" of alienation in the deepest possible manner since they remain "unredeemed," "speechless, and expressionless" in spite of the deep perfection and experience that they give to their works. No one in everyday life is therefore redeemed by the utopia of art; the redemption is an immanent, internal, closed affair of the work. On the other hand, the utopian longing of experiential reality is not fulfilled anywhere except in works of art. Paradoxically, this depiction of the utopia of art can just as easily be taken as the resigned and pessimistic evaluation of the absence of utopia and of potentially dynamic meaning, creativity, and so on, in empirical life—according to the *Philosophy of Art,* in *empirical life as such.* All art becomes, then, a symbol of the "tragedy of culture" or even the tragic nonexistence of culture.

The ontologizing of alienation was not consistent with the young Lukács's defense of subjectivity *and* culture. And ultimately, this position, too, turned out to be only that of an *essay,* even if the formal context was that of an elaborate sytematic philosophy (that indeed never surpassed the state of fragmentariness). There were two important factors that projected Lukács beyond this position: the developing perception that works of art themselves were indifferent to their possible and even probable use, aestheticizing a bad reality; *and* the development of his own ethical rebellion against the existing, historical reality that he was soon to characterize as "the age of completed sinfulness' (*vollendete Sündhaftigkeit*). We know from his letters and recorded conversations that he came to hate the "Luciferian" power of art, the power to make unbearable conditions bearable *without* changing them.

His friend Béla Balázs recorded the following in his diary in 1914: "Gyuri's [Lukács's] great new philosophy: Messianism. The homogeneous world as the goal of salvation. *Art is Lucifer's making things better!* seeing the world as homogeneous before the process of becoming so. The immorality of art. Gyuri's great switch to ethics."[37] The same idea appears in a Balázs diary entry of December 1915. And in 1916 Lukács wrote that artistic perfection itself only deepens the guilt of the artist if he has contributed to the "nonappearance of the messiah."[38] Lukács's meaning becomes clear from a letter to the German playwright Paul Ernst, a friend with whom he was about to break as a result of the latter's support of the German war effort.[39] In this very context, Lukács violently attacks all spiritual and intellectual forms—whose *power* he recognizes—that would surround the state and its physical power with a metaphysical halo. The warning is to Paul Ernst, the artist. But the eternal a priori objectifications of the soul (art, philosophy, and religion) are themselves characterized as inauthentic if brought into relation with political power. In his coming battle with the power of the state, Lukács "switches to ethics" because the philosophical weapons against the state are ethical rather than aesthetic. The occasion for this switch was, of course, the war, which would gradually and finally politicize Lukács's vision.

CHAPTER

5

The German War and the Russian Idea[1]

As LUKÁCS'S CORRESPONDENCE with Paul Ernst makes clear, he hated the war and the very phenomenon of states.[2] He saw the war as capitalist alienation raised to the level of its own concept.[3] In 1916 Ernst wrote an imaginary dialogue, which is probably an accurate picture of Lukács's attitudes. The speaker is Lukács:

> As the contemporary economy has replaced the independent, individual worker by the machine and by organized groups of workers, leading to the disappearance of the value of work for the personality, so, too, contemporary war juxtaposes not men but machines and servants of machines. From these servants one will demand more performance than from earlier warriors; this will be possible only through the subordination of personality to performance in all essentials. The result of the war will be on the one hand a further development of the capitalist economy, on the other, the emergence of a socialism of officials (*Beamtensozialismus*). . . .[4]

For perhaps obvious reasons, this contemporary document is more radical and more prophetic than Lukács's own, much later (1962), and now well-known recollection which is also worth citing.[5] "Who will save us from Western civilization?" he remembers himself asking at the end of a train of thought that gladly assented to the probable destruction of the states of the Romanovs and the Hohenzollerns. In Lukács's own context, of course, the war was a "German war," supported by the very German intellectuals with whom he once shared part or all of his cultural critique of the existing, capitalist world.[6] His answer to the war and to the expected result was conceived in terms of an uneasy combination of a utopia drawn from his work on Dostoevski and an activist, revolutionary ethics, postulating the possibility of total world transformation, derived from Fichte. That this project could ultimately take the shape of a leap to Marx and the Communist Party was, however, dependent on the emergence of a historical challenge that apparently gave flesh to both of these strands of Lukács's thought.

The justly famous *Theory of the Novel,* the representative document of this transition, poses the problem of "beyond this world" on the level of philosophy of history. Subtitled, "An Historical-Philosophical Essay on the Forms of the Great Epics," the term *essay* (*Versuch*) should not mislead us (as it has misled several Lukács interpreters): there is no question of a deliberate continuation of his earlier essayistic philosophy in the guise of literary criticism. In a text of 1918, he would insist that he was not a critic because he was interested "only in the axiology and philosophy of history of works, not in the works themselves."[7] In 1916 given this interest *and* the claim of his theory of literature that "for the epic (all epic forms), the world at any given moment is an ultimate principle . . . empirical at its deepest, most decisive, all-determining transcendental base," he had at hand intimately familiar themes and materials that would enable him to unfold a philosophy of history: the internal structure of Greek epic and bourgeois epic (the novel); the relations of the two epic forms to one another and to their worlds; and the transition from ancient epic to the novel.[8]

Lukács's total picture of Greece is a construct. To interpret and evaluate the present, he proposes a regulative principle, a formulation of the "human essence." When measured in terms of this principle, the present is found wanting. Furthermore, the complete harmony, the perfect integration, the "idealization of the unmediated communal organic and homogeneous world" are presented only on an ideal level. But there is also a historical dimension to the use of the Greek world in Lukács's analysis: any return to the supposedly "golden age" is strictly excluded. The transition between golden age and alienation is recognized, and some aspects of the golden age are evaluated negatively. Because of this factor, Lukács's notion of "human essence" as a not yet unfolded potentiality of human history, cannot be and is not drawn from ancient Greece alone. Another construct, this time purely utopian, drawn from a freely interpreted Dostoevski serves as a second regulative principle of the analysis, a regulative principle integrating a moment of freedom that (contrary to the myth of the golden age) seeks to find its own possibility but cannot do so concretely within the domain of art.[9] Thus, Lukács's philosophy of history, the body of which is a developed form of his earlier critique of alienation, minus sociological specificity, is enveloped in two regulative principles, one founded in part historically, the other purely utopian.

According to Lukács, *all* epic forms deal with empirical, historical reality. Furthermore—and here Lukács moves decisively beyond *The Soul and the Forms*—their subjects (heroes but also the artist-creator) are empirical men, empirical egos who can never be the creators of intensive totalities.[10] In the epic, the object world has primacy. For this reason "the ancient epic and the novel, these two major objectifications of great literature, differ from one another not by their author's fundamental intentions but by the given historical-philosophical realities with which their authors were confronted."[11] And now the way is open (as it never was in the essayistic philosophy) to the fusion of the theory of literature (that is, of epic forms) and the philosophy of history. To understand the relationship of the great epic forms, their historical grounds and the transition between them must be understood. This understanding relies in part on the internal evidence of epic creations. According to Lukács, the ancient epic (*Epopöe*) was the form of "totalized cultures" (*geschlossene Kulturen*). "The closedness and integration of Greek culture, in his analysis, implies the harmonious relationship of self and world, of creator and created, of essence and life, and the metaphysical totality, unity, and homogeneity of the spheres."[12]

The "closedness," ("the homogeneity," "the self-evidence") of this world is based on the intuitive certainty, evidence, and "passive, visionary acceptance" of transcendental archetypes (values) which turn out to be supported and maintained in the relationships of individual to individual in communities (love, the family, the polis) that are incorporated in the very substance of human units that are not yet free or individual. The destiny of the epic, therefore, is never personal but the destiny of a community: human fates have significance only within a "great organic life complex"—a nation or family.[13] Lukács's analysis here obviously combines the representation of natural, organic communities and the methodological idealization of these communities as one of the paradigms of nonalienation. Yet it is clear from Lukács's subsequent analysis that this dimension of nonalienation rests on a completely unfree relationship of the individual to the community and on the underdevelopment of individuals, the restricted unfolding of human potentialities—even if the artistic products of this period are aesthetically preferred to those of our own.[14]

Modern man's development has projected him beyond the closed world of the Greeks. The process and the price of development is presented by the Lukács of *Theory of the Novel* in a manner that seems to be completely analogous to Simmel's "tragedy of culture." According to Lukács, man has invented the productivity of the spirit and the creation of forms and thereby discovered individuality and an infinitely rich world. But as a direct result he has had to surrender completeness of truth and concreteness of totality; he has been forced to discover deep gulfs between theory and praxis, creator and created, self and world.[15] In this analysis, the concrete sociological presentation of the transition to the modern world found in Lukács's *Dramahistory*—and which is definitely required in that context—is absent. The step into the world of alienation is conceived not on class lines, but as a function of the productivity of the spirit. As in the *Philosophy of Art,* so in everyday empirical life (the domain of the novel): objectification once again equals alienation pure and simple. Nevertheless, Lukács has already begun here a forward movement vis-à-vis the philosophy of art because this situation is characterized, however abstractly, as historical.

Taking a step forward, Lukács synthesizes in part the dialectic of the problematic individual described in *The Soul and the Forms* with the historical-cultural ground (again, minus the sociological specificity) of the *Dramahistory*. Furthermore, there is no question of Lukács's ethical acceptance of the results of his synthesis. He makes abundantly clear that we cannot return to the world of the Greeks. At the same time, as in all his works, he is quite unwilling (unlike Simmel) to submit to the consequences of a linearly conceived tragedy of culture. In the context of the novel, the most characteristic art form of the age of alienation, Lukács generates a highly sophisticated discussion both of the phenomena of alienation and of motifs that point beyond alienation.

According to Lukács, the novel is abstract, that is, the abstract sum of unmediated, opposed, one-sided elements: the nostalgia for utopia and the prison of impenetrable social forms.[16] Every character of each novel immediately experiences this abstract dualism. The hero of the novel is a lonely, isolated, problematic man who experiences "transcendental homelessness" in a fragmented, contingent world. Transcendental homelessness is both a mark of maturity (the loss of naive faith in the old archetypes) and of the loss of substantial ties to other individuals and the world. As a consequence, the objective world is emptied of meaning and value. This objective world, in itself a human product, is no longer that for atomized, lonely unsubstantial individuals; it is for them a world of petrified (reified) conventions, "a second nature." The emergence of a second nature is the key to the alienation and deactivation of individuals in general; even the alienation (in its sentimental, contemplative, or manipulative forms) from the "first nature" is a "projection of man's experience of his self-made environment as a prison instead of a parental home."[17] The second nature is less controllable and manipulable: only a "metaphysical reawakening of souls" can overcome its stark necessities; anything less would simply strengthen the iron cage. However (and irrespective of the unlikelihood of such reawakening), it is specifically the historically emergent reification of social relationships that, in Lukács's analysis, leaves atomized, lonely individuals in a stark, unmediated relationship vis-à-vis both alienated natures.

According to Lukács, the hero of the novel (the modern individual) is the product of estrangement from the outside world; or rather "the contingent world and the problematic individual are realities which mutually determine one another."[18] The isolation of problematic man leaves his values without any intersubjective validation; they become mere ideals that cannot be realized in any way, that cannot affect the contingency of the world at all. Individuality, in this context, retreats into mere interiority, the ideal into pure negativity, and the world is rigidly divided into the "reality that is" and the "ideal that ought to be."

Thus, Lukács (utilizing a Hegelian dialectical analysis of subject and object) repeats Weber's historical derivation of the neo-Kantian theory of the two worlds of "is" and "ought" via the concept of the tragedy of culture.[19] Yet within the necessarily biographical form of the novel, according to Lukács, individuals *do* undertake self-formation and self-enlightenment (an "adventure of interiority"). But they cannot go beyond a clear recognition of the problem, a recognition that does not transcend the gulf between "ought" and "is." The ideal is now powerless vis-à-vis the interior of the individual: "dull captivity" and "clear self-recognition" are hardly the same. But perhaps clear self-recognition, when it can alter nothing, is all the more tragic. However, the biographical self-formative adventure of interiority is not as futile as it first seems because it is connected to the deepest ethical intentions of the creator of the novel, intentions that can be realized within the novel as visionary utopias.

The novel—in Lukács's depiction, "the representative form of our age" whose "structural categories constitutively coincide with the world as it is today"—reveals some motifs that point (or strive to point) beyond this world.[20] It is the first artistic form in which an ethical intention is visible and structurally operative in the creation of every detail.[21] But as the *Philosophy of Art* showed, all processes of artistic creation have a dual teleology: one stems from the intensity of the creator's experience, the other from the immanent, closed work itself. The intensity of the ethical experience of problematic subjectivity incorporated in the novel as a work of art reveals a similar duality. Lukács conceptualizes this duality in terms of a subjectivity that seeks to recognize and realize itself through opposing all alien "power complexes" and a subjectivity that recognizes the subject-object dualism but is forced to permit "the duality of the world to subsist," to consent to its own self-abolition in an ironical "distancing" from the original striving of subjectivity.[22] The ethic of creative subjectivity is thus forced to submit to an ethical self-correction that is determined by the work's content.

But this self-correction does not represent an unambiguous victory of reality over the ethical subject. The struggle against reality may be profoundly hopeless, but so is any intention to abandon the struggle.[23] Or as Márkus has put it: "not only alienation, but the active struggle against it is also a metaphysical necessity."[24] The victory of reality, from the subject's point of view, can never be a final one: "it will always be challenged by new rebellions of the idea." Furthermore, "second nature" owes its victory not to its own crude power, but to the internal disharmony and fragmentation of the subject seeking to overcome it. Thus, the fate of ethical rebellion against alienation hinges on the internal crisis of the "subjective factor."

Readers of *History and Class Consciousness* will undoubtedly recognize this notion and will not be at all surprised that, for Lukács, the crisis of subjectivity cannot be transcended *within* the novel. Nevertheless, novels incorporate the striving toward the self-realization of substantial subjectivity, and this dimension is not necessarily absent from them. The utopian dimension of some great novels is the one (and only) possible realization of the ethic of subjectivity in them so that the immanence of the work does not immediately destroy this subjectivity. But the "utopian, visionary reality" of the work cannot be pushed toward a full realization of subject-object identity; or rather, as in all art-works, the necessary distance between creative subject and the subject-object identity of the work cannot be abolished.

Thus, the Fichtean ethics of striving and utopia remain two different and unreconciled dimensions of *The Theory of the Novel.* Elsewhere Lukács clearly indicated the decisive difference between striving against the fetters of the soul and the creation of a new, utopian conception of life itself.[25] In all his writings of 1914–17, Lukács seems in the end clearly to prefer the latter, because ethical striving preserves dualism and second nature in its very structure. Nevertheless, he is not able to find novelistic utopias completely purged of the ethics of rebellion; only Dostoevski's utopias are so distinguished, but (and consequently) he "wrote no novels."

The most important utopia depicted in *The Theory of the Novel* is in Goethe's *Wilhelm Meister,* a utopia that is similar in its essential content to other humanistic utopian conceptions of the nineteenth century: Schiller's, Fourier's, and even Marx's 1844 concept of communism. Lukács undertakes a presentation and critique of this vision. In his view, Goethe offered in *Wilhelm Meister's Apprenticeship* a paradigm of a social, communal world created by free individuals. This world objectified Goethe's belief that through "hard struggles, dangerous adventures," and, most important, through a process of self-education, previously lonely and problematic individuals could succeed in developing qualities "which could never blossom without the active intervention of other men and circumstances."[26] According to Lukács, Goethe postulated communication and community—not the natural solidarity of ancient kinship or the mystical experience of community based on sudden illuminations—as the union of individuals undergoing a self-education, or *Bildungsprozess,* that freely achieved the substantality of communal, social ties in each previously lonely, isolated, and solipsistic human being. Humanism, the ideal of a democratic humanity, underlies the whole approach of Goethe's *Bildungsroman.*

And that is the rub. According to Lukács, Goethe's novel is not (or not yet) under the rubric of "transcendental homelessness"; its hero maintains "a tenuous, but not yet severed" link with the transcendental realm of values, presumably through the value of humanity. It seems to be Lukács's belief that the development of the bourgeois world is increasingly toward transcendental homelessness and the total isolation of individuals, and that Goethe's novel reveals only one intermediate and incomplete stage in this process. In Goethe's depiction, the social world ("objective spirit") is shown to be "a world of convention, which is partially open to penetration by living meaning."[27] Lukács is quite willing to defend the Goethe of *Wilhelm Meister* against the scornful attack of Novalis that presupposed a panpoetic, purely aesthetic utopia. But he feels that Goethe's synthesis cannot be protected from *second nature,* that is, a social reality that is increasingly not substantial enough to support the social action required to create a *social* utopia.[28]

Lukács has no trouble deriding the shallow class bases (nobility or nobility of the soul) that Goethe calls upon to support his conception. Furthermore, he argues, objective social development may sustain the drive to replace historically given social structures but not social structures generally. The identification of objectification and alienation, the hatred for the institutions of the objective spirit, and the disregard for the incremental liberation implied by the bourgeois era begins to play havoc with Lukács's thought. The rejection of the *Wilhelm Meister* utopia and the transition to an entirely different mode of utopian thought hardly receives adequate justification. Probably the closeness of the *Wilhelm Meister* utopia to the ideals of Western humanism and Marxist social democracy made it impossible for Lukács to give this alternative serious consideration in the "age of completed sinfulness," in the period of the betrayal of social democracy. He never completely forgot the possibility of proletarian revolution, but in 1914–15 his rejection of its possibility must have been stronger than ever. The notable absence of a stress on classes (from whom nothing can be hoped) in *The Theory of the Novel* can plausibly be traced to this rejection. So can the transition from Goethe's vision to Dostoevski's utopia of souls.

In the absence of social mediations, Goethe's *Wilhelm Meister* is, according to Lukács, an ideal, ethically founded polemic against the existing social world, a polemic that preserves the dualistic fragmentation of the world in its very structure. In his view, "the world of West European culture is so deeply rooted in the inescapability of its constituent structure that it can never adopt any attitude toward [its dualities] other than a polemical one."[29] The West, he felt, could overcome institutional heteronomy only in institutional form; thus, Lukács turned to Russia. As we have noted, he had for some years been keenly interested in both Russian literature and the revolutionary, social ethics of some of the Social Revolutionaries.[30] The intention of *The Theory of the Novel* was "to disclose the soil from which Dostoevski—that harbinger of the new man, that portrayer of a new community—emerged and which he transcended."[31] In this context (and not from the literary-artistic point of view) even Tolstoy—shifting between an uncritical nature-mysticism and a few genuine insights—is part of the soil, that is, the world, of the novel. At the same time a treatment of Dostoevski, who belongs to a new world, does not, according to Lukács, belong to the theory of the novel, the form of the age of "completed sinfulness." The possibility—concrete or mere hope—of this new world, "remote from any struggle against what actually exists," cannot be investigated in the context of the novel.[32] Within *The Theory of the Novel* this is all that we learn of Lukács's Dostoevski utopia, in spite of its important structural and regulative role in the book.

The very same utopia was actually of far greater importance in Lukács's *oeuvre,* as we now know. From the published writings, especially "Aesthetic Culture" (1910), "The Poverty of Spirit" (1911), and several essays on the writer Béla Balázs (1912–18), only the barest outlines of an overall conception emerge. The Dostoevski utopia, the "Russian Idea," in these writings was the postulate or hope of an ideal community of *individuals* completely freed from all psychological and sociological fetters, able to read one another's souls as their own, transcending the dualism of subject and object—and, thereby, of subject and world. Fortunately, we are now able to go further, thanks to Ferenc Fehér's brilliant reconstruction, from manuscript materials, of Lukács's whole Dostoevski project.[33]

The planned work, of which *The Theory of the Novel* was to be only an introduction, was to involve far more than a book on Dostoevski. Envisioned was a world-historical confrontation between objective spirit (the state, the church, law, formal ethics, the German war, Western civilization) and soul (community, religion, morality, substantive ethics, the Russian Idea). The vision projected the radical supplanting of the first by the second. For Lukács, the triumph of the state in history, anticipated and facilitated by the church, amounted to a history of the deprivation of shapes of the spirit, a kind of negative phenomenology in Hegel's sense. The analysis implicated all ideologies of the state from clericalism to democracy to nationalism and all forms of institutional life from economics to law. Undoubtedly this was the most radical version of Lukács's critique of culture. And for this reason the projected utopian alternative was also the most uncompromising of his career. Within the terms of Lukács's analysis only the abolition of all institutional life amounted to anything more than the re-creation of the original problem in different settings. The state and the institution could be fought only with weapons that differed totally from those of the enemy.

This is the content of the Russian Idea. The state, based on alienation and hierarchy, is confronted with an idea of community based on solidarity and fraternity: law and the formal ethics of duty, with a new substantive ethics based on self-sacrifice. The utopian ideal of "goodness" is reaffirmed, but it now has a collectivistic rather than aristocratic foundation. The latter shift is a result of a direct influence of the Russian Social Revolutionary terrorists on Lukács. So is his emphasis on the sacrifice of the soul, even in crimes of violence, for the sake of the soul—for the sake of the realization of the Russian Idea.

We cannot concern ourselves here with a detailed presentation or critique of the confrontation between objective spirit and Russian

Idea. Obviously, it should be pointed out that a society without institutions as well as the ethics of self-sacrifice are both quite compatible with the legitimation of state power. We can work only within the actual terms of Lukács's own thought, but even within this more narrow context, the excess of utopia inherent in the Russian Idea would take its toll. Already in *The Theory of the Novel,* Lukács had been forced to reject all actual striving, all active polemics against existing institutions because these activities themselves would have constituted participation in institutional structures. Utopia in such a context is completely removed from any possible version of this world—and in Lukács's own terms is *also* guilty of wordly complicity.

The very structure of the utopia makes the same conclusion almost inevitable. Everything hinges on the complete identity of subject and object, subject and other. This identity cannot be generated from within the world of experience; even romantic love, moving beyond individuality, breaking the walls between self and other (and self and world), had to end in renunciation, though a renunciation that pointed beyond itself, beyond the conventions that made full unity and identity of subject and object impossible.[34] This "beyond" is at various times conceptualized as mystical love and as religious atheism, but always as a community of completely liberated men for whom the higher world of the soul is the only reality, men whose souls have widened to a cosmos that substantially includes the other, all such others.[35] In other words, Lukács's Dostoevski utopia radically abolishes all sociological and institutional perspectives: "on the level of soul-reality all the fetters that bind the soul to social situation, class, origin, etc., fall away and are replaced by new, concrete ties from soul to soul."[36] The alternative that flows from the utopia of a community without social-political institutions is this: either resignation in the face of a metaphysically inevitable split between "ought" and "is," or the affirmation and acceptance of a social movement that is somehow not incorporated in institutions but in the ethical, religious parameters flowing from the Russian Idea.[37]

The Dostoevski project indeed returned to the problem of socialism, and we have Paul Ernst's 1917 testimony to the effect that Lukács at times considered the October Revolution the realization of the Russian Idea of community and solidarity that he saw (in the manner of the terrorists) deeply embedded in the culture of the Russian people.[38] Nevertheless, his verdict on socialist revolution was still not final. In 1917–18 he could write: "The ideology of the proletariat is today *still* so abstract that they are not able—aside from the military weapons of class struggle—to provide a real ethic that would affect all expressions of life."[39] In this context, the (temporary) rejection of the socialist alternative drove Lukács to a restatement of the Dostoevski utopia in which "social ties are no longer constitutive." Of course, one might continue to blame the rejection of socialism here, too, on the experience of social democracy in the war. But the expression "military weapons of class struggle" points to the Bolshevik alternative. And this, too, is for the moment rejected because a movement inspired not by *ethics* but by the political goals of institutional power cannot, in Lukács's conception, point beyond the world of objective spirit.

But the formulation itself, as we have seen, reveals a step forward. Lukács is apparently able to conceive an ethic that could "affect all expressions of life." Life could then be formed. Ethics no longer necessarily excludes realization in the world. The second great unfinished Heidelberg manuscript, the *Aesthetics* (1916–17), in fact establishes the possibility of culture, in spite of its deep internal relationship with aspects of the *Philosophy of Art*. We rely on György Márkus's impressive reconstruction of the overall thesis.[40] The new in Lukács's approach was not in the domain of the philosophy of art. By denying, however, that art is the utopia *of* experiential reality, other utopian possibilities of experiential reality are in principle rehabilitated. Everyday life is no longer seen as chaos, solipsism, irrationality, but as a dogmatic, uncritical, passively receptive attitude toward already formed materials, objectifications. Everyday life remains alienated, but now the objectifications (he calls them subjectifications) hide new dynamic possibilities.[41] The concept of "subjectification" reveals an impetus toward the reconsideration of the subject-object problem in all the spheres (everyday life, history) which materially carry the results of creative activity as such. If implicit, dormant, embodied meanings exist outside art, the possibility also exists that they can be meaningful for us. In other words, *culture*, a *new* culture, a new form of everyday life itself, is possible. This step allowed Lukács to reconceptualize his notion of politics as well.[42]

The turn to politics, to the politics of "ethical idealism," is documented by a single, important text—the summary of Lukács's contribution to a 1918 debate.[43] This lecture posits a further purification of the aesthetic sphere, including it in the realm of the contemplative, and an explicit inclusion of politics (for the first time) in the sphere of the practical. This great if only partial step into the Aristotelian-Kantian tradition implies a refusal of the separation between the ethics of the individual and the politics of the community. According to Lukács's definition, the practical spheres, instead of excluding objectivity (as in the most formal versions of Kantian ethics), intend to change their object. The inclusion of politics in the realm of the practical implicitly draws the objectifications of the objective spirit (institutions) into the problematic of self-transformation. While ethics intends direct self-transformation, politics intends to create or change the institutional context for self-transformation.

Nevertheless, Lukács tries to maintain the separation of ethics and politics by postulating an ethical *action directe,* a self-transformation independent of the whole institutional question. As we will see, he preferred this alternative in principle, yet he could not adhere to it, given his concrete interest in outlining a progressive and revolutionary politics. According to Lukács, the structure of both practical spheres requires that ethics (self-creation and self-transformation) take primacy, that politics and institutions be *instruments* of ethics, not values in themselves. Yet politics has an important function, namely, to overcome the resistance of the externality of the second nature that tends to demolish the project of social self-education. At the same time (and here lies Lukács's continuity with his early doubts), politics can be objectified only in institutions which become part of second nature as soon as they are considered values in themselves, that is, as soon as politics becomes autonomous. According to Lukács, even progressive movements—he mentions social democracy explicitly—become conservative when their institutions become ends in themselves. On the other hand, a Kantian or Fichtean primacy of ethics in politics guarantees a constant revolutionary thrust against *all* institutions (even revolutionary institutions), a "permanent revolution" aiming at the concrete, empirical realization of the categorical imperative forbidding the instrumentalization of men.

Clearly, Lukács took the necessary step that finally pointed beyond the ontologization of the condition of the revolutionary without a revolution. Instead of aiming at a utopia without any social institutions whatsoever he now expressed his continued hatred for all institutions differently. Ethics is still the goal, politics is only a means. But ethical direct action on its own is socially inconceivable. Politics therefore receives an important supplementary, preparatory function. Instead of a society without social institutions, Lukács now postulated the creation of new institutions which would eliminate the obstacles to a new culture of ethical freedom *and* would promote a permanent revolution against the institutions of revolutionary creation, because even these serve freedom only before their rigidification as *stable* institutions.

An entirely new potential relationship to Marxist theory is visible here. To transform institutions we must know their developmental tendencies and objective possibilities. The combination of a resigned Marxist sociology of cultural decline and an ethical posture based on the uneasy blending of Kant, Fichte, Kierkegaard, and Dostoevski yields everything but this. Equally, the reception of Marxism as dialectical theory did not have to mean the disappearance of Lukács's own hatred for institutional-political life—given the dreams of Marx, Engels, and even Lenin (for a moment) about the disappearance of politics along with the state. The path had been charted for the assimilation of dialectical theory to his own ethical-cultural objectives. But this path was not completely open until Marxism in all its dimensions as a world view was rehabilitated for Lukács by the revolutionary wave that finally engulfed him.

CHAPTER

6

Wager on Communism: Lukács in the Revolution

LATE IN 1915 Lukács returned to Budapest, where he was declared physically unfit for active military duty and assigned for a time to a post in the offices of the government's mail censor. He made several trips to Heidelberg, leaving it for good—physically if not intellectually—in 1917. The Weber circle had begun to break up during the first year of the war and on his initial return to Budapest, Lukács and several close Hungarian friends called together a new group which began to meet on Sundays in the apartment of the dramatist, Béla Balázs.[1] The group nicknamed itself *Szellemkék* ("little spirits"), referring to their trust in *Szellem* (*Geist,* spirit).

Only slightly less impressive than its Heidelberg forerunner, the Budapest *Szellemkék* group was a gathering of intellectuals, virtually all of whom soon emerged, if they had not already done so, as important figures in Central and Western European cultural life. In addition to Lukács and Balázs, the initial participants included the writer Anna Lesznai and several younger intellectuals, Béla Fogarasi, Karl Mannheim, and Arnold Hauser. In 1917 the little group organized itself into the Free School of the Cultural Sciences, a title which indicated its links to the German school of the *Gesiteswissenschaften* developed by Dilthey, Simmel, Windelband and Rickert. The Free School of the Cultural Sciences consisted of a lecture series which served as an ongoing forum for collaborative intellectual work. With the formation of the School the initial circle of associates expanded to include, among others, the composers, Béla Bartok and Zoltan Kodaly, the art historian, Friedrich Antal, the poet, Josef Révai and not least of all, Ervin Szabó. With the exception of Szabó, they were young intellectuals between their mid-20s and mid-30s in age; most but not all were Jews; all were from prosperous, urban middle and upper-middle class families.

Lukács was the dominant figure in the group, which concerned itself with analysis of the crisis of modern culture and the prospects of cultural renewal. The participants shared a philosophical hostility to materialism, positivism and relativism; in opposition to the fatal expansion of *Zivilisation* and *Gesellschaft* they sought to uphold a tradition and vision of authentic *Kultur* and *Gemeinschaft*. Dostoevski, Kierkegaard, Simmel, Kant, Hegel, Meister Eckhardt, Lask, Ernst, French Impressionism, Hungarian popular-folk culture, the German journal *Logos*, and its Russian counterpart of the same title (whose contributors included Nicholas Berdyaev and Vladimir Soloviev), stood among the Free School's past and contemporary kindred spirits.

The group defies clear-cut political categorization. Nearly all its associates believed, like Lukács, in an ethical or mystical utopian socialism which, while devoid of any and all practical elements, entailed an intellectually sweeping rejection of capitalism. And Erwin Szabó's occasional presence and lectures provided a substantial source of theoretical orientation in revolutionary Marxism. More basically, however, the Free School was simply and emphatically nonpolitical, more of a religious than a political group, as one of its members has recalled.[2] For this reason, but especially because of the group's rejection of materialism, the historian Zoltan Horvath places it in the right wing of the Hungarian intellectual opposition of the war years; to the right of the liberals and reform socialists around Oskar Jászi and the older Social Science Society, as well as of the younger bohemian-anarchist tendencies associated with the avant-garde literary journals, *A Tett* (*Action*) and *Ma* (*Today*), which began to appear in 1917.[3]

In this connection one of the signal features of the group was its self-consciously hermetic character, its principled refusal to recruit large numbers of affiliates or to disseminate its ideas to a wider audience.[4] This contrasts sharply with the Free School of the Social Sciences, set up by Jászi in 1906, which functioned as a center for workers' education. According to at least some of the members of the Free School of the Cultural Sciences, popularization contradicted the very principles of these sciences. The group was, in other words, a conscious vanguard of a regeneration of *Seele, Geist,* and *Kultur* which not only lacked a "mass base" but also carefully refused to find one.

A glimpse into Lukács's own outlook on the eve of his departure from the Free School and his entrance into the Communist movement is provided by his eulogy-essay on the occasion of Georg Simmel's death in September 1918.[5] Most significantly, this essay indicates that Lukács considered himself—and the very movement of thought—to be on the verge of a new and total theoretical synthesis which he, however, was unable to elaborate. Simmel, he notes, was the most important "transitional figure in the whole of modern philosophy." When Simmel first appeared on the scene, the state of philosophy was hopeless: the great tradition of classical German idealism appeared to have dissolved while the most important "outsiders of that period (Nietzsche, Hartmann) stood without roots or impact in a tidal wave of the most banal and soulless materialism and positivism." Simmel's greatness lay in his capacity to make the most minute and obscure phenomena of everyday life philosophically conscious.

He is, Lukács states, the "true philosopher of impressionism"; his work is the "conceptual formulation of the impressionist world view." Like every impressionism, however, Simmel's philosophy is transitional in its very essence, rejecting conclusions and final formulations on grounds of principle, rather than incapacity. His philosophical work, again like every great impressionist movement, is "nothing but a protest of Life against forms which have become occluded and thus incapable of imbibing the fullness of life." As such, his labors are transitional to a "new classicism" which will grasp the fullness of life in "firm and stringent, but all-encompassing forms." This, then, was where Lukács stood in what were to be the final weeks of the Free School of the Cultural Sciences.

The year in which the initial *Szellemkék* circle declared itself the Free School of the Cultural Sciences was also the year of the Bolshevik Revolution. The Free School's work proceeded virtually without taking notice of developments in Russia. Nor did its members play any role in the "October events" in Hungary in 1918, the fall of the Hapsburg crown, and the emergence of a bourgeois-democratic revolution which brought to power a coalition government under Count Kārolyi.[6] With revolutionary ferment seething not only across Europe but in their own city's streets, however, it became increasingly difficult even for intellectuals such as those in the Free School to remain entirely oblivious and detached. Lukács's name made its first appearance in a public-political context early in November 1918, when he and several friends from the Free School joined a large list of Hungarian intellectuals as signers of an open letter in support of Oskar Jászi's call for a "Free State-League of Nations" between Hungary and other democratic states.[7] Later that month, Lukács published his first political article in the pages of *Szabad Gondolat* (*Free Thought*), the journal of the revived, bourgeois-radical "Galileo circle." Under the title, "Bolshevism as a Moral Problem," he voiced his opposition to the imposition from above of a revolutionary regime by the Russian Bolsheviks.

Lukács's political career, then, began with what could be called a flirtation with democratic socialism. This phase, however, lasted roughly only a month. In late November–early December 1918, Lukács was approached by Béla Kun, the leading member of the Central Committee of the newly formed Communist Party of Hungary (CPH). In mid-December he joined the party. Of the inner circle of the Free School, only Fogarasi accompanied him while Révai, who was only an associate, joined the CPH independently. By January 1919 Lukács was an editorial associate of the party's theoretical organ, *Internationale;* a member of the staff of its Central Agitator School in Budapest; and a member of the Committee for Student and Working Youth Groups, which was a subcommittee of the Central Committee. When, in late February, the Karolyi government declared the CPH illegal and jailed the Kun Central Committee, Lukács became a member of the underground Second Central Committee.[8] At this time, Lukács wrote a brief letter to his close friend in Germany, Paul Ernst, a line from which reveals his understanding of the novelty *and* familiarity of his situation: "In view of all our discussions of politics, you will after all not be surprised that I am where I am, only that I am in so high a position."[9]

Others, however, were surprised. His close friends in the Free School met the news of his "conversion" with utter disbelief and so must have his German friends, associates, and readers.[10] In this regard, it is ironic that in 1918 Lukács's aesthetic studies received laudatory mention from Max Weber in his speech to students in Munich on "Science as a Vocation," which sought to separate science from "Politics as a Vocation"—a separation Lukács was shortly to overcome; and he received warm praise from Thomas Mann in the latter's cultural hymn to German nationalism and power, *Reflections of an Unpolitical Man.*[11] No less surprised by Lukács's entrance into the CPH were numerous of his new comrades. One of the party's leading functionaries, for example, has recalled his and others' impatience and disgust with what they considered the opaque and irrelevant metaphysical Marxism of Lukács, Révai, and Fogarasi.[12]

As Lukács himself noted, however, his leap into the Communist movement and Marxism was not as extraordinary as it first appeared to be. In broad terms and from the vantage point of recent revolutionary situations, for example, sudden and far-reaching personal-intellectual transformations of previously nonpolitical or variously conservative individuals into political-social revolutionaries are not unfamiliar. Moreover, there is a basic sense in which Lukács's pre-1919 thought as a whole, and its final, most hermetic phase in particular, virtually cried out for an entirely new type of thought and action. While it cannot be said that his transformation from idealist philosophy and cultural criticism to Marxism was simply a product of the inner logic of the development of his thought, and thus a necessity, it nevertheless remains true that—as Lukács himself as well as both critics and sympathizers of his Marxism have recognized—the fundamental continuity of his thought between the early years of the century to 1971 is its most distinguishing feature.

If, at the theoretical level, Lukács's transition to communism and Marxism is to be viewed, as Istvan Mészáros has recently emphasized, in terms of a dialectical *Aufhebung* and not a "radical break," the latter is the only possible term to apply to the existential dimensions of Lukács's move.[13] He suddenly and decisively rejected the comfortable, *haut bourgeois* intellectual world, which was the only world he had known since his youth and the one whose higher echelons he had reached before the age of thirty. In its place he chose the uncomfortable world of an embattled revolutionary party, embracing its risks and hardships and sharing them with men and women to whom not long before he might have denied the right to walk in the shadow of a Stefan George.

Finally in this connection, the theoretical and the existential dimensions of Lukács's transformation are, in fact, integrally linked through a series of basic elements. First among these is the radicalism of Lukács's cultural critique of capitalism. Further, there is little doubt that in the days or hours in which Lukács made his decision, he did so by glimpsing total, radical revolution as the concrete, social expression of the deepest impulses of his thought: the "dream of the whole man"; the supersession of alienation and the "tragedy of culture" (Simmel's term for the defeat of life and spirit at the hands of their own objectified products); the realization, at last, of a world in which man is "everywhere at home," of the "new world epoch" evoked at the close of *The Theory of the Novel.*

Moreover, there are specific and central motifs of Lukács's pre–1919 thought which not only shaped his Marxism in its long-range development but also had a more immediate bearing on his initial decision for radical revolution. Expressed in aesthetic and moral-philosophical rather than social-political terms, for example, his early work pushes at every point toward the realization of integral *action* which, if not capable of abolishing the alienated world, at least makes possible a momentary elevation above it in a unity of subject and object, knowledge and activity, values and their realization—as in the "gnostics of action" in "On the Poverty of Spirit" and the achievement of the whole man in "The Subject-Object Relation in Aesthetics." Similarly, the realization of authentic *community*—of collective culture and experience—is one of the deepest imperatives of his early work, even in its most elitist and individualistic moments.

With regard to the suddenness of his transformation, the concept of the "leap"—the radical decision in the name of absolute self-realization—was a vital philosophical and personal-psychological category for Lukács well before his own "wager" on Communism, and can on one level be viewed as having prepared the way.

For all these reasons and with the admitted advantage of hindsight, it is possible (though difficult) to imagine Lukács's continued abstention from the burgeoning revolutionary developments around him in 1918–19 on the ground that they remained utterly inadequate to the inner and truly spiritual needs of man. What is absolutely impossible to imagine is Lukács seriously and for any length of time opting for the Social Democratic or any other reform movement which did not proclaim as its goal the immediate, revolutionary transformation of "the whole of existing reality."

Lukács's essay, "Bolshevism as a Moral Problem," appears at first to contradict such a claim, arguing as it does against Bolshevism and for democratic socialism.[14] And since Lukács opted precisely for Bolshevism shortly after he wrote this essay, the essay seems to give his "leap" an irrational and arbitrary character. The actual picture is more complicated and more fascinating. On the one hand, the structure of the argument has much to do with his philosophical past. On the other hand, a few months later, he justified his choice of joining the CPH in "Tactics and Ethics" by many of the same arguments.[15] "Bolshevism as a Moral Problem" maintains that the central Marxist notion of the proletariat attaining general human liberation by realizing its own class interests (its own liberation) is constructed on the Hegelian model of the "Cunning of Reason." But without a suprahistorical subject guaranteeing a favorable outcome, at the moment of any political decision, the construct splits into "soulless empirical reality" and "utopian ethical will." Thus Lukács argues that Marxism is both a sociology involving class analysis and class conflict and a philosophy of history resting on the utopian postulate and ethical "ought" of a socialist world order. Indeed, he continues, the victory of the proletariat is the objective conclusion of the sociology, but the democratic socialist world order for which this is a precondition can only be the result of the moral will of the proletariat. All of Lukács's subsequent articles (until 1920) on communist morality include some form of this dichotomous search for the moral subject of the world transformation. In the article in question, Lukács decides against the Bolsheviks because he cannot yet convince himself that the democratic world order (and this is the first time he depicts the future as democratic) can be willed by nondemocratic means and that the "sudden heroism" of Bolshevism involves more self-sacrifice than patient democratic work. He admits that both alternatives entail great dangers, great "sins."

When, in December 1918, Lukács reversed his choice and joined the Communist Party, he did not abandon his criterion of self-sacrifice. "Tactics and Ethics," written presumably between January and March 1919 (the first piece of writing justifying his entrance into the Communist movement), argues that the essential criteria of socialist means are only the requirements of building the consciousness of the new world order. Thus, for a brief moment Lukács renounces the demand that the new "means" of revolutionary practice satisfy democratic criteria. On the other hand, he does not simply replace democracy with its abstract opposite; he turns instead to the dialectics of consciousness, that is, to Hegel (a turn Lukács did not complete until 1920). In his view, "means" that satisfy the criterion of building consciousness are hardly just "means": they are the gradual realization of ultimate ends. But in his view, as against the standard utilitarian Marxist position, the ethics of revolutionary acts cannot be similarly derived. That is, they cannot be derived from their potentially beneficial value to the overall economic and spiritual advancement of society. Rather, Lukács argues that ethics present the individual conscience with the imperative that one must act as if a change in the world's destiny hinges upon his action or inaction. In ethics, he insists, there is no neutrality; whoever decides not to decide to act must equally answer to his conscience for the inaction. Thus, the individual who chooses communism must assume the same individual responsibility for every human life lost in the revolutionary struggle as if he had taken every life. Simultaneously, however, everyone who chooses the other side—the defense of capitalism—must likewise assume individual responsibility for the annihilation caused by imperialist war and for future oppression of nations, classes, and peoples.

Yet, Lukács continues, ethics can neither resolve nor deny the "insurmountable, tragic conflicts of human destiny." On the contrary: ethical self-consciousness reveals that "there are situations—tragic situations—in which it is impossible to act without being guilty. But at the same time, it teaches us that, in cases where we must choose between two forms of being guilty, there is still a criterion for correct and false actions. This criterion is: sacrifice." Thus the individual, faced with two forms of guilt, chooses the correct action when he "sacrifices his less-significant self on the altar of higher ideas." When these ideas take the form of "a command of the world-historic situation, a philosophical-historical (*geschichtsphilosophische*) call,'' sacrifice is also the standard of judgment of collective action.

What, finally, of the question of ''individual acts of terror''? Here Lukács follows Ropshin, the Russian terrorist and novelist, in arguing that ''murder is not permitted; it is an unconditional and unpardonable sin; it 'ought' not to be committed, but it 'must' be committed.'' The acts of the revolutionary terrorist have no moral justification, but their ''finally moral nature'' lies in the fact that the terrorist ''not only sacrifices his life for his fellow beings, but also his purity, his morality, his soul. In other words, only the murderous acts of the man who, unshakably and without doubts, knows that under no circumstances is murder sanctionable, can be of a moral—tragically moral—nature.''

This passage provides the key link between Lukács's philosophical past and his transition to revolution and Marxism. In his early criticism of Kantian ethics, most notably in ''On the Poverty of Spirit,'' he had affirmed that, to keep one's hands clean in *this* world can be the greatest sin of all. Conversely, he believed that sin itself, involving the greatest personal sacrifice, can be the preparation of the individual for that ''goodness'' that was for Lukács a utopia of a new type of solidarity. As Ferenc Fehér shows in his reconstruction of Lukács's 1916 notebooks for the never-to-be-written book on Dostoevski, the meaning of ''goodness''—under the impact of the ''Russian Idea'' from Dostoevski to the messianic ideologies of self-sacrifice in populist terrorism—had moved from the aristocratically conceived ''soul community'' of ''On The Poverty of Spirit'' to a democratically reconceived community of human solidarity.[16]

As late as 1918, Lukács's ethics contained a central tension of several unresolved elements: individualism versus community; democratic versus aristocratic forms of solidarity; self-sacrifice versus terror; ethical activism (Fichte) versus a nonpolemical attitude toward the world of reification (Dostoevski). From this standpoint, the common elements between ''Bolshevism as a Moral Problem,'' which rejected Bolshevism, and ''Tactics and Ethics,'' which embraced it, are as important as the differences. In both, evidently, Lukács made a choice for a community he believed could embody a new type of solidarity: as he put it soon afterward, speaking of the moral basis of the new society, ''the mutual love and solidarity of all human beings."[17] In both he believed that the proletariat could become the vehicle for the realization of this community and had already incorporated some of its elements; in both, as well, he had opted for ethical activism, even revolutionary activism, maintaining that the individual criterion for action pointed to a new type of solidarity: self-sacrifice.

The decisive point of tension between the two essays seems to be situated in the difference between the Russian Idea and the Russian reality. The Bolsheviks appeared to satisfy the requirements of self-sacrifice and violence, but unlike the earlier Social Revolutionary terrorists, their methods and political actions did not anticipate the solidarity of the new world. In the frame of his own moral evolution, however, rejecting the Bolsheviks would have pushed Lukács into the camp of the Social Democrats, on whom he lost no love. Nor had he had anything but scorn for bourgeois legality. Embracing the Bolsheviks, on the other hand, entailed the risk of a new aristocratism, that of the elite party. The unfolding events in Hungary saved him from this consequence—for awhile.

"Tactics and Ethics," it should be noted, was written prior to the formation of the Socialist-Communist Hungarian Soviet Republic (March 21, 1919), although it was published as a pamphlet during the short-lived "dictatorship of the proletariat." In a note to the published edition Lukács indicated that the new, revolutionary order issued in a "change in the function of ethics." As a result, his arguments were of a primarily documentary interest, although we will see that the change pointed to a democratically interpreted ethics of creation and self-creation. The issue of the "Red Terror" was a major one during the several months of the revolutionary regime, although it was grossly inflated by the regime's enemies and employed as a legitimation for a far more extensive "White Terror." In connection with the "Red Terror," however, Lukács, who as Deputy Commissar of Public Education (or Culture) was not averse to methods of moral coercion in scientific, literary, and educational matters, also argued that the era of proletarian dictatorship entailed the elimination of executions and organized class terror by political police and revolutionary tribunals.[18] This is worth indicating in view of the numerous references to Lukács in conjunction with "Tactics and Ethics" and his role in the government as an alienated aesthete turned resentful and blood-thirsty executioner.[19]

With Marxism, Lukács argues in "Tactics and Ethics," the end goal of socialism is utopian in the sense that it can be realized only in the annihilation of the whole economic, legal, and social framework of existing capitalist society; but it differs radically from all other utopias in that the road to this end goal is not "an absorption of ideas which float outside and above this society." The Marxian theory of class struggle, which "in this connection completely follows the Hegelian conceptual scheme," transforms the end goal to be reached from a transcendent to an historically immanent goal: "the class struggle of the proletariat is the goal to be reached and simultaneously its realization." In other words, Marx is no longer the Fichtean he had been in the *Dramahistory,* although it is reasonably clear that Lukács himself would remain so in many respects. His own thought between 1919 and 1923 would remain antinomically suspended between a stress on the creative, revolutionary will derived from Fichte and a teleologically conceived theory of history drawn from Hegel.

Lukács's writings of his period of transition to Marx (late 1918 and early 1919) reveal a voluntaristic concern with the decisions of the subject (first of the individual, then of the class, and finally—after 1920—of the party), decisions that are gradually integrated within the context of "objective" historical possibilities. As his thought developed, he attempted to historicize the Kantian antinomy between objectivistic determinism (age of necessity) and voluntaristic subjectivism (age of freedom as introduced by a free act) without, however, being able (or perhaps wanting) to overcome the very antinomy that Hegel, Marx, and at times he himself as a young man desperately wanted to resolve. Indeed, the central meaning of *dialectic* must imply such a resolution.

Thus, at this juncture it is essential to turn to Lukács's understanding of the Marxian materialistic dialectic. As we have seen, already in his 1915 article on Croce—that is, even before he became a Marxist—Lukács had attacked the exaggerated claims of the objectivistic, deterministic "dialectic" of social democracy—the understanding of dialectics as the natural laws of motion of history and *all* reality, a version of dialectics that excluded human subjectivity. The first version of "What is Orthodox Marxism?"—written perhaps days before the declaration of the Hungarian Soviet Republic in March—states more strongly than ever its opposition to Kautsky's determinism and Bernstein's empiricism.[20] However, part of the article surprisingly reaffirms essential aspects of Engels's (and hence Kautsky's) version of the theory, and there is throughout a somewhat uncritical mixture of "dialectics of subject and object" and "objectivistic dialectics."[21]

Much of Lukács's early Marxist work is in a sense a commentary on the "Theses on Feuerbach"; here, too, the motto is: "The philosophers have only *interpreted* the world differently; the point is to *change* it." Consequently, after defining orthodoxy in Marxism as it relates only to method and not to dogmas, he identifies this method as the revolutionary dialectic. A theory can be revolutionary precisely to the degree that it ends the distinction between theory and practice, to the degree that it helps to bring about essential changes *in its object*.

Thus far, Lukács is merely drawing out the implications of the "Theses on Feuerbach" as they relate to the subject-object problem. But the next few steps actually have more to do with Engels. Lukács, like Engels, stresses those Marxian texts that are themselves plagued by a mechanical, objectivistic concept of dialectics. Referring to the end of *Das Kapital* I, Lukács argues that for Marx

> capitalism represents the negation of individual property, based on the individual's own work. The same capitalism brings about with the *necessity of a natural process* its own negation, the negation of the negation: the higher unity. [Emphasis added.]

Lukács, however, also had to do battle with Kautsky and, without being fully conscious of it, with Engels. In another article written at the same time, "The Problem of Intellectual Leadership and the 'Intellectual Workers'," he sought to modify the rigidity and blindness of capitalism's "natural laws" by the first version of his concept of class consciousness in the age of the bourgeoisie.[22] According to Lukács, Marx had anchored his conception of history's final goal by "appropriating unchanged the greatest legacy of Hegelian philosophy: the idea that *Geist* unfolds itself in a unified manner from complete unconsciousness to a clear coming-to-consciousness of itself" (*Sich-Bewusstwerden*). In this connection, Lukács announces the core of his critique of Marx's "orthodox" followers during the period of the Second International: failing to grasp the Hegelian conception of history, they viewed historical development as an automatic process, independent and qualitatively different from human consciousness. For the "vulgar Marxists" the difference between Hegel and Marx is fundamental: namely, a substitution of materialism for idealism. For Lukács these are "mere phrases." What is decisive in the Hegel-Marx relationship, he contends, is that Marx's critique of Hegel is a "modification" of Hegel: that is, "a radical deepening of the Hegelian standpoint: [Marx] sought and found, in the unified process of development of society, the consciousness that seeks itself."

That Lukács's own position was in part suspended within the movement between Hegel and Marx is made dramatically clear in his view of the relationship between Hegel's *Geist* and Marx's class consciousness. *Geist,* he asserts, departs from its unconsciousness and becomes conscious of itself in the Marxian concept of class consciousness—a statement which indicates that proletarian class consciousness is a manifestation of the "world spirit." In virtually the same breath, however, Lukács proclaims that Marx's concept of class consciousness is the self-consciousness of the "real moving force of history": class struggle. And this latter statement, for Lukács, embodies Marx's "modification" and "deepening" of Hegel, while it points in the direction in which Lukács was beginning to move.

But if the "vulgar Marxists" viewed the development of history as an automatic process, separate and different from human consciousness, does Lukács's own view as outlined above not imply that the development of history is a logically determined process of the movement of consciousness itself? His emphatic rejection of this possibility rests on two basic propositions. First, he maintains that, for Marx, in flat contradiction to the claims of his followers, consciousness is a real and constitutive, not an epiphenomenal component of historical development. Second, Lukács explicitly insists that the emergence of class consciousness is not an automatic or necessary development but—and here he employs a concept adopted from Weber's sociology—an "objective possibility."

In the form of immediate consciousness of class membership and of class interest conflict in capitalist society, the emergence of proletarian class consciousness is, in Lukács's view, a spontaneous process. There is, however, "one more decisive step" which cannot be spontaneous: the "coming to consciousness of the class consciousness of the proletariat" (*das Bewusstwerden des Klassenbewusstseins des Proletariats*). Beyond its immediate and spontaneous class consciousness, the proletariat must come to consciousness of "the world-historic process and its own world-historic mission of realizing the classless society." Thus, the "truly epochal significance" of Marx's social theory, Lukács asserts, is that it *is* the theoretical articulation of this final step in which the whole development of society is made conscious of itself in proletarian class consciousness. That is, Marxism is the knowledge that the "law-like character of social development, its complete independence from human consciousness, its similarity with the play of the blind forces of nature, is a mere appearance [*ein blosser Schein*] which can continue to exist only to the point at which these blind forces . . . are brought to consciousness."

But within this framework and in his writings through and including *History and Class Consciousness,* Lukács refused to grant that the "realm of freedom" could issue from history's logic or reason's cunning. It had to be willed freely. Moreover, the Marxian theory of history and its large-scale dialectic could demonstrate only the presence of a revolutionary *situation,* not the necessity of the revolutionary entrance into the realm of freedom. In this regard, Lukács in 1919 did not possess even the rudiments of a social theory that would enable him to answer the *facts* adduced by Bernstein and other Social Democrats to show the impossibility of such a transformation. For the moment, he adopted a highly voluntaristic attitude toward facts: decision precedes them. No facts in themselves, he insisted, would ever justify a revolutionary decision. When the overall interpretation of historical unity pointed to a revolutionary situation (as in 1919), one could say in the face of contrary facts: "so much the worse for the facts." What we have here is the emphatic primacy of ethics over theory and, thereby, the continuing tension within Lukács's thought between will and knowledge, freedom and necessity.

The two major theoretical essays written during the second half of the Soviet Republic, however, begin to indicate the steps Lukács would take toward working out this dilemma. His "Old Culture and New Culture" of June 1919 represents the summation and radicalization of his previous critiques of culture.[23] The heart of his view here is that while capitalism (to a greater extent than all previous epochs) embodies the domination of individuals and their relations by the economy, under communism the economy will be subjected to the conscious control of associated individuals. We have seen how, in Lukács's earlier efforts, the idea of a free creation of a new, absolute culture remained a tragically abstract dream, rarely connected to any social subject or process. "Old Culture and New Culture" resonates with the excitement of the breakthrough: the proletariat may lay the foundations for a totally new culture.

The vision was radical; indeed, in Lukács's own subsequent view it was mythological. Following the failure of the Hungarian Soviet Republic and the marked decline of revolutionary prospects in Western Europe, he would come to consider "Old Culture and New Culture" utopian. It was otherwise with the powerful thesis of "The Functional Change of Historical Materialism."[24] In the capitalist age, he maintains, historical materialism functions as a weapon in the class struggle, from which a certain dogmatism is inseparable. In the age of freedom, which Lukács believed to have begun with the Soviet Republic and the revolution in Russia, the function of historical materialism would be that of scientific research. The political locus of the change is the transitional period of the proletarian dictatorship; its theoretical locus is self-criticism, the application of historical materialism *to itself.* The result is that historical materialism turns out to be an ideology of the capitalist epoch, a function of the age in which the autonomous economy reduces everything to its laws. The truth of historical materialism is thus absolute within its own era but relative to that era. It cannot, therefore, be applied in any strict sense to precapitalist societies where the economy is not completely independent of ideological interference and where there exists a leisure class producing absolute culture. Nor can it be applied to the new "realm of freedom," where the economy, as he argues in "Old Culture and New Culture," would be dominated by an absolute culture produced by all individuals.

The literal red thread running through Lukács's 1919 reflections is the attempt to formulate a conception of relations between economics, politics, and culture in the deeply problematic "transitional period" between capitalism and communism. If, in retrospect, we can see that here, too, his efforts are packed with internal tensions and problems, we also must insist on their originality and often astonishing farsightedness. At the core of his perspective stands the lapidary phrase, "politics is merely instrumental; culture is the goal."[25] In "The Functional Change of Historical Materialism'' he contends that the very opening of the period of the proletarian dictatorship reverses the relation between economics and politics that had prevailed under capitalism. That is, it initiates a period of the primacy of politics, of political action over economic laws. Although formulated very differently, this position is essentially close to that of the contemporary policies, if not the theory, of Bolshevism.

But this is only a part of Lukács's position. For him the primacy of politics over economics cannot itself define and guide the ''period of transition''; it is only the means of reversing the relation between economics and culture. As he argues in ''Old Culture and New Culture,'' the very fulcrum of the transition to communism is a new, democratic, communist culture which, as a freely willed self-transformation of individuals, initiates the final abolition of commodity fetishism and the subordination of production to communally and rationally determined human needs. So, for example, while Lukács is not especially critical of the traditional Marxist view of the central role of state planning, he nevertheless rejects any inflation of state planning into the primary meaning of the transition to communism. The primacy of politics (here, planning) over economics may eventually guarantee the material welfare of the mass of individuals, but, according to Lukács, it cannot insure their self-determination. He is seeking, in other words, to integrate at the center of the ''transitional period'' tendencies that will nourish the Communist future within the present. And this anticipation of the future is for him precisely the increasing self-determination of the proletariat—its free moral will, in his terminology.

This view, as we shall soon see, was not easily concretized within the then-existing political realities. Nevertheless, Lukács's perspective was designed in part to solve the problem of grounding freedom in necessity. The reversal of relations between economics and politics prepared the way for the subordination of economy to a level of human freedom *higher* than that offered by politics, namely culture. But the existing political realities were not the only source of problems. The very manner in which he posed the concept of the primacy of the political was itself filled with internal contradictions, rich in both hopes and dangers.

The desperately precarious situation of the Hungarian Soviet

Republic constituted the terrain on which Lukács developed these ideas. We need not survey the story of its 133 days in existence nor that of Lukács's role as Deputy Commissar of Public Education, in which he confronted emerging problems quite concretely.[26] Central to our concerns, for the moment, is Lukács's theoretical insight into what was perhaps *the* fundamental crisis of the whole—and in Hungary very brief—experience of the transitional "proletarian dictatorship": the danger of consolidation into an end in itself. He addressed himself to this problem in the essay, "The Role of Morality in Communist Production," which was probably written in June 1919.[27] Its immediate purpose was to exhort Hungarian workers to intensify labor discipline and production. The result of Lukács's effort, however, was an astonishing text which critically and prophetically anticipated the subsequent Stalinization of the Russian Revolution, even as it expressed the theoretical concepts that enabled Lukács eventually to accommodate himself to Stalinism.

The aim of communism, he begins, is the construction of a society in which the "freedom of moral decision replaces the compulsion of law in the regulation of all activity." And this final aim must determine the means by which it is realized. The root cause of the crisis of commodity shortages and the price rise, whose effects are felt by every worker, is "the slackening of labor discipline and the decline in labor productivity." To extricate itself from this crisis of communist production, there are, according to Lukács, two possible paths open to the proletariat. On the one hand, every individual worker, recognizing that the situation depends on himself, can voluntarily strengthen his discipline and productivity. And, Lukács indicates, when the proletariat itself creates labor discipline, "when production in the proletarian state is placed on a moral foundation, then with the abolition of class divisions the external compulsion of law will cease automatically; the state will wither away . . . and the real history of humanity . . . will begin."

When, however, the proletariat is not capable of acting voluntarily, "it must create institutions which are capable of realizing this necessity." In this instance the proletariat must create a legal order through which it "forces its individual members, the proletarians, to act in accord with their class interests." The proletariat, in other words, "applies its dictatorship to itself." Such a measure is "a necessity for the self-preservation of the proletariat when the correct knowledge and voluntary fulfillment of its class interests are lacking." But, Lukács adds, "it cannot be denied that this course contains great dangers for the future," because "when the proletariat takes this road, it must create a legal order (institutions) which cannot be abolished automatically by the historical development." The institutions thus created will push the development of proletarian dictatorship in a direction that endangers "the appearance and realization of the final goal. For the legal order which the proletariat was forced to construct *must be overthrown*—and who can say what convulsions and suffering would result from a transition which took such a detour from the realm of necessity to the realm of freedom?"

Here Lukács implicitly foresees the basic outlines of the development of the Russian dictatorship *of* the proletariat into a bureaucratic dictatorship *over* the proletariat. At the same time, however, this critical insight prefigures the ideology with which that new bureaucratic power would legitimate itself: namely, the idea that it is the proletariat which applies "its" dictatorship to itself. The difference between Lukács's standpoint in 1919 and both the emergent Leninist and subsequent Stalinist positions, though, is that he calls a dictatorship over the proletariat by its own name. And, in the immediate context of 1919, Lukács's deepest hopes lie with the other alternative—that in which the blind rule of the economy over man and the power of law and institutions over free moral choice will be abolished. It is impossible, he concludes, that the proletariat, which "heretofore has remained true to its world-historic mission under the worst circumstances, will betray its mission at the very moment it is at last in a position to fulfill it in action."[28]

For all of its pathos and radicalism, Lukács's concept of proletarian self-determination entailed not only utopian but also mythological elements. Unfortunately, if the free self-determination of the proletariat was a myth, if the replacement of law by morality was nonsense, the only alternative left was the one Lukács feared. The case turned out to be similar with his view of the role of the revolutionary party during the Soviet Republic. The only essay Lukács wrote on this problem in the four and one-half months of the new regime—"Party and Class"—can be located readily in the tradition of revolutionary syndicalism, at least in part reflecting the influence of Ervin Szabó.[29] It was even more deeply linked to the special terms in which Lukács sought to disclose the ways in which the emergent revolution provided resolutions to the fundamental problems his whole intellectual and ethical *oeuvre* had raised. To get at the meanings and problems of his conception of the party's role, a brief sketch of the political setting will be helpful.

In mid-March, 1919, the government of Count Károlyi resigned. After five months of inept efforts to bring Hungary's severe domestic and foreign affairs crisis into some sort of order, power passed into the hands of the Social Democratic Party. The latter's initial task was to gain room in which to operate, which meant first of all neutralizing the increasingly militant activity in the streets of Budapest by the unemployed and *Lumpenproletariat,* among whom the Communists had their social base and, second, putting an end to the CPH's attempts to penetrate the trade unions. Béla Kun, it will be recalled, was in prison at this time, but the underground Second Central Committee, of which Lukács was a member, continued agitation, especially for popular demonstrations.

One month after having assisted in the imprisonment of the Communist leadership, the Social Democrats invited Kun and his comrades into a governing alliance. In return for releasing them from jail and granting them key posts and even a dominant voice in shaping the new regime's programs, the Social Democrats gained Communist agreement to the principle that both parties would submerge their ideological and organizational identities into a unified proletarian dictatorship. Lenin, who viewed this turn of events as a harbinger of the revolution over Europe, was also quick to question Kun's willingness to enter the alliance on the terms he did. In Lenin's view, the Social Democrats were not only proven opponents of revolution but far and away the stronger of the two parties.

Regarding practical results, Lenin was not far off the mark. Neither party dissolved itself, which meant that the CPH, now severed from its initial social base, found itself incapable of penetrating, let alone seizing control of, the trade union movement and the Red Army, both of which remained Social Democratic strongholds. Increasingly intense struggles between the two parties, along with the dismal failure of the program to nationalize industry and agriculture and the collapse of the war of revolutionary national defense against invading Czech and Rumanian armies, resulted in the fall of the Hungarian Soviet Republic on August 1,

1919, after 133 days in existence. The counterrevolutionary terror which followed left the Hungarian working class movement in a shambles, and the way was opened to the solidification of a right-wing dictatorship under Admiral Horthy.

Lukács's "Party and Class" greeted the March 21 declaration of unity between the Communists and Social Democrats and the creation of proletarian dictatorship as the "cancellation of the conditions of existence" of both the Communist and Social Democratic parties. The proletarian party, he argues in the essay, is the organizational expression of the central contradiction and crisis within the proletariat as a class in the advanced stages of class struggle. On the one hand, the proletariat has become too powerful to avoid political struggle in realizing its numerous immediate interests, while on the other it is not strong enough to impose its will on society as a whole. As the expression of this dichotomous situation within the proletariat, however, the proletarian party is not itself the solution to the dichotomy: those who would claim it is, Lukács contends, are opportunists. Rather, as the syndicalists have consistently stressed, the party stands in a contradictory relation to the proletariat. It is, by its very nature, a political formation which is not only separate from the proletariat, but which, in this separation, reproduces the separations of body and mind, consciousness and labor, theory and practice which constitute the social relations of capitalism. Yet, Lukács argues, the syndicalist critique of the party fails to recognize the "dialectical character" of the contradiction between party and class: the power relations of the class struggle require the organization of the party, even as these same power relations turn the party organization into a real hindrance to the autonomous action of the proletariat.

Thus, Lukács proceeds, the proletarian party is a necessity, but a necessity only as a transitional form to a "higher unity," namely, the "unified proletariat as the ruling class in society." The dialectical opposition between the party and the class is ultimately based upon the "power of self-preservation of the bourgeois state" which, he specifies, hinges on the proletariat's continued belief in that power. And "as soon as the proletariat has convinced itself to seek the destruction of capitalism, this power is already in ruins." Such, he argues, is the new historical epoch opened by the events of March 21. The new unity of the proletariat and the prospect of its dictatorship, then, has been created "by the proletariat itself," which had "set itself in motion as a unified force"—not, in other words, by the mere fact that the proletariat's leadership had entered into an alliance.

The *principle* guiding Lukács's defense of what he took to have been the new proletarian unity in the Hungarian Soviet Republic, was in fact the same principle that had informed his critique of the Russian Revolution in "Bolshevism as a Moral Problem": from the very outset of its dictatorship, the proletariat's action must be "pure proletarian action, a total break with every action delimited by the party organization." Needless to add, his position in March 1919 was also in harmony with his numerous appeals to the proletariat to initiate the age of freedom by free acts. But if, as we have suggested, his perspective on the role of the party in relation to the proletariat amounted to a kind of Lukácsian variant of revolutionary syndicalism, we can also glimpse a more purely Lukácsian theme—and Lukácsian problem.

It appears that his concept of the revolutionary party has its ultimate theoretical roots in his ethic of self-sacrifice and the ideal of community that had begun to emerge in his writings with "On the Poverty of Spirit." The party was to play the role of the "gnostic activists of goodness," representing the realm of freedom, the age beyond alienation and economic necessity, even though it remained no more than an ideal suspended above necessity so long as the proletariat itself did not act freely. The party, in other words, represented the holding action that the incognito nature of the revolutionary without a revolution always seemed to require.

In the spring of 1919 he believed (briefly) that the need for the holding action had been overcome. But he could believe this only at the cost of a full-fledged mythologization of the proletariat's role in the actual events, with whose details he was intimately familiar. But even as political metaphor aimed at providing ideological legitimation for the Soviet Republic, Lukács's position implied a description of the real state of affairs in March 1919 that was hopelessly wide of the mark. Nowhere was this more clear than in his concluding assertion that the self-dissolution of the parties would be a natural task for the Communists, who had organized themselves into a party in the first place "only in order to abolish finally the party form as such." Once again, we have a remarkable paradox emanating from the deeply antinomic structure of Lukács's thought. For on the one side, his position, as an ideal formulation of relations between party and proletariat, was an original and radical criticism of any attempt to hypostatize the party into *the* instrument of proletarian revolution. But on the other, Lukács could not abstract his idea of the party from the existing parties as empirical and instrumental realities. And, while his essay, "Party and Class," hailed the dissolution of proletarian parties, it also contained the opposite tendency: that of idealizing the empirical Communist Party.

CHAPTER

7

Wager on the Party: Lukács in Exile

WITH THE COLLAPSE of the Hungarian Soviet Republic, Lukács, more often than not in spite of his intentions, began to emerge as the founder of "Western Marxism." To escape the White Terror that succeeded the 133 days, the recent convert to revolution, after remaining in Hungary to do illegal work, followed most of the other leaders of the Communist Party to Vienna. Arrested shortly after his arrival and threatened with extradition to Hungary, which would have meant certain death, Lukács was released toward the close of 1919, thanks largely to an appeal to the Austrian authorities by some of Germany's leading men of letters.[1] Vienna itself at the time was an international focal point of exiled and otherwise itinerant revolutionaries; militants from the Balkans, Poland, Russia, Italy, France, Germany passed through the city and discussed and debated the unfolding events.[2] On his release from prison, Lukács directed himself to the task of interpreting—and transforming—the fact that "in the middle of the fatal crisis of capitalism wide masses of the proletariat continued to experience the bourgeois state, law, and economy as the only possible environment of their being, which could of course be improved ('increasing production'), but which nevertheless remained for them the only 'natural' basis of society as such."[3]

In late 1919–early 1920 in Vienna the exiled Hungarian party, in conjunction with the Austrian Communists Gerhard Eisler and Ruth Fischer, founded the journal, *Kommunismus*. It was to serve as the official theoretical organ of the Third (Communist) International for Southeastern Europe and began weekly publication in

February 1920. Lukács, a member of the journal's editorial collective, promptly emerged as its most active and influential contributor. Three of the eight essays he would include in *History and Class Consciousness* appeared originally in *Kommunismus*.[4]

From a distance of nearly half a century, Lukács characterized his own work in 1920–21, as well as that of *Kommunismus* as a whole, as "messianic sectarianism": the attempt to take the most radical position on every question of the day by always announcing the necessity for a total break with all bourgeois institutions and habits.[5] This tendentious reappraisal reflected the decades-long "maturation" of Lukács's Marxism—a process which began, as he himself suggests, in the *Kommunismus* period, when he also began to understand Lenin. In fact, copies of the journal came to Lenin's attention early in 1920, and he promptly condemned it, singling out one of Lukács's articles as a characteristic expression of the "infantile disorder" of "left-wing Communism" or "ultra-Leftism."[6]

From a different point of view, *Kommunismus,* and Lukács's contributions in particular, can be viewed as expressing the hopes and perspectives of a group of revolutionary Communist internationalists in confrontation with the first signs of the phenomenon that would become known as "socialism in one country." The proletarian-democratic, cultural-revolutionary, and ultramilitant vision of Communist revolution upheld by the journal, however, quickly came into conflict with the two dominant facts of the period: the progressive dissolution of the revolutionary movement in Europe and the unanticipated survival of the Russian Revolution in isolation. And as events developed, *Kommunismus* had to choose between its other ideals and its loyalty to the Russian Communist Party and the Third International, a loyalty which ultimately proved to be unflinching.[7]

More specifically, the main thrust of the journal was in opposition to the Leninist trade-union and parliamentary-participation tactics as obstacles to the development of clear proletarian class consciousness and autonomous proletarian action. Numerous articles, including several of Lukács's own, were also highly critical of the increasing hegemony exerted over the International by the Russian party and upheld the necessity of a more federalized organization which would nurture local and regional initiatives.[8] *Kommunismus* was in contact with the international ultra-Left and ran articles by some of its spokesmen: the Dutch "Tribunists," Anton Pannekoek, Henriette Roland-Holst, and Hermann Gorter; the Italian group around Amadeo Bordiga; and representatives of the Workers' Opposition in the Russian party.[9]

The history of *Kommunismus,* which covered a period of slightly under two years, consisted of the rapidly deepening contradiction between its loyalty to the Russian Bolshevik Party on the one hand and its independent, critical, and "ultra-Left" conception of Marxism on the other. From its founding in early 1920 to mid-1921, when it was closed down by the Executive of the Third International, the journal looked with increasing concern at both the internal occlusion of the Russian Revolution (centering around the transition from "War Communism" to "N.E.P." and the suppression of the Kronstadt Revolt in early 1921) and the Russian party's retreat from "revolutionary offensive" on the international plane (as announced at the Third World Congress of the Third International in the summer of 1921).[10] Moreover, Lukács and his close comrades, Révai and Fogarasi, were emphatic in their warnings against the visible tendencies toward bureaucratic sclerosis within the everyday life of the European revolutionary movement.[11]

By the fall of 1921 the political situation was such that to have pursued the logic of these perspectives would have entailed a break with the Russian party—a step that had already been taken by other ultra-Left groups. The Moscow Executive of the Third International had concluded at the Third World Congress that victorious proletarian revolution would be a matter of years, not months, and that the new circumstances required "reaching the masses" rather than revolutionary vanguard actions as well as a more centralized and disciplined ordering of Communist ranks. The ultramilitant tactical proposals, the decentralist organizational principles, and the philosophical heterodoxy of *Kommunismus* could not be sustained within the framework of this emergent new course.

The dilemmas of *Kommunismus,* which led to its ceasing publication in October 1921, were also and, in the immediate context, more closely bound up with the crisis within the exiled Hungarian party. Political differences within the CPH had emerged in the period prior to the founding of the Soviet Republic and developed into open factional struggle during the Viennese exile, when the causes for the failure of the revolutionary government were debated. The split revolved around the Béla Kun and Jenö Landler factions, with Lukács as one of the latter's main representatives. Kun's opponents within the party viewed him, as a contemporary observer has recalled, as an "incarnation of intellectual inadequacy, uncertainty of will, and authoritarian corruption" and placed the burden of the party's unresolved dilemmas on his leadership.[12]

The Moscow Executive, however, took a different view. Kun, who had been groomed by the Russian Bolsheviks during the war and remained a pliant protégé of Zinoviev, retained recognition as the legitimate head of the CPH. To keep the factional battle from getting out of hand, the Comintern dissolved not only *Kommunismus* but the Hungarian Party in the fall of 1921. With these developments Lukács, along with Révai, Fogarasi, and others from the original *Kommunismus* group, moved between Vienna and Berlin, working primarily in the offices of *Die Rote Fahne* and *Die Internationale,* the main publications of the German Communist Party. Lukács's political role as a member of the anti-Kun faction in the Hungarian party and as a spokesman of the ultra-Left tendency in the International was sufficient to establish his reputation as a troublesome dissident. But his positions on tactical and organizational questions emanated from the philosophical-theoretical interpretation of Marxism that he had begun to develop in 1919. On this level his work, culminating in the essays collected in *History and Class Consciousnes,* presented the most radical challenge to the communist movement—and to Lukács himself.

His work in exile proceeded through a complex developmental maze. According to Lukács's own autobiographical recollections, the trajectory of his political theorizing and activity in the 1920s moved along a path from "messianic left-sectarian" theory of world revolution combined with a pragmatic, almost populist, united-front ideology and practice within the Communist Party of Hungary, to the more coherent unity of theory and practice at the end of the decade, when he presented an explicitly antisectarian, united-front concept of the democratic dictatorship of workers and peasants. Leaving aside the various simplifications contained in his retrospective account, the decisive missing variable within it was the "Bolshevization" of his thinking. Paradoxically, this increasingly pronounced dimension unfolded simultaneously with the deepening of Lukács's critique of bureaucratization, which in turn had its roots in both his messianism on the world scale and his pragmatic, populist tendency in Hungarian matters. The "Bolshevization" of his thinking was peculiar enough in its own right, postulating a concept of the party that corresponded only to the utopian roots of his own thought. Yet, as it did for virtually all Bolsheviks, this "Bolshevization" constituted an internal limit to Lukács's critique of bureaucratism.

Thus, after the fall of the Hungarian Soviet Republic and under the shadow of the leadership of the Third International, no syndicalist or Luxemburgist theory could continue to disguise the fact that the idea of a free, spontaneous, democratic self-determination of the real proletariat was a utopian myth. Between 1920 and 1928, Lukács would criticize various aspects of this myth, although he did not abandon his belief in the more or less immediate possibility of world revolution. But he grounded this belief, and the whole ethical dimension of his thought, in a new mythology: that of the Communist Party. And this rendered him and his group ideologically powerless against the emergent Bolshevization of the non-Russian sections of the Third International, even as Lukács proposed a decentralized structure for the International and, within the Hungarian party-in-exile, fought against the representatives of the Moscow-based Executive.

Nevertheless, with all of its contradictions and dangers, Lukács's view of the party had a different origin and teleology from the view presented by Leninism. Quite remarkably, after the collapse of the Soviet Republic in Hungary, Lukács managed to maintain the logical structure of his earlier view of the party form, even as he undertook a prescribed self-criticism (August 1920) of his call for the self-dissolution of the Communist and Social Democratic parties.[13] His error, he implied, lay in not recognizing that the Leninist type of party was not open to the same criticisms that could legitimately be leveled against both the "opportunistic" Social Democratic and the very first forms of the European Communist parties. He had, in other words, not abandoned either the neosyndicalist views of 1919 or the Fichtean ethics of self-creation and self-determination. Earlier in 1920, prior to his "self-critique," he had in fact published two essays that confirmed the deep continuity of his positions of 1919, one on "Parliamentarianism" and another on "The Moral Mission of the Communist Party."

"Parliamentarianism" maintains most of Lukács's earlier reservations vis-à-vis the bourgeois party form and rejects the struggle for votes and parliamentary representation as mechanisms for integrating the proletariat and for legitimating the class rule of the bourgeoisie. Admitting parliaments to be at times effective loci for a defensive tactic of the proletariat, Lukács rejects all parliamentary activity for the period of the "revolutionary offensive," when the real unity of the proletariat is attainable.[14] In a revolutionary moment the parliamentary involvement of the revolutionary party endangers the spontaneity of the masses and restricts the ability of the party to raise spontaneous mass actions to the level of class consciousness. But here Lukács places as much emphasis on the workers' councils as he does on the party, viewing the former as organs of proletarian spontaneity. The very existence of these organisms of the proletariat's own unity, he argues, makes parliamentary participation superfluous, indeed, dangerous.

Yet, for all of his interest in syndicalism and workers' councils in 1920, Lukács was prepared to make the councils only co-equal partners of Communist revolution. Viewing them as proletarian counter-institutions which initiated the overcoming of the bourgeois and Social Democratic separation (i.e., reification) of economic and political struggles, Lukács also considered them powerless by themselves to accomplish a political revolution.[15] Only the party could lead the movement, preventing the councils from backsliding in legalistic, reformist directions.[16] In his analysis of the failure of the factory councils in Italy in 1920, Lukács criticized syndicalism and clearly affirmed the official theses of the Communist International: "only the party is capable of seizing, organizing, and directing political power."[17] In all of this, he stood between Rosa Luxemburg and Lenin, perhaps closer to the former. Yet his final decision in the latter's favor was facilitated not only by the de facto structure of power in the parties of the Third International, but by his own philosophical concepts. Unexpectedly, it was his earlier stress on the need to ground the moral, free will in the present realities (first linked to a Luxemburgist faith in the proletariat) that initiated his transition to Lenin. But the transition would satisfy only Lukács, never the orthodox Leninists.

While the self-determined activity of the proletariat began to take on mythical features in Lukács's own eyes after 1919, he nevertheless did not abandon his attempt to solve the problem of a transition from the realm of necessity to the realm of freedom by way of an appeal to moral freedom. His essay "The Moral Mission of the Communist Party" (1920) makes this clear—as it also discloses how much of his original hopes he has renounced.[18] Within its sustained conceptual structure, there is a new voice: all demands for an internal transformation of individuals as a precondition of communism, Lukács announces, are not only utopian but, finally, a form of petit-bourgeois conservatism. Demanding too much from difficult objective conditions and from individuals educated in egoism, such views relegate all prospect of liberation to the distant future.

Against this type of utopianism, Lukács juxtaposes an article by Lenin praising the initiative of Russian workers in working on the new "Communist Saturdays." Lukács views this "free initiative" as the seed of freedom's realm within what remained necessity's age, a claim that lay well inside the theoretical frame of his 1919 essay on "The Role of Morality in Communist Production." But, with the Russian experiment as a model to be followed by others, Lukács has introduced a new agent of the free moral act: "The Communist Saturdays . . . *are in no sense institutional deeds of the Soviet Government; they are, rather, moral deeds of the Communist Party*" (emphasis in original). The institutional compulsion he had warned against in 1919 would still be dangerous, but the Communist Party, he now argues, is *not an institution.* It is instead the *"organizational expression of the proletariat's revolutionary will"* (emphasis in original). The free will of the proletariat, missing in the proletariat itself, has now been found by Lukács.

From this point, he wrote nothing on communist morality but much on the party, apparently having achieved this conflation of the two concepts. One has to wonder whether he actually believed that the implicitly revolutionary moral will of the proletariat could be externalized in history in such a manner. The man who, not long before had proclaimed the primacy of revolutionary will over apparently obdurate facts, was beginning to take account of them. "Delays" in the coming of world revolution and Hungary's fall into the throes of bloody counterrevolution eroded many of Lukács's original expectations and facilitated his compromises with the specific realities of an exile party protected and financed by the Moscow Executive of the International. This was implied in his transference of the moral dimension of revolutionary subjectivity from the proletariat as a whole to the party. But the problems involved entailed more than mere readjustment of the voluntaristic aspects of his Marxism. Lukács was in fact forced to reconsider the entirety of his Marxian social theory which had incorporated a belief in an objective and necessary process leading to world revolution.

The major product of this reevaluation would be *History and Class Consciousness,* which Lukács completed at the close of 1922, and which we shall examine in Part Two. The immediate results, however, appeared in 1920, when Lukács introduced the two concepts that would play the central roles in his magnum opus: class consciousness and reification. It goes almost without saying that they refer, once again, to the problem of relations between freedom and necessity, the driving force of his entire *oeuvre*. The key text here is Lukács's 1920 essay, "Class Consciousness," which he would revise slightly for inclusion in *History and Class Consciousness*.[19] In it he confronts, in the context of the immediately pressing problems of the revolution, the dilemmas imposed by objective developments in the emergence of proletarian class consciousness.

The issue, as Lukács sees it, is this: "As soon as the moment of the transition to the age of freedom is objectively given . . . the blind forces drive with apparently irresistible force toward destruction, and only the conscious will of the proletariat can save humanity from catastrophe. . . . As the final economic crisis of capitalism begins, *the fate of the revolution* (*and with it, humanity*) *depends on the ideological maturity of the proletariat, on its class consciousness*" (emphasis in original). He is seeking, in other words, to situate the crucial moment of class consciousness in a fully automatic historical process which, left to itself, would result in destruction. The crucial moment, moreover, would arrive only at the final state of the ineluctable objective process.

Without developing it, Lukács introduces the concept of reification to account for the *absence* of proletarian class consciousness throughout the long period of capitalism's development and impending crisis: "The proletariat as the product of capitalism is necessarily subjected to the forms of existence of its progenitor. This form of existence is inhumanity, reification." The proletariat is the living negation of capitalism, but this negation is expressed only in the form of critiques of segments of capitalism (wages, working conditions, and so forth)—a fragmented critique that is precisely the expression of reified consciousness. Economic aspects of the proletarian situation are most readily graspable, Lukács indicates, with the political dimensions less so, and the cultural dimensions virtually opaque. Class consciousness, however, can be nothing less than a grasp of the totality of these otherwise fragmented moments. But Lukács does not indicate how and under what conditions consciousness of the totality can emerge and merely points to such signs of its approach as the appearance of workers' councils, "the political-economic overcoming of capitalist reification."

Nor can he readily disclose the path to its emergence since the keystone of his effort is a definition of class consciousness according to which it is what the proletariat *would think if* it were able to comprehend all interests flowing from its social position, interests relating not only to immediate action but to the whole structure of society. Neither a psychological nor mass-psychological category, class consciousness, in Lukács's view, is independent of what a member of a class or even an entire class actually thinks in any given historical situation. It is, rather, a concept that is "imputed" or "ascribed" to the class.

Between the not yet conscious class and the concept of class consciousness, then, stands the party. Lukács's position here recalls that of Lenin in *What Is to Be Done?* In both instances, the general role and particular actions of the revolutionary party are legitimated by its supposedly absolute or total knowledge of history. And in the essay "Class Consciousness," Lukács's epistemology, which distinguishes between empirical and true proletarian consciousness, resolves the tension between the party and the workers' councils just as it was resolved in the Russian reality: in favor of the party which used the "soviets" in the overthrow of the old regime, suppressing them thereafter.

This, however, was only one side of Lukács's position, one pole of the antinomic whole of his theory. His stress on the workers' councils, although weakening, and his critique of bureaucratization within the revolution pointed in the other direction—the one plotted by his continuing belief in proletarian self-determination. An adequate response to this range of questions called for a deepening of the concept of reification. Yet the evolution of Lukács's view of the party was an implicit attempt to answer the same questions, which history was hurriedly piling on the table.

The workers' councils were no longer the empirical base on which the theory could be built. By late 1920 they had been obliterated in Hungary, while in Germany they were legalized and made powerless in revolutionary terms. The Russian soviets were gradually eliminated at the factory and military levels and transformed into components of the emergent "Soviet government." When Lukács counterposed the "moral act" of the Russian Communist Party to the "institutional acts" of the Soviet government, he had tacitly recognized that politics had reverted to an isolated sphere in the reified world. In the same vein, he endorsed an article by Vladimir Sorin, the Russian "Left-Communist," who in 1920 had demanded that the party cleanse the soviets of bureaucratic elements endangering the proletarian internationalism of Russian politics. The Left-Communists were in fact critical of the existing leadership of the Russian party, although they, and Lukács as well, saw the party (suitably interpreted) as the guarantor against a "return of reification."[20] To be sure, Lukács was not alone in understanding "bureaucracy" in a limited way, confining it to the "parasitic" administrators of government in part left over from the old regime. Of course such a stress seems curious from the much more sophisticated point of view of *History and Class Consciousness*. The paradox is solved if we recall that the Leninist concept of bureaucracy (till Trotsky's 1923 *New Course*, written in conscious opposition to the party) always confined the problem to the institutions of the state, necessarily exempting the party, and expecting remedy from it and only from it. Lukács himself never seemed to understand or even consider the bureaucratic nature of the Leninist apparatus as such, though he came to be suspicious of the leaderships of Comintern and the Hungarian Party. But these suspicions were themselves to be stillborn in the theoretical sense because he was *unwilling* and *unable* to confront the source of the problem, the Russian Communist Party.

From our historical standpoint, Lukács's party myth was hardly a way out of the dilemma of bureaucratism. But this is not the only standpoint from which it ought to be judged. We have, for example, already touched upon a number of respects in which his perspective deviated from Leninism: his insistence on proletarian self-determination and the need for federalized structure within the International; his belief in the moral rather than institutional character of the party; his critique of bureaucracy, and so forth. Moreover, between 1920 and 1922, in connection with the bitter and protracted factional fight within the exiled Hungarian party, Lukács gained direct experience of the Moscow Executive's authoritarian techniques. Far from having been, as a common misconception would have it, an abstract intellectual quite out of place in the field of political infighting, Lukács was immersed, if unsuccessfully, in sustained and vigorous struggle against Béla Kun, the Executive's pliant and unsavory favorite in the Hungarian party.[21]

Nevertheless, Lukács's position vis-à-vis the whole process of Bolshevization was ultimately hopeless. Nor is this only a matter of the political weaknesses of his own and other antibureaucratic currents in the Communist movement. Rather, the hopelessness stemmed from the inner tensions of his whole standpoint. He was, on the one hand, perfectly capable of formulating highly critical views on key questions of the revolution, emphasizing throughout that the party's role was limited to raising all the consequences of the proletariat's situation and action to the level of class consciousness.[22] On the other hand, and in spite of his genuine desire to criticize the forms of bureaucratism in the Communist movement, his mythology of revolutionary subjectivity, his concept of "real" class consciousness and his dogged adherence to the Russian Idea as supposedly realized in the October Revolution, all prejudiced him to support the ultimate bases of the bureaucracy, the Leninist party. The ultimate principle having his implicit support, Lukács was powerless against the Bolshevized Comintern and its Hungarian agents.

As he continued to demand a high degree of class consciousness, willingness to sacrifice, and a "complete subordination of each individual to the fateful question of the revolution," Lukács in 1921 was in fact emerging as an increasingly vigorous advocate of a highly centralized and disciplined vanguard party.[23] To be sure, he believed that a party of *his* type could only emerge from a dialectical process of interaction with the proletariat, in which questions of organization were never separated from those concerning consciousness: he spoke in 1921 of the necessity of the party's "constant interchange with the subjective and objective revolutionary development of the class." Yet in virtually the same breath he defined organization in a highly voluntaristic manner as "in its essence . . . the conscious and free act of the vanguard."[24]

The following picture emerges: for Lukács, if organization was not understood as a process nurturing conscious political action, the consciousness of individual party members could not be raised to the level necessary for a dynamically centralized party. In that case—and Lukács knew the real consequences—centralization would be achieved only in a bureaucratic manner, and all bureaucracy represented the intrusion of reification into proletarian organization. But the voluntaristic definition of organization, combined with the insistence on centralized controls from the outset, would subvert the very possibility of a dynamic process of development within the party. The conscious and free activity of those who were, by his own criteria, not yet class conscious reduced itself to mythology. And by way of this mythology, voluntarism turned into *bureaucratic voluntarism*.

Class consciousness, revolutionary organization, and the reified world—these were the terms of Lukács's dilemma, and that of the postwar revolutionary movement. He would spend the year 1922 revising and deepening his analysis of the terms. The result was a text whose remarkable originality nearly compensated for its tragic and fatal flaws.

PART 2
HISTORY AND CLASS CONSCIOUSNESS

Prologue

LUKÁCS'S CRITIQUE and reconstruction of Marxist theory are the substance of the essays in *History and Class Consciousness* (1922).[1] Our mode of procedure will be presentation, analysis, and immanent critique. That is, we will reproduce the theoretical trajectory, the major concepts, *and* the internal limits and antinomies of Lukács's thought. We intend to question him with concepts that flow from his own analysis, only occasionally introducing points of view that emerged later within the tradition he founded, "Western Marxism." In general, we believe that after more than fifty years of neglect, misinterpretation, and a very short period of enthusiastic acclamation, the internally engendered self-oppositions of the theory show forth from behind an incredibly agile dialectic of concepts. The standards for judging Lukács, therefore, emerge from within his own work.

This, too, is a sign that he is one of the very few great thinkers of the twentieth century. What he said of classical German philosophy could now be said of himself: "Classical philosophy is able to think the deepest and most fundamental problems of the development of bourgeois society to the very end—on the plane of philosophy. . . . And—in thought—it is able to drive all the paradoxes of its position to the extreme point where the necessity of going beyond this historical stage in mankind's development . . . can at least be seen as a problem" (p. 134). For us, then, Lukács is a major representative in the tradition of the philosophy of praxis—a tradition that has much to say to us in spite or even because of its antinomies. His own aim was to express, realize, or incorporate the philosophy of praxis, or philosophy of history with practical intent, in a critical, dialectical social theory. This attempt, whatever its power and originality, was a failure. Nevertheless, the elaboration of the projected synthesis between philosophy and theory made and still makes *History and Class Consciousness* the fundamental text of Western Marxism.

CHAPTER

8

Theory of Reification

WITHIN *History and Class Consciousness,* only the reification chapter ("Reification and the Consciousness of the Proletariat") represents a systematic attempt to formulate a dialectical social theory. Lukács leads up to this in three steps, producing a unique combination of sociology, philosophy of praxis, and social theory. The sociology attempts the synthesis of Weber's theory of rationalization and the historical sections of *Das Kapital,* which Lukács transposes into a conceptual movement based on Marx's fetishism of commodities. The philosophy of praxis, on the other hand, represents Lukács's own reconstruction of the history of German classical philosophy, culminating in a Marxian reformulation of the concept of the "identical subject-object" as the social subject of historical practice. The purpose of Lukács's history of philosophy is to derive from the works of Kant, Fichte, and Hegel in particular a "philosophy of praxis" that could become the regulative principle of social theory and could begin to mediate the seemingly frozen immediacy yielded by the sociology. As a result, social theory can begin with the results of the sociology, but under the mediation of the concepts of the philosophy of praxis. The frozen, reified realm of objectifications that affects all subjectivity was conceived by Lukács as becoming a dynamic "objective spirit" which would point to the conditions and possibilities of the release of historical subjectivity. While in the end, the possibility of working out a new social theory was subverted by Lukács's inability to undertake the self-critique of all the categories required by his own understanding of the concepts of "category" and "mediation," one would be ill-advised to look at the outcome alone. The *process* of the development of Lukács's theory of reification is itself of the greatest interest.

The Immediacy of Reification

What is involved here is a powerful synthesis of dialectical theory with Max Weber's sociological analysis of "Western rationality." Yet for Lukács, it was never a question of simply utilizing Weber's concepts. Rather, his originality lay in showing the identity of several key categories of Marx's critique of political economy and Weber's analysis of the development of Western rationality. Weber had intended to show that historical materialism was only one powerful system of "ideal types" among many such possible systems. The convergence of Weberian and Marxian categories was therefore all the more dramatic. Lukács developed Marx's treatment of reification toward an overall social analysis and showed the economic categories to be explicit forms of being, determinations of existence. He thus seeks to transcend Weber's analysis with a dynamic theory that would ultimately anchor social theory itself in the "objective possibility" of the historical transformation of capitalist society.

Lukács pays particular attention to the fact that the concept of commodity is the first economic category that Marx unfolds in his two published analyses of capitalism. Within bourgeois society the abstract economic categories (especially those of commodity and abstract labor) correspond to the *immediate* form of appearances of economic conditions. To be lost in these abstractions, to estrange them from all historical ground, is vulgar economy. But to disregard them as merely "subjective" is methodological nonsense. The world of commodity exchange, according to Lukács, constitutes a "second nature" of appearances, of the phenomena of reification. Although *illusion* (*Schein*) has a systematic place in this world, it is not merely a world of illusions. The appearances (*Erscheinungen*) do take on the form of illusion when, for instance, they appear to be historically unchangeable.[2] But as appearances, they are the historically necessary forms of existence in which their likewise historical "inner core," their essence, is manifest. This essence is identical to the substratum of the historical action of men in a given social framework which is, in turn, the foundation of the concrete totality to be synthesized.

What is important is that the dialectical moment of recognition of the world of commodities reveals to Lukács that reification is not only the central problem of the economy, but "the central structural problem of capitalist society in all aspects" (p. 94). As a result, the moment of overcoming becomes more problematic than ever before. Lukács had previously argued, in 1919, that the extension of capitalist economy reduces all values to exchange value. But in those days Lukács was optimistic that the "free decision" of the proletariat could create a total transformation commensurate with total reification. In *History and Class Consciousness* the voluntarist moment often returns, but now the main argument moves forward through a far more complicated dialectic.

Lukács's analysis of reification moves through the moments of "alienated labor," the reification of capitalist society as a whole, and the reification of consciousness in bourgeois science and philosophy. Because of this conceptual movement, it is misleading to identify the concepts of alienation (*Entfremdung*) and reification (*Verdinglichung*). In Marx's work it was in fact the notion of commodity fetishism, not a developed concept of alienation, that enabled Lukács to see that the problematic of reification lies at the center of the Marxian critique. From commodity fetishism, Lukács deduced a concept that, as a student of Simmel, he had been utilizing at least since 1910: the concept of the alienation of labor. Lukács argues that labor (labor power and labor product) becomes a system of objective, independent things—commodities—whose autonomous laws control and subjugate the laborers. On this basis Lukács investigates the consequences from both the objective and subjective sides. From the objective point of view "commodification"—"reification"—means the creation of a second nature of pseudo things. From the subjective point of view, it means the estrangement or alienation of human activity and the deactivation of the men who are forced to face and work within this second nature (p. 98). Thus, Lukács deduces from "reification" the notion of "alienation," which is important both in the work of the young Marx and, according to Marx, in the history of the species.

From the alienation of labor Lukács at once moves to its specific historical form under capitalism: the *abstraction of labor*. The category of abstract labor is not merely a conceptual construct, but a social, historical product; according to Marx it is a moment of all labor, which is required and produced in its pure form by the increasing universality of the commodity form. This is the case because while commodity exchange tends to guarantee its own labor supply by attacking the bonds of all natural communities, large-scale commodity production is only possible if the abstraction of labor becomes the principle "governing the actual production of commodities" (p. 98). That is, labor power is abstracted under capitalism both in the sense of being sold as a commodity on a par with other, qualitatively different, commodities and in the sense of being reduced to a partial, quantitative shadow of itself in the factory.[3] It is in this context that Lukács fuses the Marxian category of abstract labor with Weber's category of formal rationality, which rests on quantification and calculability. In contrast to substantive (material) rationality, formal rationality, according to Weber, excludes all norms and values. Thus, mechanical, repetitive, standardized, easily defined, and isolated sets of action are the most quantifiable and calculable. But this means (as Weber knew) that the modern trend toward industrial rationalization is the trend toward the "progressive elimination of the qualitative human and individual attributes of the worker" (p. 99).[4] Lukács sees the final culmination of this trend in the Taylor system, which Weber accepted within the context of industrial rationality, though he understood its meaning as the mechanization of the psyche of the worker, that is, the separation of "his psychological attributes from his total personality" and their rational, statistically calculable integration into the system of production.

The full rationalization of the work process means, according to Lukács, the fragmentation of the object of production, originally an "organic whole," into mechanical elements each of which is the predictable result of specialized partial operation. The subject of production, the worker, is even more fragmented: one specialized partial operation, partial skill is selected in the case of each worker; it is developed at the expense of all other actual and potential skills and is set against his total personality. Marx, contrary to some misinterpretations of his work, calls attention to this process, in *Kapital:* "The laborer is mutilated into a fragment of a man" and "the intellectual potentialities of the labor process are estranged from him."[5] But Lukács goes further. On the one hand, he argues, the worker's activity becomes purely objective; on the other hand, the worker's remaining subjectivity is reduced to "contemplation" of his own (and other workers') alienated activity. This contemplative stance implies mechanical passivity toward a work process that "conforms to fixed laws and is impervious to human intervention" (pp. 100–101).

According to Lukács, the fragmentation of the subject of production must also be understood in a wider sense: it means not only the destruction of the subjectivity of the individual worker, but also the atomization, the isolation of workers from one another. Commodity production requires and stimulates the separation of workers from natural communities, while commodity exchange establishes social relationships among things but not among men. The historical passage from *Gemeinschaft* to *Gesellschaft,* which is itself stimulated by early capitalist forms and commodity exchange, is the prerequisite for the large-scale supply of free labor (labor power as commodity) that is necessary for a *system* of commodity production resting on abstract labor.

While Lukács leaves the historical analysis of the interrelated development of free labor and commodity production to others, he seeks to make a systematic point that will drive the analysis beyond Marx and, implicitly, beyond the stage of capitalism Marx had confronted. He argues that free labor in itself is not enough to allow the complete self-realization of capitalist production or even the total rationalization of a single factory. The culmination of capitalist rationality is only possible when "the fate of the worker becomes the fate of society as a whole," when the "internal organization of the factory" becomes the microcosm of "the whole structure of capitalist society" (pp. 101–113; p. 106). Behind this analysis lies Weber's insistence that a rational (capitalist) economy is not possible without rational administration of law, politics, and, ultimately, every day life. For Weber, rational administration is bureaucracy. The bureaucratic administration of the state and of law, which he considers the inexorable fate of Western man, is to him sociologically identical with the capitalist organization of the factory. It is, moreover, the prerequisite of a completely developed form of this capitalist organization. This means, according to Lukács, that all aspects of life are standardized and reduced to their elements, that is, to easily calculable partial systems that will obey formal laws. Not only work but gradually all human activity is therefore alienated and made part of a second nature impervious to human control (p. 110).

This satisfies Lukács's initial criterion for total capitalist rationalization. When a whole society is dominated by a factory-like administration—when, as Weber says, a whole civilization experiences "the absolute and complete dependence of its existence, of the political technical and economic conditions of its life on a specially trained *organization* of officials"—then the fate of the alienated worker indeed becomes the typical human fate.[6] Furthermore, the members of the bureaucracy themselves are no exceptions. Lukács maintains that one-sided specialization, the intensification of one faculty at the expense of all others, is most dehumanizing in the case of the bureaucrat: a single aspect of his mental faculties is detached and mechanized, and under the apologetic headings of "honor," "responsibility," and "consciousness," even the realm of ethics is drawn into the realm of the salable commodity—bureaucratic service (p. 111).

If this is the immediacy of capitalist rationalization, of reification, the fundamental question is that of its limits, that is, the mediations which release its potential (and powerfully disguised) dynamic. As a preliminary answer, Lukács reproduces the Marxian formulation of the irrationality of the capitalist system as a whole. He points to the problem of "realizing" surplus value (a problem that forcibly synthesizes the system of production with the system of distribution) and to the crises that tend to result from this. The underlying problem in this regard was also noticed by Max Weber: "The maximum of formal rationality in capital accounting is possible only where the workers are subjected to the authority of business management. This is a further specific element of the substantive irrationality of the modern economic order. . . ."[7] Since Weber defined substantive (material) rationality in terms of human values that were arbitrarily chosen, his analysis was not the same as Lukács's. The category of totality was indeed epistemologically closed to Weber, yet it is clear that Weber noticed the opposition of capitalist economic rationality and the satisfaction of basic human needs. Without the category of totality, and under the influence of economic theories of marginal utility, however, he could not consider that the nonsatisfaction of many basic human needs in hierarchically structured modern social and political systems might be an element of "formal" irrationality from the point of view of the system as a historical whole. Weber disregarded, in other words, the whole problem of crisis.

However, as it is painfully clear from our historical experience, the problem of reification that Lukács raised from the economic level to the level of total society cannot be answered by pointing to economic crises alone.[8] The whole content of *History and Class Consciousness,* indeed Lukács's whole intellectual history to 1923, demands (but does not fully accomplish) a general critique of deterministic Marxism. Yet his analysis of reification reveals the deep structural problem of the subjective dimension under advanced capitalism: "Just as the capitalist system continuously produces and reproduces itself economically on higher and higher levels, the structure of reification sinks more deeply, more fatefully and more definitively into the consciousness of man" (p. 105).

The Reification of Consciousness

The reification of consciousness is the passive, contemplative intellectual reproduction of the immediacy of reification. According to Lukács, this form of reification also moves on the total social level. The worker becomes the passive individualized spectator of a process in which his fragmented activity is the object of a process that he can observe, but not control or transform. Bureaucratic administration reproduces this scheme on the level of everyday life. The result everywhere is passivity and isolation in face of a world that is only seen in fragments: a world that appears fundamentally unchangeable. Marx's basic critique of the science of political economy was that it "scientifically" reproduces (represents and reconfirms) these illusions of bourgeois society's everyday life. Lukács extends this double critique of everyday consciousness and of naturalistic science in the direction of all of modern science and philosophy.

It would be a mistake, however, to seek a fully developed critique of modern science and scientific philosophy in *History and Class Consciousness*. Instead, Lukács presents several important insights, as well as some rather problematic claims. First, on the formal level of the sociology of science, he integrates the "setup" of all modern sciences into his overall framework. All of modern science is dominated by specialization and, organizationally, by forms of increasingly bureaucratic administration. On the level of scientific content, the sciences are first characterized by their fragmentation of reality and, consequently, by their loss of both totality and any ontological substratum: "The more intricate a modern science becomes and the better it understands itself methodologically, the more resolutely it will turn its back on the ontological problems of its own sphere . . . the more it will become a formally closed system of *partial laws*. It will then find that *its own concrete underlying* reality lies, methodologically and in principle *beyond its grasp*" (pp. 115–116. Emphasis in original).

Second, the sciences are characterized by their freezing of the immediate factuality of the given reality because its dynamic is visible only from the point of view of totality. The modern sciences are thus criticized for three reasons: (1) loss of totality; (2) loss of ontological (*historical*) substratum; (3) freezing of the given. The freezing of the given means that appearances are taken as ultimately irreducible and unchangeable. The structure of facts, that is, their *historically dynamic* "substratum" is not interrogated—the asking is considered unscientific. This historical dynamic lies (in the case of the human sciences) in the conscious and unconscious actions of men within the boundaries of the structures of a given social stage. The exact sciences must destroy the totality of the world because the totality cannot be synthesized from unmediated abstractions and facts. Conversely, only a deliberate movement toward the totality begins to mediate and historicize dead facts and abstractions.

At the first stage of his analysis of reification, Lukács has not introduced his understanding of the subject-object dialectic, the great concern of his pre-Marxist period. However, even his analysis of immediacy is unfolded from a double point of view: the deactivization of the human subject and the increasing "naturalization" of his objects (which are aspects of reified subjectivity). The analysis of immediacy culminates in a total split between the remnants of subjectivity of isolated individuals and an independent object world. Yet we were just forced indirectly to anticipate a stage of analysis that sees a dialectical relationship in this context. This was necessary because otherwise Lukács's view of the natural sciences could not be understood at all. On the level of formal sociology, Lukács's critique applies to all sciences. On the level of method, furthermore, the natural sciences have become historically the models for all the other sciences. Yet we must be more careful when relying on this method. Lukács's critique of the loss of ontological substratum and totality is valid only if a method of their recapture is available or at least definitely possible. But Lukács is extremely critical of those Marxists (such as Engels) who, "following Hegel's bad example," applied the dialectic to nature because "the interaction of subject and object, the unity of theory and practice, the historical change in the reality underlying the categories as the bases of the change of categories in thought are absent from our knowledge of nature" (p. 17, fn. 1).

Lukács is certain that Engels's dialectics of nature (the basis of Engels's understanding of dialectics in general), cannot overcome a purely contemplative stance toward objects (pp. 15–16). For similar reasons, Lukács rejects the late Engels's (and without knowing it, Lenin's) copy theory of knowledge, particularly his illusory solution of the Kantian *thing in itself* problem (pp. 145–146).

While the whole problem of science is hardly given an adequate solution by Lukács in 1922, he nevertheless extends his sociological critique of the reification of consciousness to all the sciences, drawing a conclusion that is less convincing, given his difficulties with "nature": through the "specialization of skills" the sciences destroy "every image of the whole." For the natural sciences both parts of this statement may be valid, but not the causal link. It is questionable, therefore, whether a genuine homology can be affirmed between the commodity form and the factory structure, on the one hand, and the logic and the organization of the sciences on the other. The same problem exists and, for our purposes, is even more serious in the case of legal and political institutions and ideologies. Once again the historical origin of rationalization/reification in these spheres predates the general extension of the system of commodity exchange, not to speak of the factory system. Once again it may be answered that the dramatic extension of the rationalization of everything traditional in these spheres receives its tremendous impetus from capitalist-bourgeois society, which in turn needs the rationalization of all spheres. But can this mean that natural science, law, parliamentary-party institutions, and political bureaucracy are nothing (for good or for ill) other than the homologous forms of rationalization/reification pervading all of them?

Lukács's long-standing hatred of the *objective spirit* blinded him to all possible distinctions here, and the reductionist logic of the Marxian primacy of the economic that he accepted for at least high capitalism met him half way. But, in the process, he made his own task immeasurably more difficult. Not finding any elements or traces of possible emancipation in the various spheres of the social world, he was not only drastically confined to the Marxian answer that proletarian revolution will dissolve the dynamic center of reification, the factory-based capitalist economy, but he was also forced into a dramatically mythological version of the thesis of proletarian subjectivity. This was not because he was an "idealist," however, but because he was a more sophisticated and more radical follower of Marx—in other words, because he discovered, through the help of Weber to be sure, the first intelligent and intelligible link between capitalist economic reproduction and the reasons of the "superstructure." Since the realm of the superstructure was, however, conceived according to the most rigorous standards of the Weberian concept of "rationalization," he could not (and, of course, did not want to) squeeze any element of potential subjectivity and creativity or even dynamic possibility out of law, science, bureaucracy, technology. As a result the theoretical burden on the revolutionary proletariat became impossibly great.

The problem was not simply, as Lukács was later to put it, that he identified all objectification with reification. From this, only a false understanding of labor and technology would have followed. Nevertheless, he poses the question of whether or not a philosophy can sum up the results of the sciences into a coherent whole. According to Lukács, the summing up of partial formal systems, no matter how encyclopaedic, is only the duplication of the process of Western rationalization. The sum of special sciences which are formally independent of one another and treat their content as eternally given does not in any way approach the createdness and the dynamic of the content. Philosophy as "sum" treats the special sciences as they treat their own content, as something ahistorical (pp. 121–122). The most recent schools of philosophy do not rise beyond the reification of consciousness: "The reified world appears henceforth quite definitely as the only possible world, the only conceptually accessible, comprehensible world vouchsafed to us humans" (p. 122).[9] Thus, modern rationality appears as the expanding, all-encompassing reason of the capitalist world, creating increasingly impenetrable and opaque fetishes. The price seems to be human activity, "praxis," all potential levels of subjectivity from work to philosophy. Yet it is obvious that, from the outset, Lukács's methodological claims imply that he is looking for the mediations beyond this immediacy, for the practice confronting and abolishing reification. Therefore, after describing the "phenomena of reification," Lukács turns toward the *dynamic of reification*. First, he attempts to mediate historically the immediacy of the abstract possibility of the *Aufhebung,* and to generate the conceptual outlines of a dialectics of practice. In this context, he examines the historical structure of the concept of a completely formal reason—Weber's formal rationality—as the final product of an intellectual tradition of "rationalism," German classical philosophy, whose original intentions were radically different from those of most modern guardians of "reason." To conceptualize a paradigm capable of surpassing reification in the present, he turns to the philosophy of the past.

The Conceptual Dialectic of Subject and Object

It may seem strange that a Marxist should turn to the history of philosophy to elucidate problems dealing with the dynamic of the capitalist world. Yet, in this context, Lukács is following some clues from Marx and Engels. "The proletariat can only be abolished by the realization of philosophy," wrote Marx in 1843, and this argument was concretized by Engels as late as 1888: "Only among the working class does the German aptitude for theory remain unimpaired. . . . The German working class movement is the inheritor of German classical philosophy." Both statements (and the essays in which they appeared) treat classical philosophy as one of the basic sources of dialectical theory (and, therefore, practice). On the other hand, one can find statements in Marx and Engels that refer to philosophy (in general) as a mere epiphenomenon; their statements tend to reduce the history of philosophy to the history of the modes of production. In general, the Marxism of the Second International adopted the latter attitude toward philosophy. But the reduction of all forms of subjectivity was, for Lukács, only the expression of the logic—and in a revolutionary period, the defense—of capitalist reification. The conservative political behavior of official Social Democracy in the twentieth century was well balanced by the passivity implied by its theoretical presuppositions. Lukács was impressed that the Russian Revolution disregarded the canons of Social Democratic practice. Therefore, he returned to the dialectic of practice worked out in the "Theses on Feuerbach," which he was certain remained the philosophical basis of the unfinished critique of political economy.

The first thesis on Feuerbach, which contains the subject-object dialectic, is decisive. Marx wrote: "The chief defect of all materialism up to now . . . is that the object (*Gegenstand*), reality, sensuousness, is understood only in the form of object (*Objekt*) of contemplation (*Anschauung*), but not as sensuous human activity, as praxis; not subjectively. Hence it happened that the active side was developed . . . by idealism, but only abstractly, since, of course, idealism does not know real sensuous activity as such." Lukács's reconstruction of the history of German classical philosophy represents an extended commentary on this passage. He was indeed seeking "the active side," the dialectic of praxis disregarded by official Marxism no less than by classical materialism. On the other hand, Lukács knew that the dialectic of subject-object that would emerge from the works of Fichte and Hegel would ultimately remain a conceptual dialectic, abstracted from concrete historical activity. But, given the immediacy of reification involving frozen and fragmented subject-object relations, he believed that it was an important step to present what could be called the *subjective possibility* of a dialectic of practice. Furthermore, he regarded German classical philosophy as a self-conscious microcosm of the problem of reification and its overcoming, even if the manner of this overcoming (in spite of all practical intentions) was always fated to remain contemplative, conceptual, abstract, and hence itself ultimately reified: "Classical philosophy is able to think the deepest and most fundamental problems of the development of bourgeois society through to the very end—on the plane of philosophy. It is able—in thought—to complete the evolution of the class. And—in thought—it is able to take all the paradoxes of its position to the point where the necessity of going beyond this historical stage can at least be seen as a problem" (p. 134).

"The Antinomies of Bourgeois Thought," section two of the Reification chapter, amounts to the first serious Marxist treatment of modern philosophy. Nevertheless, Lukács disclaims any intention to present a systematic history of philosophy. He is concerned with a limited number of problems, although he considers *these problems* historically the most significant. The Kantian problematic of the thing-in-itself is the center of his concerns, which is not surprising for the theoretician of reification. For there is a general coincidence between the problematic of human relations frozen into apparently impenetrable, unchangeable, and opaque thing-relations, and the Kantian notion of a "realm" of incomprehensible, unapproachable, and yet limiting *things-in-themselves*.

Lukács's analysis of modern rationalist philosophy represents, as we have said, an overall search for the *subjective possibility* of the dialectic of reification. Nevertheless, even *within* this *subjective* dimension, it is possible to speak of subjective and objective sides. The first level of the claim of reason to subsume all of reality is that of contemplation. This level emphasizes the side of the object. Of course, even here the problem is posed in terms of the attempt of the rational categories of the subject to create (*erzeugen*) the object world. But contemplation can mean only *formal* creation. The object world is not really acted on. Furthermore, the subject of contemplation, its rational forms and faculties (what Hegel called Kant's "soul-bag"), are assumed to be given, to be the only ones possible, until at least Fichte. The dynamic of this stage of analysis comes not from the side of the subject, but from an objective reality that again and again refuses to be subsumed, penetrated, and produced by the given rational forms. The various functions that Lukács assigns to the Kantian thing-in-itself exemplify this refusal, this subsistence of "irrationality." In his view, the *thing-in-itself* has two basic functions in Kant's philosophy. The first is the representation of the ultimate impenetrability of the sensuous contents subsumed by the categories of the "understanding." This signifies the inaccessible nature of the ultimate "source" of the data of the senses. The second function represents the inability of the categories of the understanding to synthesize a rational totality (pp. 126–127).

Hegel, in his lectures on the history of philosophy, points to the conflict between the demand of Kantian reason (*Vernunft*) to synthesize all of existence and the self-contradiction that the categories of understanding [*Verstand*] get involved in when they seek to satisfy this demand. This distinction between reason and understanding (although it has medieval roots) points to the courageous beginning of modern rationalism and its cowardly end. Kant himself, Lukács points out, honestly and explicitly presents this contradiction. "The Antinomies of Pure Reason" demonstrates the inability of the categories to synthesize the totality of being in space and time, to penetrate the ultimate construction of substances, and to uncover the ultimate ground of causality (and necessity). Furthermore, Kant himself attempts to probe beyond a mere statement of the contradictions resulting from the problem that "Reason, in the continuous advance of empirical synthesis, is necessarily led up to them [the dialectical play of ideas] whenever it endeavors to free itself from all conditions and apprehend in its unconditioned totality that which according to the rules of experience can never be determined save as conditioned."[10] Kant probes further because, as he says, practical reason demands ultimate answers.

Lukács will follow him, but first he wants to make clear that the antinomies represent the dissolution of the rationalist project on the level of contemplative system building. This was, of course, Kant's point also. But Lukács's thesis about German classical philosophy fuses with his sociological analysis of the newest schools of philosophy. The renunciation of the ideal of systematization did not mean the end of the contemplative stance toward the world. On the contrary, at the end of the process, most positivist schools of philosophy (functionalism, nominalism, conventionalism, pragmatism) explicitly renounce the metaphysical and systematic claims of concepts and yet find themselves much further from the understanding of practice in the world of men than the supposedly "speculative" thinkers of German classical philosophy.

As we have already implied, and in contradistinction to "positivism," Kant sought a solution to at least some of the antinomies of contemplation in the direction and for the sake of practice. But, and this is crucial, Lukács interprets this attempt as a *turn inward.* We should recall that Lukács was quite familiar with the category of "inwardness" which he combatted in his pre-Marxist days but which at times reappeared in his writings as the "solution" of the subject-object problem.

Now, in a powerful critique of Kantian ethics, Lukács brings together the problem of "inwardness" and reification. In Kant's philosophy, he argues, the quest for a new subjectivity on the level of practice succumbs to the thing-in-itself. The formalism of Kantian ethics does not allow the "internal freedom" of the individual subject to be externalized, to confront the necessity of the external world. Even worse, the structure of necessity penetrates the individual subject himself: his psychological nature obeys external laws, and the subject is split into noumenon (thing-in-itself) and phenomenon according to the solution (or nonsolution) of the third antinomy (p. 137).

The overall coherence of Lukács's procedure can be easily illustrated in this context. Through a solid interpretation of Kantian moral philosophy he is able to show that the destruction of subjectivity in the factory, the integration of even the worker's psychological being as an alienated mechanism, is anticipated by the categories of an eighteenth-century moral philosophy that could conceive of practice only on an individual and abstract level. This enables Lukács to examine historically the categories of practice that claim to overcome the destruction of subjectivity. That is, to be able to say something about the possibilities of future practice, he penetrates the subjective dimension of the past. Thus, he correctly argues that German classical philosophy *did* recognize that it was not enough to discover the "freedom" of subjectivity to transcend a purely passive, contemplative attitude toward the world. Freedom must be externalized to become substantial freedom: practice must not remain indifferent to the "concrete material substratum of action" (p. 139).

It is not a contradiction but a further corroboration of Lukács's theses that already in the work of Kant the notion of practice becomes more concrete in context of a consideration of history. In spite of the ultimately unresolved character of the antinomy of internal freedom and external necessity, Kant did not reduce the external historical world to objectivistic laws of nature. In his *Strife of the Faculties,* he asks, "How is history *a priori* possible?" And his answer is, "If the diviner himself creates and contrives the events which he announces in advance," history is deliberately related to politics. Lukács makes clear that Kant did not attempt to "perfect his system" through a systematic philosophy of history, but through his philosophy of art. In his view, Kant and, more specifically, Friedrich Schiller, a follower of Kant in philosophy, tried to delimit art as a realm where the subject of action "could be seen to be the maker of reality in its concrete totality" (p. 153). In Schiller this was a conscious attempt to conquer the fragmentation and dehumanization of the modern era. But Lukács repeats an earlier argument from his second Heidelberg Aesthetics (1917): vis à vis the nonaesthetic world, the point of view of art is alienated. Lukács rejects all aesthetic solutions to the problem of reification for two fundamental reasons: (1) *within* the aesthetic relationship, the creation of the subject of art, of the artist, cannot be posed; (2) *within* the aesthetic dimension, the historical relationship of subject and object falls away.

In Hegelian terms, within the framework of art we cannot concretely understand the problem of subject or the problem of substance. According to Lukács, the notion of the *creation of the subject* is first posed by Fichte; for Kant, the subject and the categories were given. But the object world, as Lukács shows, continues to resist the eternal categories of an eternal Kantian subject, and this means that the gulf between subject and object remains unbridgeable. In Fichte's philosophy, Lukács claims, there is a drastic reversal. And it is here that we finally reach the philosophic spirit of *History and Class Consciousness*. Fichte postulates an identical subject-object from which and by which, in accord with rationalism's original claim, all of reality, including the empirical split between subject and object, can be synthesized. This identical subject-object must be forged through activity (pp. 136–137). In Fichte, this problem is posed epistemologically and ahistorically, although he contributes to a historical solution by no longer limiting practical subjectivity to the individual ego. Nevertheless, Lukács's consideration of Hegel's discovery of the historical dialectic does not amount to an abrogation of the Fichtean roots of his concept of "subject."

Hegel's *Logic,* in Lukács's view, represents an attempt to ground the movement of concepts in the dynamic of the concrete totality of existence (p. 142). This dynamic was presented in Hegel's *Phenomenology* as substance-becoming-subject. If the dialectical method is to overcome all ossified antinomies (and as Hegel remarked, there are antinomies everywhere), then it must first retrace the *genesis* and *creation* of the subject of this overcoming.

But, second, the genesis of the subject becomes concrete only if the substance that is the dynamic source of this genesis—the substance that will become the object of the subject—is uncovered. In Hegel, history turns out to be this substance, both as source and as object (p. 158). The historical process produces, and is produced by, the subject. This is how Lukács interprets Hegel's demand to grasp and express "the true not only as substance but also as subject."

As soon as the historical dialectic, "the dialectical identity," of subject and object is discovered, the discovery demands further concretization: "To comprehend this unity [the unity of subject and object] it is necessary . . . to exhibit *concretely* the 'we' which is the subject of history, that 'we' whose action is in fact history" (p. 161).

Lukács considers one of Hegel's great achievements to be the completion and historicization of Fichte's decisive break with the individualistic notion of subjectivity in Kant's philosophy of practice.[11] However, he states that, in Hegel, the attempt to concretize the 'we' of history results in a chain of false concretizations leading to a conceptual mythology. Hegel, in his lectures on the *Philosophy of History,* indeed locates a subject-object dialectic in nations: the spirits of nations (*Volkgeister*). Lukács is right in pointing out that this is only an apparent dialectic. The spirits of nations turn out to be only instruments of one world spirit (*Weltgeist*): as Hegel says in the *Philosophy of History,* they are "steps in the development of the one universal Spirit, which through them elevates and completes itself to a self-comprehending totality."

At this stage, Lukács points out that Hegel's conceptual mythology negates history and historical practice. If history is the work of an absolute subject, then it remains alien to human reason and reifies (instrumentalizes) human subjects. For all intents and purposes the subject-object dualism is reintroduced. Furthermore, the notion that history has an end (a notion arising not from the dialectical method, but from positing an absolute subject that becomes self-conscious in the philosophy of the present), negates the historicity of the future. But the practice of the present can only be directed toward a future that is historical. Otherwise, the result is either extreme voluntarism (practice is completely free) or extreme determinism (there is no practice in the sense of praxis, that is, subject-object dialectic).

Marx's critique of Hegel always pointed out that, given the reintroduction of alienation, of the subject-object duality into all of history past, present, and future, reconciliation becomes possible only in thought. Lukács fits this critique into his analysis and draws the conclusion: within the realm of philosophy, contemplation cannot be transcended after all. The only aspect of German classical philosophy that points beyond a contemplative stance vis-à-vis reification is the dialectical method, although the method itself can only receive antinomic expressions in a philosophy that is ultimately not open to the concrete historical ground of subjectivity, its social ground. Nevertheless, Lukács argues, it is possible to continue the methodological project of German classical philosophy outside philosophy. The continuation and concretization of "the dialectical method was the true historical method reserved for a class which was able to discover within itself on the basis of its life experience [*Lebensgrund*] the identical subject-object, the subject of action, the 'we' of genesis, namely, the proletariat" (p. 164).

Thus, Lukács reaches the proletariat by way of the analysis of German philosophy. Even if the parallel to the development of the young Marx is striking, two critical comments can be risked.[12] The concept of the identical subject-object derives from the quest of classical German philosophy to express *all substance* and in particular nature itself as the deed of a *subject*.[13] As such, it is the subjective counterpart of total reification. It also well expresses what the thesis of total reification required of Lukács. To be sure he characterizes all historical versions (except his own) of the theory of the identical subject-object as conceptual mythology. Because the proletariat is a sociological reality (unlike the nation), he claims success (in the name of Marx) where Kant, Schiller, Fichte, and Hegel have failed. His claim involves the presupposition that the historical process, or at least the present as history, has become transparent to theory. But here the task of social theory to catch up with the conceptual speed of the philosophy of praxis (the dialectic of the subject-object) has become difficult indeed. The mere sociological existence of an exploited, dehumanized class and the ability of a conceptual dialectic to present this class as an identical subject-object do not add up to revolutionary practice. The agility of a conceptual dialectic can easily turn into a new conceptual mythology in the face of the opacity and density of history, in the face of reification. Historical practice, or praxis, can replace conceptual mythology only if the dynamic of the historical process, in this case the hidden dynamic of reification, produces the objective possibility of this praxis. And given what had to be possible for this heir of German idealism and Marx, namely the free creation of history henceforth, the line between social theory and conceptual mythology turned out to be very thin.

The Dialectic of Immediacy and Mediation

The dialectic of the identical subject-object (the center of the "philosophy of praxis") and the dialectic of immediacy and mediation (the bases of all dialectical social theory) seem to flow from different conceptual presuppositions. Systematically, the first (which Lukács developed before *History and Class Consciousness*) proceeds from the side of the subject: the problem is to find (or create) a subject that is the identical subject-object—for example, the absolute subject of Fichte and Hegel or Lukács's proletariat. The second dialectic, that of mediation (first investigated by Lukács in *History and Class Consciousness*), proceeds from the side of the object, that is "objective" historical possibility.

"Reification and the Consciousness of the Proletariat" culminates in an attempt to discover the objective possibility of proletarian subjectivity. In this context the pair of categories, immediacy and mediation, provides the most crucial methodological insight. Mediation for Lukács is the release of "immanent possibilities" that do not appear on the level of immediacy and, therefore, escape reified thought. But even this release can be truly important only if the meaning of history enters the consciousness of the only possible agent of "praxis" Lukács could conceive: the proletariat. The question is whether or not the proletariat is ready to understand history and the historical mission that Lukács attributes to it. In this context, we must also determine whether Lukács's crucial reference to the proletariat is the product of an implicit dogmatism that pretends to understand the totality of history before any process of mediation or of a methodology that is analyzing one category of historical materialism, itself an ideology, as Marx analyzed the categories of political economy, that is, as the beginning point of mediation.

Lukács's discussion of the "point of view of the proletariat" begins rather radically and indeed critically. What change is brought about by a proletarian perspective? he asks. The answer is: "In the first instance nothing at all." The forms of proletarian existence are the most reified and dehumanized. Therefore, "the objective reality of social existence *in its* immediacy is 'the same' for both proletariat and bourgeoisie" (pp. 165–166). However, Lukács says, the categories of mediation are fundamentally different for the two classes.

The essay "Class Consciousness," composed in 1920, distinguishes between the social existence of bourgeoisie and of proletariat in terms of class interest. The reification essay of 1922 briefly presents this argument as a possible solution to the problem of reification. The historical concept of class, Lukács asserts, implies class interest. Bourgeois class interest and the world of reification define one another; to the bourgeoisie the reified world appears and must appear eternal. For the proletariat, however, reification is not a definitional but merely a historical limit, a limit that conflicts with the proletariat's historical interest in liberating itself. Yet this interest is in principle not part of the empirical consciousness of the proletariat. Unfortunately, even for the proletariat, the limits of reification are internalized, and the dynamic conflict of immediacy and interest, of "empirical consciousness" and "class consciousness," cannot easily be made conscious. "Class Consciousness" projects the solution from a combination of (1) the process of the objective disintegration (collapse) of capitalism and (2) a voluntaristic agent (the class or the party) intervening near the end of this process to break through the reified consciousness and, finally, through the political institutions of capitalism (pp. 82–83, 92). In "Reification and the Consciousness of the Proletariat," however, Lukács is not quite satisfied with this rather schematic solution (which is, nevertheless, a philosophically adequate statement of Leninism). The notion of class consciousness based on something wholly external to the proletariat—universal interest—was not Lukács's only statement on the dialectic of proletarian class consciousness. In the reification essay, for example, the consciousness of interest is replaced by self-consciousness.

According to Lukács's theory of reification, the social existence of the proletariat—of the proletarian individual and of the class—

contains the "objective possibility" of the overcoming of reification. The first relevant aspect of this social existence is the absence of the illusion of subjectivity. At this point, Hegel's master-slave dialectic functions on the level of the immediacy of reification. For the bourgeoisie—the master—there is an illusion of subjectivity ("owner," "entrepreneur," "manager," "thinker") in face of things (worked by others) although the bourgeoisie is ultimately subjected to the laws of nature and "second nature." This illusion appears in bourgeois thought in the form of a subject-object split. The proletariat, on the other hand, is itself reduced to a mere object—"consciousness in the shape of thinghood"—and its illusions of subjectivity (if such illusions ever exist for the proletariat) are dissolved by progressive integration into the objective mechanism of production (pp. 181–183). Lukács is gradually introducing the Hegelian qualification most stressed by Marx, that the proletariat—the slave—can recognize itself in the world because of its reification in the work process. But in *History and Class Consciousness* Lukács does not stress the creative, objectifying moment of all (even abstract) work as a crucial determinant of this recognition.

In Lukács's analysis, the reduction of the proletariat to object of production is almost total. Only the barest minimum of the contemplative subjectivity of the mere spectator is given to the worker. His qualitative, creative activity is alienated, mechanized, and quantified. But the relation of quantity and quality is presented as dialectical. Here Lukács is not thinking of one of Engels's laws of the dialectic. He admits that there are possible examples of quantitative changes at a certain level passing over into qualitative changes. He claims, however, that there is a far more important aspect of the relation between quality and quantity. In contexts involving subject-object relations, the transformation of quantity into quality "means the emergence of a truly objective form of existence" (pp. 181–183). In these contexts, "*every* change is one of quality in its innermost nature" (pp. 183–184). Thus, the quality-quantity relation turns out to be a special case of an essence-appearance dialectic of the emergence of the *essential* from the web of mere appearances.

It is worth noting that Lukács's analysis here corresponds to Husserl's defense of a phenomenological *Lebenswelt* against naturalistic quantification. But in Lukács, quantification is an element of a capitalistic rationalization; hence, it is by no means only a scientific falsification of reality. His analysis of labor time makes his critical perspective clear. It is perfectly rational for the capitalist to treat labor time, its increase and decrease, as a merely quantitative problem. The worker, too, may (even must) think of labor time and its wage "equivalent" in this way. But in all aspects of his everyday life he is affected by all changes in his labor time qualitatively. Labor time is the "determining form of his existence as a human being" (pp. 183–184). The worker's labor time is integrated into the objective side of production, but it can never become wholly quantitative for the worker. This means that the worker alone *recognizes* something qualitative on the objective side. This does not alter his alienation, but it has made one aspect of it conscious. Lukács builds the objective possibility of a rupture in the reified world based on the necessity of what we would call a minimal consciousness of alienation. He argues that the worker's minimal consciousness of a qualitative aspect of the commodity labor time represents the beginning of the dissolution of fetishistic forms. In this commodity the worker can recognize himself and his domination by capital. This recognition is the self-consciousness of the commodity; the "substance" of capitalist society thus begins to become-for-itself.

Lukács further argues that when self-consciousness is added to the commodity structure, "when the worker knows himself as a commodity," this self-consciousness "*brings about an objective structural* change in the object of knowledge" (pp. 184–186. Emphasis in original). Lukács clearly has in mind Engels's argument that the "laws" of history are operative only because of the unconsciousness of the historical agents. The very plausible converse of this is that the beginning of consciousness begins to make these laws inoperative. Lukács also puts this another way: the addition of self-consciousness to the commodity structure is an objective change in the commodity structure. It is the first complete objectification of the special nature of labor as a commodity. The abstract labor component still appears as a thing, but now the human (qualitative) component, the source of surplus value, appears as the beginning of consciousness.

Lukács's discussion of the problem of labor explicitly follows the overall structure of Marx's conception of the struggle over labor time. Yet there is a crucial difference. Lukács also wants to get from the problem of the workday to the class struggle. However, his analysis implies, very likely unintentionally, that from the point of view of early twentieth-century politics, Marx's discussion has a tendency (if taken only abstractly and dogmatically) to culminate only in an economic struggle and not in practice directed at the totality of bourgeois society. Of course, the problem of labor time remains intrinsically more fundamental than that of wages. But even from the struggle over labor time, we cannot mechanically derive revolutionary consciousness. Thus, Lukács feels obligated to add one additional dimension to the analysis. As we have seen, even under the veil of quantification the worker can become (and in our minimal sense, must become) conscious of the qualitative aspect of labor. In the absence of this consciousness, Lukács argues, "the special nature of labor as a commodity . . . acts as an unacknowledged driving wheel in the economic process." But he has already explained that with the advance of capitalist reification, the total reduction of the worker to object implies the beginning of self-consciousness. This does not yet mean that something can be done about transforming the capitalist system, but it does mean that the objective possibility of overcoming is added to the immediacy of the social existence of the worker as object.

If the qualitative, living core of one fetishized quantitative relationship is made conscious, is revealed, then, according to Lukács, it becomes possible to recognize the fetishistic character of all commodities and to penetrate to the human and social foundations of all of the reified structures of capitalist society (pp. 185–186). But this recognition, this "self-consciousness of the commodity," means only that the proletariat is conscious of itself as object (and victim) of the economic process (p. 198). We can be more precise. The individual worker recognizes himself as object in one commodity, in his labor power. This implies the possibility of the recognition of social labor as object in the commodity system, that is, the possibility that the class recognizes itself as the object of commodity exchange. This recognition means that the rigidity of social things begins to dissolve into human processes. In the sphere of commodity exchange nothing more is possible, but in the sphere of production the objective possibility of recognition is richer in meaning. One particular fetish must be penetrated, must be seen as a process, for the proletariat to recognize itself as the subject (in the past unconscious) of the economic process: the fetish of the wage labor-capital relationship: "If the reification of capital is dissolved into the unbroken process of its production and reproduction, it is possible for the proletariat to discover that it is itself the subject of this process" (p. 198). The worker's minimal consciousness that something of his own has been integrated into the objective process is now supplemented by a consciousness that precisely this human element, living labor, is the source of the surplus value (that is, unpaid surplus labor)—the driving force of the production and reproduction of capital and capitalist society. We have shown that, in Lukács's analysis, the minimal consciousness of the worker of himself as object is necessary, but the self-consciousness of the class as object is only an objective possibility. It must be added that the self-consciousness of the class as subject is a possibility predicated on the possibility that the whole system of commodities dissolves into processes.

Lukács's theory of the dialectic of class consciousness is presented in terms of two enormous gaps: one is between the minimal consciousness of alienation of proletarian individuals and the self-consciousness of the class as the potential subject of history oriented toward the totality of capitalist society. The other is between the process of defetishization inherent in the life and work of the proletariat and the defetishizing movement of revolutionary theory itself. In both cases the analysis is debilitated by an egological ("I," "we," "theory of totality") model of subjectivity (excluding interaction, intersubjectivity in work, everyday life, institutional existence) that flows from both the uncompromising totalization of the logic of reification to all social spheres and from the complementary conceptual myths inherited from classical German philosophy. Notwithstanding the care with which the dialectic of mediation was first unfolded, the gaps will be bridged by the myth of proletarian freedom that the theorist posited even before the analysis. The dialectic is thus a pseudo dialectic or, at best, an incomplete one.

As we have shown, the empirical consciousness of workers is not presented in "Reification and the Consciousness of the Proletariat" (as it is in the essay "Class Consciousness") as mere psychological or mass psychological consciousness. It is indeed a minimal consciousness of alienation. But this minimal consciousness is said to be "only the beginning of a complex process of mediation whose goal is the knowledge of society as a historical totality"; that is, in Lukács's terminology, "class consciousness" is this goal. The minimal consciousness of alienation is defined by Lukács as necessary within the framework of reification. But class consciousness and the revolutionary praxis of which it is a "moment" are only objective possibilities that presuppose this necessity.

In the Marxist tradition, the emergence of the proletariat as a class generally appears as a consequence of industrial centralization and of the reduction of all workers to the same standardized state of social existence. Lukács does not reject this model but calls it one-sided. The isolation and atomization of workers cannot be overcome without industrial concentration, but other factors are also crucial. "The self-consciousness of commodities" represents the recognition of the social character of labor, but even this recognition is only a prerequisite for the abolition of the isolated individual. Common interests and a common situation can be recognized and defined relatively early by workers (also by other groups), but this does not immediately imply a total challenge to the society that continually tends to reproduce atomization.

What Lukács came to understand very well was that the mere physical proximity—concentration, centralization—of a sociological stratum does not overcome the atomization, fragmentation of its members. Nor does the struggle for interests (themselves heterogeneous) unite heterogeneous strata as a class. The problem is only that the self-consciousness of the single worker as an alienated commodity also does not accomplish the necessary task. It is unclear how the self-consciousness of atomized individuals leads, in other words, to either their consciousness of the subjectivity of the other or to a drive toward the understanding (in common) of the capitalist totality. The first question is excluded by the theory of reification even as a problem. The second, however, is clearly thematized—demonstrating its insolubility.

The problem of totality is understandably first raised from the point of view of theory. Lukács reiterates that the contradictory dynamic of society is revealed only when the necessary abstractions are synthesized into wholes. But he also continually reminds the reader that totality is never immediately given. Reality presents itself in terms of isolated, abstract units (categories). Only a complicated process of mediations attains the whole. Theory does not deal with a given totality; it gradually synthesizes it, and "wholes" are attained on different levels. The scope of the totality is ultimately relative to the given stage of our theory and practice. This stress on totality enables Lukács to argue that the real, objective dynamic of history can be understood. Objective possibility is *objective* only in the context of this understanding.

History, for Lukács, has laws ultimately because of the unconsciousness, "false consciousness," of the historical actors. False consciousness is the function of being lost in the immediacy of the given, the abstract, the partial. Objective possibility means a break in the structure of necessity, but for Lukács this break can be meaningful only when theory and consciousness are directed toward the totality of society: "By relating consciousness to the whole of society, it becomes possible to infer the thoughts and feelings which men would have in a particular situation if they were *able* to assess both it and the interests arising from it in their impact on immediate action and on the whole structure of society" (p. 62).

Thus, theory first provides understanding of the dynamic of society which is implicit in the possibility of the historical actors themselves becoming conscious of this dynamic. Dialectical theory establishes the relationship of the historical actors to society as a whole, and because theory arises from and interacts with the historical dynamic, its mere existence already represents the objective possibility of consciousness becoming practical. But this is true only if the distance is bridged between a theory of praxis and practical theory. Indeed, Lukács seeks to interact theoretically with the possibilities of the present for the sake of future praxis: "As long as man concentrates his interest contemplatively upon the past *or* future, both ossify into alien existence. And between the subject and the object lies the unbridgeable 'pernicious chasm' of the present. Man must be able to comprehend the present as becoming. He can do this by seeking in it the tendencies out of whose dialectical opposition he can *make* the future" (p. 223).

The transformation of the category of objective possibility is presented by Lukács in the context of his theory of praxis, but a theory of praxis obviously cannot "make" the future. It becomes a moment of praxis itself only when it becomes a "practical theory," and this is only possible when theory "has become part of the consciousness of the proletariat and has been made practical by it." Objective possibility can be realized only by the practice of the possible subject of historical transformation. On the other hand—and this is what distinguishes Lukács's concept of practice from all pragmatism—the reverse is also true. Praxis is not possible without theory. In other words, Lukács's concept of the projected unity of theory and practice comprises two complementary and parallel movements, each striving toward the other. Theory defetishizes reification by totalization, by the synthesis of totality or totalities. The empirical practice of the proletariat defetishizes in terms of the emergence of the minimal consciousness of alienation. To Lukács, only the fusion of these two movements would attain that class (self-) consciousness that would practically change the structure of its object (the hitherto atomized proletariat) by constituting it as a class for itself. What is highly unclear is how the theory of revolutionary intellectuals is to supply the missing parameters of intersubjectivity (a problem Lukács does not admit) and how, under what modes, what institutional, organizational, and educational forms that theory is to enter into the structure of proletarian consciousness. Not only has all this never happened, but if one reads and rereads *History and Class Consciousness,* the fundamental thesis turns out to be incoherent unless one solves these questions. But given the Lukácsian conception of the theory of totality and the minimalization of subjectivity in work, in everyday life, and in institutional life, the questions do not have an answer, even in principle.[13]

In this overall context, the fact that Lukács's concept of praxis is presented in an emphatically nondeterministic manner is only an apparent gain. The continued absence of proletarian class consciousness is said to be objectively possible. This would mean that the "contradictions [of capitalism] will remain unresolved and will be reproduced by the dialectical mechanism of history at a higher level, in an altered form, and with increased intensity." Thus, the theory is at least open to the coming reality of the twentieth century, the reconstruction of capitalism, and the emergence of new forms of domination.

But Lukács's whole theoretical effort is directed toward the discovery, the facilitation, the enlightenment of that historical agency which would realize what historical Marxism expected from necessity. And here Lukács failed. His philosophy of praxis was not ultimately concretized as a dialectical social theory for our time; indeed his philosophy (insisting on a mythological conception of subjectivity) and his sociology (yielding a totally closed, petrified world of reification) subverted the possibility of such a theory. For he presented the parameters of the constitution of a self-conscious revolutionary subject that can push contradiction into social transformation only very schematically, in terms of a chain of objective possibilities. The dynamic that he uncovered was thus an ultimately artificial, illusory dynamic. He replaced historical analysis with a static system of the objective possibilities of the present. But not satisfied with such a solution (in a historical period that still seemed revolutionary), Lukács tried to improve the case with a generous dose of voluntarism: "Any transformation can only come about as the product of the—free—action of the proletariat itself" (p. 228).

Lukács's theoretical development from 1919 to 1922 clearly illustrates that the illusory concretization of his theory of praxis and his inability to overcome the antinomy of freedom and necessity, culminate in a party myth. The use of the category of objective possibility only exacerbates this problem in the context of a partial (or dogmatic) class analysis. Anything at all can become an objective possibility when a mythical power is assigned to a class or a party. The conceptual dialectic of subject-object, after all, makes Lukács assume, in spite of his own theory of reification, that the dynamic of immediacy is more or less transparent.

The whole problem of class analysis is indeed solved in a dogmatic and mythological fashion by Lukács. He views the industrial proletariat, in spite of his inability to truly mediate its social existence, as the identical subject-object of the capitalist stage of history; thus, the analysis is intended to support what he believes in the first place: namely that the absolute subject, the industrial proletariat in the West, could and would make a fundamental social revolution, incorporating that freedom in the present which would be the seed of an emancipated future. This dogmatism is especially problematic in light of the fact that no unitary class analysis emerged from the work of Marx;[14] that already by 1923 the industrial proletariat in the West seemed to have a tendency to become less rather than more revolutionary; and that Lukács's own theory of reification seemed to exclude the possibility of proletarian freedom. This problem was only deepened by the chapters of *History and Class Consciousness* on revolutionary organization, where Lukács was forced to scale down his myth of the proletariat. But because of the requirements of his philosophy of praxis and sociology of reification, he was able to do this only in terms of another myth.

CHAPTER 9

Theory of Revolution

LUKÁCS COULD NOT fully cope with either the profound implications or the real problems of his theory of bourgeois society in the more directly political sections of *History and Class Consciousness*. The essay "Reification and the Consciousness of the Proletariat" was ultimately too radical, too far reaching (but implicitly also pessimistic), from the point of view of most of his political concerns in 1922. Furthermore, the missing or incomplete mediations of this chapter had to be worked out during the harried existence of the day-to-day struggles of the workers' movement rather than at the more luxurious pace that is historically associated with the development of great concepts. The thinker, adopting the perspective that the Marxist workers' movement was the heir of German classical philosophy, had to propose solutions that were temporally and conceptually plausible in terms of the practice of the movement. Of course, to be lost in the immediacy of the empirical state of the movement was a great danger. But Lukács, because of his own intellectual past, tended to fear instead the opposite danger: that of intellectually moving far beyond the political possibilities of the proletariat; his many critiques of utopianism can always be understood as critiques of his own past.

The concept of reification did, however, enter Lukács's revolutionary theory in the concept of ideological crisis (roughly a political equivalent of the reification of consciousness), which distinguishes his position from those of both Luxemburg and Lenin. Lukács's conception is both a restricted use of the concept of reification and one that, in its organizational consequences, depends upon the antinomic formulation of the free act of the proletariat in the context of total reification. As a result, in terms of the proletariat as a whole, the concept is used far too generally and dogmatically: "The human material with which the revolution must be made . . . consists necessarily of men who have been brought up in and ruined by capitalist society" (p. 337). In terms of the party, on the other hand, the negation of the concept is totally uncritical and dogmatic, culminating in a myth of a self-created organization that overcomes reification and the subject-object dualism within its own limits. In practical terms, this use of the concept of reification would come to mean two different things: in the context of the Communist Party of Hungary it was a critique of the bureaucratic opportunism and careerism of the Béla Kun Central Committee. But in the context of the Third International, it meant an apology in advance for political (not theoretical) Bolshevization (since the Russian party supposedly approximated his theoretical model). Having lost the slight critical edge toward the Russian developments that he still maintained in 1920, Lukács was now in danger of being lost in a new immediacy. Furthermore, we should note that in the German context this was an immediacy that was externally imposed and was therefore increasingly without an internal dynamic.

When all this is said, the harshness of this description must be immediately modified. Lukács's theory of revolution in *History and Class Consciousness* was a comprehensive and to some degree an original synthesis. And his ability to penetrate as deeply as he did in so many contexts does not give us the privilege of condemning him too harshly when he loses himself in the immediate conditions of his time. We must also remember that in the Hungarian party, where he did have some political weight, he maintained a critical role longer than anyone—until 1928 at least.

As to the particulars of Lukács's theory of revolution, he did not reject the underlying polarity of bourgeoisie and proletariat under capitalism. Indeed, he argued that only these two classes have the objective possibility of developing class consciousness. Furthermore, in parts of *History and Class Consciousness,* he also accepted Rosa Luxemburg's thesis that the collapse of capitalism on the purely economic level was inevitable because even the international possibilities of capital accumulation were finite in space and, therefore, time. However, Lukács at no time combined the fundamental polarity of classes and the certainty of economic collapse into a theory of the inevitable victory of a pure proletarian revolution. First, relying on a few Marx texts, he insisted that the automatic economic process tends to lead toward the collapse not only of capitalism, but of all civilization into barbarism, to the destruction not only of the bourgeoisie but of both great classes. Of course, he maintained, before the final disaster, the "free action" of the proletariat can save civilization and establish socialism. This, indeed, is the world historical importance of proletarian revolution.

Second, relying on the historical experience of the period from 1917 to 1922, Lukács argued that at the outset of revolutionary insurrection, the proletariat alone is generally not strong enough to gain and maintain political power successfully. In Russia and Hungary the most important reason for this was the relative weakness of the proletariat within the total social constellation. Without the alliance of the peasantry (and the lasting support of peasant soldiers) the Russian revolution could not have succeeded, while the Hungarian revolution (not having the peasantry, although for a time having the soldiers) had to fail.

On the other hand, the "ideological crisis" of the proletariat, which caused internal division and stratification of the working class itself and was a factor in both Russia and Hungary, was the main reason for the relative weakness of the proletariat in the West. And, finally, the relationship of the proletariat to subject or dependent nationalities was a third cause weakening it in all three contexts. Lukács believed that Rosa Luxemburg's hostility to the Leninist party came from a failure to emphasize these three factors, that is, from a mistaken stress on the necessary development of a pure proletarian revolution. Because if revolution involves many classes, the proletariat's immediate spontaneity may at various stages come into conflict with the spontaneity of the other classes or nationalities and even of some proletarian strata; hence spontaneity can be no guide at all to revolutionary action (pp. 312ff). The Leninist party, actively leading the proletariat, becomes the only mode of leadership at an advanced stage of revolutionary development. Furthermore, if the ideological crisis is one of the great limitations on the revolutionary activity of the proletariat, reformist or opportunist elements must be expelled from the revolutionary party.

Once again Rosa Luxemburg's model, which would use only the

weapons of mass enlightenment against Bernstein and Kautsky, is rejected by Lukács. Instead of enlightenment and debate, only exemplary or offensive actions wholly initiated and organized by the party can break through the passivity, the ideological crisis of the proletarian masses. Lukács consistently argued that no automatic objective process will produce the revolutionary ideology necessary for total social transformation. A breakthrough in this sphere would be produced not by necessity, but by freedom. We have seen how Lukács's notion of freedom came to culminate in a party myth. In the chapter on organization in *History and Class Consciousness,* this myth received its most detailed exposition.

Here the subject-object dialectic, the overcoming of reification, is temporarily restricted to the process of the free self-organization of the revolutionary vanguard. Lukács's insistence on the total involvement of the personality of party members in political activity, his attack on all traces of bureaucratic rationality, and his notion of free self-creation were demands derived from his theory of reification. On the other hand, the logic of his argument forced him to accept and justify a party that in fact satisfied few of the implicit requirements of his theory. To be sure, there were important differences between Lukács's revolutionary theory and Lenin's, and for these we must turn to a more detailed exposition of this whole problem.

Lukács's theory in *History and Class Consciousness* weaves through three central movements: (1) the revolutionary class; (2) the revolutionary process; (3) the revolutionary organization. These are not his own divisions, and we propose them for analytical purposes only.

The Revolutionary Class[1]

Ultimately Lukács accepted the traditional and dogmatic Marxian identification of the industrial working class with revolutionary subjectivity as such. In the context of his theory of revolution, he turned out to be more flexible, however, even if once again he did not really succeed in overcoming dogmatism. To be sure, stratification within the working class could hardly be doubted, especially by a sociologically sophisticated friend of Max Weber. Even Lenin's thesis of a worker's aristocracy erected on the proceeds of imperialism recognized this, as did Eduard Bernstein. Lukács, however, was uncertain of the explanatory value of the Leninist thesis and its reductionist logic. However, within the Marxist tradition he could find few alternatives that could explain the empirical behavior of the working class *and* point to some of its revolutionary possibilities. Neither Bernstein's empiricist dissolution of the notion of class nor Luxemburg's messianic faith in the revolutionary proletariat was satisfactory. But the problem went deeper. Turning back to Marx himself to confront the original formulation of the theory with a new social world, what he found, or must have found, was highly ambiguous.

In parts of *Kapital* I, Marx structurally integrated the praxis of the working class into the history of capitalist development. But when it came to extrapolating the long range future tendencies of capitalist development (especially in *Kapital* volumes II and III), Marx almost wholly neglected the dimension of sociological class analysis and described these tendencies only from the point of view of the category of capital. Lukács explicitly complains that the fragmentary third volume breaks off just when Marx comes to the topic, "class." Thus, the first volume of *Kapital* could have provided at least a model for Lukács, while the other two testified only to the fragmentary state of Marx's own social theory.

In Marx's earliest works, especially in the published works of 1843, Lukács found a definition of the working class based on the possibility of revolutionary praxis, a possibility founded on the radical needs of the class that are at the same time universal human needs. Lukács implicitly recognized the deep Hegelian foundations of this notion.

In the *Communist Manifesto,* Lukács found the well-known two-class model of the capitalist world, which located revolutionary class consciousness in progressive impoverishment but defined the total society as the object of class consciousness. This two-class model was, of course, especially paradoxical from the point of view of the changed social situation.

Partially in the *Manifesto* and especially in the *Poverty of Philosophy,* he found the notion that the revolutionary class already exists in itself—implicitly, potentially—on the level of sociological description but that it has yet to constitute itself for itself.

The question is whether or not Lukács was able to synthesize his theory of class consciousness with the various meanings of class in Marx in a wholly new historical context. However, after the experience of the Russian Revolution and the failure of the Hungarian Soviet Republic, Lukács was absolutely certain that political practice in terms of the sociologically false two-class model was pernicious.

Nevertheless, Lukács insists here that only the bourgeoisie and the proletariat are capable of any level of class consciousness, that is, knowledge and action in terms of the total situation (p. 71). Furthermore, only the proletariat is capable of historical subjectivity in the positive, constructive sense of overcoming all reified objectivity. The other classes (or strata), the peasantry, petit bourgeoisie, and so forth, act on mere spontaneity—and can only be the objects of the historical process. Whether any of these classes is important for a revolutionary movement depends on the given historical situation, but the role of one or more generally tends to be crucial. When such a "spontaneous" class or stratum is historically important, its mass psychological consciousness must be so influenced that it acts in a progressive direction. And mass psychological consciousness can only be affected through a certain amount of respect for the immediate interests of the class or stratum (pp. 309–310).

As we will see, in Lukács's analysis it is precisely the task and justification of the Leninist party to influence "mass psychology" in the appropriate way. The question is, however, whether or not the relationship of the Communist Party to the proletariat, especially when the socialist goals of Marxist ideology are subordinated to *Realpolitik* in practice, will be itself (equally or partly) manipulated. Lukács knew that the compromise on socialist principles for the sake of *Realpolitik* was dangerous, even if necessary. He believed, however, that a class-conscious, unified proletariat could clearly risk a temporary diminution of its aims. But was the proletariat for Lukács everywhere unified and class conscious? For him economic and social development of the capitalist world provided the objective possibility of socialist revolution, but the proletariat's stratification, disunity (often fragmentation), and lack of class consciousness have blocked the emergence of revolutionary subjectivity. Lukács fuses these factors into his concept of the ideological crisis.

Ideological crisis is the continued hold of reification and

bourgeois ideology over the mind of the workers, in spite of the social-economic crisis of the bourgeois world. Ideological crisis is, moreover, organizationally objectified in reformist and opportunist (centrist) parties and unions that tend to work for limited political or economic gains, separating the political and the economic struggle. They work exclusively within the established boundaries of the existing system (pp. 311–312), sponsoring modes of thought that methodologically presuppose the existing world as eternal (p. 17). The result is that, on the subjective level, workers continue to treat the system as unchangeable, while on the objective level they continue to be atomized, and passive, struggling only in isolated and rigidly defined directions. Lukács presents the Leninist theory of labor aristocracy as a partial explanation of the sociological ground here.

Workers of the developed capitalist world benefit from the "super exploitation" of colonies and, hence, become more integranted into the existing capitalist system (pp. 307–308). Lukács was never overly sympathetic to any reductionist and determinist explanations of class consciousness. Indeed, he argued, while labor aristocracies do exist (as Lenin explained) they can in no way fully explain the ideological crisis of the proletariat. There is no evidence that when the prosperity of a given stratum of workers is undermined, class consciousness increases. Furthermore, there had never been an overall correlation between revolutionary activity and poverty of workers. Thus, Lukács noticed the connection between the theory of labor aristocracy and the unsophisticated pauperization thesis and was not inclined toward such ad hoc attempts "to save the phenomena" (that is, the dogma of the *Communist Manifesto*). He meant to present his theory of reification as an alternative to the whole framework connected to the pauperization thesis. Accordingly, Lukács locates the "ideological crisis" in the increasing pervasiveness of the commodity form, implying the atomization and deactivation, but also the fundamental homogenization of the working class.

Lukács does not, as we have said, dispute the empirical existence of stratification in the proletariat (pp. 325ff.). But he rejects the notion that it generates final or fundamental divisions. There is stratification regarding immediate interests and empirical consciousness. But there is underlying unity in terms of historical consciousness (pp. 327–328). The strata within the proletariat in his theory, then, are defined in terms of the comparative ease or difficulty with which they can acquire class consciousness. Lukács defines the Communist Party, as we have seen, as the independent *Gestalt* of the "imputed" or "ascribed" class consciousness. One of the party's roles is to navigate through the vicissitudes of the unequal development of class consciousness, battling (or purging) the organized representatives of false consciousness; by overcoming the ideological crisis, the party enables the proletariat to become a revolutionary class for itself. The conclusion here is inescapable: without the party, the proletariat cannot overcome its ideological crisis. From the standpoint of class analysis, this means a division of the class into a small, relatively active part and a large, relatively passive part, which brings to mind Marx's important question: Who educates the active part, the educators? But before considering Lukács's confrontation of his ideal type of the party with the world of reification, we must analyze the role he assigns to the ideological crisis in the process of revolutionary development.

The Revolutionary Process

By revolutionary process we mean primarily the interrelationship of politics and economics in the period of socialist transformation. Lukács's work in this area is best understood in terms of a series of confrontations with the theories of Rosa Luxemburg and the Bolsheviks. Indeed, most of his own theory of revolution was presented in the form of a critique of Luxemburg's various theses. But we should not be misled; he accepted Luxemburg's theory of capitalist collapse as a better analysis of the immanent tendencies of capitalist development than the Engels-Kautsky-Lenin (imperialism) thesis of the linear movement through monopolization and state capitalism to socialism. However, his methodological critique of a deterministic interpretation of historical materialism—that restricted the "primacy of the economic" to a period of capitalism well before its "final" period of crisis—permitted Lukács to accept Luxemburg's theory of development (restricted to economic tendencies) over those of Engels and Kautsky and at the same time to begin a critique of Luxemburg herself from the Leninist point of view of the "primacy of the political," which was the specific Bolshevik contribution to the orthodox Marxist theory of revolution.

Lenin's *Imperialism, the Highest Stage of Capitalism* (1916) seems to contradict this claim. The book is distinguished by an almost unconditional acceptance and extension of the Engels-Kautsky thesis of monopolization into socialism. Lenin explicitly argues that the very meaning of monopoly capitalism lies in a socialized mode of production in the context of private, capitalist appropriation. For Lenin, the capitalist mode of production is characterized not by the domination of the class of wage labor by the class owning the means of production but by the anarchy of production that defines a competitive system of commodity production. He defines socialist production exclusively on the basis of overcoming the anarchy of production through centralization and planning.[2] The key idea of Lenin's model of imperialism, in distinction to most Social Democratic theories, predicts no automatic breakdown of the system, but points to the increasing tendencies toward war and national struggle for liberation as the fundamental weakness of the imperialist world system. Thus, Lenin breaks with one aspect of the classical Engels-Kautsky interpretation of Marxism: its deterministic structure.

It is exactly the problem of the deterministic framework of Rosa Luxemburg's theory of capitalist development that allows Lukács to side with Lenin in good conscience. To be sure, as we have said, on the level of immanent economic tendencies Lukács accepted Luxemburg's theory. But he did not believe that the revolutionary process took place on this level. Not an original economic theorist himself, he was somewhat ambiguous on the problem of crisis and collapse. In some contexts he clearly implies that without proletarian revolution, capitalism will collapse, but the result would be in this case "barbarism" (p. 82). This particular formulation belongs to 1920, however. His 1922 view seems to be that on the pure economic level, capitalism would always find a "way out," and the success or failure of these "ways out" in the concrete world of the class struggle would depend on the proletariat (pp. 308–309). Thus, the process of capitalist development as described by Rosa Luxemburg receives a Leninist twist from Lukács: the objective economic development yields not automatic collapse, but a situation in which the political-military struggle of the two classes decides the continuation or the destruction of the capitalist system. "Violence," Lukács states, "becomes the decisive economic factor in the situation." (pp. 249–254).

Nevertheless, the full acceptance of the specifically Leninist perspective on the primacy of the political (or the state), entailed more than just a rejection of economic determinism. The Engels-Kautsky model saw state capitalism as the logical culmination of the tendency toward monopolization, and Lenin tended to accept this notion. Furthermore, in the context of his theory of imperialism, he managed to extend it: imperialist expansion and war are the affairs of capitalist states which are forced to plan, control, and rationalize production to the highest extent possible in moments of emergency. On the other hand, and as a result, in the context of war and national struggles for liberation, the advanced sections of the proletariat must confront the state directly, and socialism becomes a question not of the development and breakthrough of a new force of production (that has already been created by monopoly capitalism), but of the struggle for political power. In this sense *Imperialism, the Highest Stage of Capitalism* established the economic foundation of the Leninist thesis of the "primacy of the political." The political side of the thesis was developed elsewhere. Its extreme poles are well represented by Lenin in *State and Revolution* (1917) and, to chose the best example, in Bukharin's *Economics of the Transformation Period* (1920), perhaps the most important theoretical work of "war communism."

But Lukács himself in 1919 clearly indicated the poles of possible interpretation: either the utopia of proletarian self-determination or the harsh reality of the institutional constraints of the proletarian state (over the proletariat as well as other strata) could supply the element of political primacy over economics. This insight, originally formulated in terms of a myth of proletarian freedom, was, as we have seen, progressively mythologized in his work—the party being presented by 1920 as the unitary expression of the "will" of the proletariat as well as of a "noninstitutional" political constraint from above.

The myth was the veil of a harsh reality. And yet Lukács's replacement of the freedom of the proletariat with a new mythology never managed to please his Leninist opponents, whom the party myth nevertheless legitimated. The curious thing was, however, that the issue was never clearly posed by either side. The reluctant founder of "Western Marxism" apparently did not notice, or want to notice, the transformation of the meaning of the primacy of politics both in Leninist theory and practice between 1917 and 1922. In particular, Lukács did not notice any discrepancy between the nearly libertarian *State and Revolution* and Lenin's subsequent pronouncements on the state, which corresponded far more adequately to the actual practices of the Russian Communist Party. In *State and Revolution,* Lenin argued that the capitalist form of the state is totally unsuitable to a socialist transformation toward a stateless society and thus is to be smashed and replaced by new political forms (for example, workers' soviets). One could interpret the primacy of the political dimension expressed in *State and Revolution* as having culminated in a utopian dream of virtually direct democracy—a dream that veiled (perhaps from Lenin himself, at least in 1917) the drastic political necessities of revolutionary transition to socialism in Russia.

But on one level at least—that of relations between the new state and labor—Lenin remained consistent with his earlier conception in *Imperialism,* even extending it from the economy to society as a whole. As he wrote in *State and Revolution:* "The whole of society will have become . . . a single factory, with equality of labor and pay. But this factory discipline, which the proletariat . . . will extend to the whole of society, is by no means our ultimate goal. It is only a necessary step. . . ." Elsewhere in the booklet, he speaks of the population in its entirety as workers of "*one* huge syndicate, the whole state."

What we have here is that very extension of the factory form (and the worker's fate) to society as a whole (that Lukács characterized as the specificity of reification) with one proviso that will disappear in practice and in theory: the political form of this state was for a moment presented as radically democratic. Lenin's first (theoretical) model (1917) of the society of socialist transition was, therefore, of a society organized as a single, ultrademocratically managed firm or factory. The model leaves the capitalist structure of labor untouched, and therefore its democratic emphasis, confined to the realm of general social administration, bifurcates each individual into citizen and subject in the manner of the political theory of the bourgeois revolution. This was the model criticized by Marx as political alienation par excellence, except that in this case the position of the worker in society-as-a-factory cannot even achieve and sustain the integrity of a private sphere.

To complete the analogy with the bourgeois revolution, the political theory soon degenerated into the mask of a new Jacobinism—this time permanent. Of the citizen-subject dualism, Leninism preserved only the second half. Lenin soon began to speak of a state capitalism armed with the Taylor system not as the last stage of capitalism, but as the first stage of the dictatorship of the proletariat.[3] His most famous statement on state capitalism and Taylorism came when discussing the opposition of Bukharin and other Left Communists to the reestablishment of the old forms of the capitalist state, an opposition basing itself on *State and Revolution:* "The need to destroy the old state . . . was a matter of yesterday."[4] Two years later in *Economics of the Transformation Period* Bukharin himself echoed this perspective when he argued that the demand for workers' control was useful and important to dissolve capitalist discipline but was to be strongly rejected (and replaced with centralized control and planning), given the demands of socialist discipline. The authoritarian, militarized factory provided the *second* and *final* Bolshevik model of the primacy of the political dimension.

The various forms of the interparty opposition until 1922 continued to revive themes of political democracy, antibureaucratism and workers' self-management but without any success. While their critique of bureaucratic and authoritarian centralism was usually quite perceptive, their own substantive position tended to rest on dogmatic and utopian beliefs in the immediate realizability of pure proletarian or pure socialist programs.[5]

The position developed by Lukács and the group around the Vienna-based journal, *Kommunismus,* was suspended somewhere between the position of the antibureaucratic Russian Left (fairly close to Lenin's first model) and the dreams of war communism (the second Leninist model). Lukács's case was somewhat unusual because he alone understood and explicitly criticized the factory model of society which was at the base of both alternatives. Nevertheless, his own conception of the "subject" of the primacy of the political shifted in a manner that was extremely close to that of Bukharin, with whom he had no special political connection or theoretical sympathy.[6] But unlike Lukács, Bukharin was less able and less interested in shielding the implications of his position by a recourse to the language of German idealism. In the context of the incredibly difficult period of the civil war and war communism, he openly admitted that "extra-economic" political force could be exercised only by the workers' state, while the workers themselves were increasingly a part of blind economic tendencies to be restricted, disciplined, and welded together by political force.

The spontaneity of the proletariat was increasingly seen by both Bukharin and Lukács as a danger to the project of socialist revolution. The political element that was to achieve its revolutionary primacy had to come from some other source. Lukács's complicated position between Lenin and Rosa Luxemburg is not to be seen merely in the context of his juggling with freedom and necessity, party and class, but even more in terms of his attempt to specify the subject of the primacy of politics in the age of revolution. In his view, Luxemburg's stress on organic economic development, spontaneity, and proletarian self-determination, subsumed the proletarian revolution under the supposed model of the classical bourgeois revolution, thus losing the primacy of politics. He could, nevertheless, not bring himself (anymore than could Luxemburg) to acknowledge the Leninist model of the militarized factory as the paradigm of socialist transition. There were in fact three models of the transition that Lukács now (1922) rejected: (1) the myth of proletarian self-determination as the content of the primacy of the political (Lukács's position in 1919; in part Lenin's in 1917; and indeed fairly close to that of Luxemburg herself); (2) the primacy of economic development, yielding the spontaneous political revolution of the proletariat and the emergence of a new mode of production from the womb of the old (what Lukács took to be Luxemburg's position); and (3) The primacy of the political dimension in the form of the authoritarian-military organization of society as a factory.

The rejection of the last was a consequence of the theory of reification. For Lukács, the logic of the commodity form under advancing capitalism was precisely to impose—through the mechanism of rationalization—the factory structure on all spheres of society. For Lenin and Bukharin on the other hand, the social economic system of capitalism remained irrational precisely because it was not fully rationalized, the anarchy of the market representing precisely the target of the further extension of reason in the sense of calculation, prediction, bookkeeping, and so forth. Only central planning could fully rationalize society. By this future projection—that their heirs were to realize without attaining economic rationality itself—the Bolsheviks were confirming Max Weber's judgment that socialism ("the rule of the official") would only strengthen the "iron cage" by subsuming all of society under a single, unified bureaucratic hierarchy. The question for us, of course, is whether Lukács, an early rebel inside the iron cage, who indeed executed a Marx-Weber synthesis of social theory, managed to provide another alternative.

The answer, of course, is yes and no. His critique of bureaucracy, his violent rejection of a capitalist factory model of labor (not to speak of society), his continued use of the concept of proletarian self-determination, the ever-present traces of council communism in his work, were at least the negative preconditions of a new answer. Of this, his Bolshevik enemies were to have no doubt. And yet, because he extended reification to absolutely all spheres of capitalist society, because he continued to hate indiscriminately objective spirit—all institutions and all law—and because he understood all "objectification" as alienation unless at the heights of the absolute spirit, he could neither discover the presence of creative subjectivity in the various spheres of society nor embody the meaning of emancipation in different political institutions.

The single key to the dissolution of reification, the dialectic of labor time and consciousness, failed him, as we have seen. The gap between the "minimal consciousness of alienation" and "class consciousness" remained enormous. To be able to postulate the surpassing of reification, therefore, he continued to have recourse to a proletariat as the absolute subject of history. But his sociologically precise interchange with Luxemburg's class theory revealed this as an untenable myth. To represent the proletariat, to represent the planning of the future in the present, to represent freedom in the realm of necessity, another agency, another subject, had to be found. It was, of course, the same agency reversing in the end the logic of the substitution of the party for the proletariat.

What Lukács could not face, as is shown by the relative shallowness of his critique of actual bureaucratic phenomena in the Communist International, was the self-perpetuating tendency inherent in "representation" and "substitution." To hide this possibility from himself required further mystification. The utopian and mythologizing character of his treatment of the party was both a tacit admission of the magnitude of the danger and an ultimate, self-delusive surrender to the source of the danger. He was unable to find an original, alternative conception of the primacy of the political dimension. What he did was to reconceptualize his own early myth of self-determination in the terms of an entirely illusory model of Leninist politics. The result could satisfy neither the intrinsic needs of his own theory nor the scrupulous anti-intellectualism of his bureaucratic enemies.

Revolutionary Organization

The final chapter of *History and Class Consciousness*, "Towards a Methodology of the Problem of Organization," begins with a critique of utopian attitudes towards the proletariat. Lukács criticizes even a utopian understanding of the workers' council, seeing it as "the panacea for all problems of the revolution" (p. 313). Nevertheless, the chapter culminates in a totally utopian, mythologized view of the Communist Party. This conclusion is less paradoxical if we realize that Lukács's own utopianism already had traveled a road from class to council to party.

Lukács's ideal concept of the Communist Party—and the term "ideal" here has an un-Weberian moral dimension—must be understood as a vantage point of critique. Once again the critique of Rosa Luxemburg's views plays a central role. Lukács did believe that, vis à vis social democracy, Luxemburg's notion of the party represented an advance because she understood that the party must first of all become the leadership of the whole proletarian mass movement, instead of becoming the repository of independent organizational interests that have a special relationship to the trade unions and the relatively small well-organized sections of the proletariat (pp. 301; 305).

But Luxemburg insisted on the ultimate subordination of this leadership to the spontaneity of the masses. According to Lukács, this overestimated, first of all, the strength of the proletariat in the beginning of the actual revolutionary period. When the task is to coordinate the proletariat with other classes, strata, or nationalities, spontaneity must be replaced with conscious direction. Second, Luxemburg conceived the primary ideological task of the party as teaching and enlightenment. This view, said Lukács, misunderstood the depth of the ideological crisis of the proletariat, a crisis taking place not only in the subjective consciousness of the proletariat but also in objectified reformist parties and labor unions which tended to reproduce and perpetuate an atomized and deactivized proletariat (pp. 307; 312–313). The ultimate conclusion of this line of argument is, as we have shown, that the proletariat is wholly integrated in the world of reification.

Given the fact that Lukács was presenting himself a problem that was impossible to solve, it is not surprising that his solution ends in mythology. What is the solution to the ideological crisis? "This crisis can be resolved only by the free action of the proletariat" (p. 313). This answer corresponds to the general point of view of Lukács's writings as early as the Hungarian Soviet Republic, but here it is no answer at all. Free action hinges on class consciousness, and the proletariat is caught in an all-pervasive ideological crisis. But, according to Lukács, it would be utopian to expect that in the transition from the age of necessity to the age of freedom, total freedom could suddenly burst upon the historical scene. The seeds of freedom must dialectically grow within the age of necessity. The sociological appearance of the proletariat is the first step; the organization of the proletariat into a class is the second one. But these are not yet conscious steps, and the age of freedom must be attained consciously. The organization of a truly revolutionary party is the first conscious step within the age of necessity toward the age of freedom (p. 317). The Communist Party is an independent *Gestalt* of proletarian class consciousness in its most advanced forms or, more precisely, of the objectively highest possible level of class consciousness at any given moment.

Lukács is insistent that he is not creating phraseology here for a sect isolated from the masses. Although the party attributes its own consciousness to the class as a whole, it does not tactically disregard the fact that the empirical consciousness of the masses is generally far less advanced. The Communist Party must, therefore, constantly interrelate with the growth of the masses, providing leadership when they are in motion and exemplary actions when they are passive. In both instances Lukács rejects the Blanquist, or sectarian, idea that the party can make the revolution. Rather, he sees even vanguard actions of the party as responding to and overcoming only the ideological crisis. Lukács conceives of party organization as a process of dialectical relations with the development of the masses, but he insists that this dialectic must be "consciously deployed" (p. 330). Briefly, the creation of the vanguard must be a free act, the free self-creating act of the vanguard itself (p. 332).

Lukács believed, in other words, that, because of the new relation between theory and practice, the formation of Communist parties everywhere presented "the permanent assault on and gradual disappearance of the purely *post festum* structure of the merely contemplative, reified consciousness of the bourgeoisie" (p. 320). No bureaucratic party, then, can be part of an assault on reification. Yet he defines the absence of bureaucracy only by way of the "classical" position Lenin had presented in *What Is to Be Done?* But Lukács surely must have known that Lenin's original justification of this model relied on nothing so elevated and elaborate as a critique of reification—the basis on which Lukács articulates his model of Lenin's model. The reified world fragments life and work; the party engages the total personality. The reified world atomizes individuals by offering egoistic freedom as the goal (meaning in reality freedom only for a few); the party demands individual discipline, assigning freedom to the organization as a whole. The reified world compartmentalizes society; party work reintegrates politics, economics, and culture. Reification deactivates individuals; the party activates them as participants in history, and so forth.

Specifically, in Lukács's view, the reified world projects bureaucracy and the cult of leadership as the only forms of the organization of power; the party combats both, vigilant always against the formation of internal hierarchy. Indeed, Lukács introduces the idea of the purge to deal precisely with these problems—implicitly admitting their presence in the best party. In every respect, the party must consciously create itself, for it is no less than an empirical realm where the subject-object separation must be overcome before it can be abolished in society as a whole.

With this in mind, it is worth recalling that, in the context of the Communist Party of Hungary, Lukács's party-ideal has a sharp, critical edge. Yet his many references to the Russian party seem to suggest that this party came closest to the ideal. Here, the power of the Russian Idea (realized in the October Revolution) remained undiminished. Nevertheless, for the non-Russian parties, such a cult of Russia and "October" could serve only as an apology for Bolshevization. One might argue that Lukács attempted something analogous to the Russian Left-Opposition groups of the first years of the 1920s. After all, he knew well enough that the Russian party was itself becoming increasingly bureaucratic. From this angle, his idea of the party is an implicit critique of all existing parties, including the Russian. But this would mean that he had once again retreated to a utopian critique, for in *History and Class Consciousness* there is *no* discussion of the internal dynamics between the existing parties and something more advanced.

The charge against Lukács of utopian mythologizing is in any case unavoidable here. But are we dealing with an emancipatory or an authoritarian utopia? We have seen that the idea, according to which a realm of overcoming alienation can be created in the midst of the alienated world, has deep roots in Lukács's past. The "whole man" of his early aesthetics, experiencing catharsis while facing a unified project; his "Dostoevskian" ideal of subjectivity purified of psychical and sociological determinations; his notion of a subjective internality so deep that it will, in face of all necessity and alienation, establish intersubjective human ties; all these notions were now in a sense revived in his concept of the party.

We have already argued that, implicitly, through his concept of subjective freedom, Lukács admitted an opaque, impenetrable, unchangeable historical necessity. But we have also tried to show that one of the main projects of *History and Class Consciousness* was the working out of a dialectic of *mediation* that would overcome the antinomy of freedom and necessity. Nevertheless, its theory of the party, derived both from the main theoretical premise and from the immediacy of a political world about which Lukács was less and less hopeful, returns to a mythologizing concept of subjectivity. And once again, this concept must be interpreted in terms of its duality—the myth implies, after all, not only extreme voluntarism, but also its opposite. A mythologizing concept of subjectivity, according to criteria that Lukács worked out against Hegel's absolute subject, meant that at last the objective historical process has become *both* opaque and fully deterministic. Lukács's party concept finally vitiated his whole social theoretical project. But, given the *philosophical* demands and assumptions of this project, it was open to exactly this outcome from the beginning.

We have arrived at a negative assessment of the outcome. So did the ideologues of the Communist International—but for a different reason. To us Lukács's mythology was a debacle because it justified them; to them it was dangerous because they understood the critique that had not meant to penetrate quite so far. The International, moreover, needed an ideology that not only legitimated it, but that no longer contained the tension between norm and fact, "ought" and "is." Such a one-dimensional ideology could not be found in the storehouse of German idealism, crammed as it was with the antinomies, hopes, and dangers of emancipation. The deep-seated antinomy of Lukács's own theory, flowing from the innermost sources of his project, was in summation this: a relentless critique which, sparing neither Engels nor, implicitly, Marx or the Bolsheviks, pointed beyond the Marxian tradition itself; *and* a philosophy of history that sought to discover the macrosubjects capable of anticipating and achieving a society of absolute freedom and transparency. It is this antinomy that makes Lukács Marx's greatest heir and interpreter. It is also what made his early work the origin of "Western Marxism." Finally, it is what made his synthesis unacceptable to both the Bolsheviks and—ultimately, in spite of everything—to any future tradition in revolutionary thought.

PART 3

THE FATE OF A BOOK, 1923–1933

CHAPTER

10

The "Lukács-Debate"

LUKÁCS'S TRANSFORMATION from bourgeois philosopher and cultural critic to revolutionary Communist was a remarkable event, although in its singularity his conversion can now be seen as representative of the political "radicalization" of intellectuals in this century.[1] No less striking is the fact that his conversion proved permanent, a lifelong committment to the Communist cause in an age when the more typical phenomenon has been that of intellectuals donning and shedding an array of faiths and despairs. The unwavering character of Lukács's decision is especially notable since, from the outset, his newly chosen career was not crowned by success. He performed effectively, even heroically given the circumstances, as cultural commissar and military commandant during the Hungarian Soviet Republic. While this is a matter of record, so, too, is the disastrous failure of the whole experiment. Then, in the imbroglio of factional battles within both the exiled Communist Party of Hungary and the Third International, Lukács was consistently in the losing camp. From his "ultra-Leftism" of the early 1920s to his "Right-deviation" near the end of the decade, he regularly ran afoul of prevalent party positions. That he managed to adapt himself to them with almost equal regularity is, among other things, a sign of his political ineffectiveness.

Yet when it came to Communist politics, the former Hegelian-Dostoevskian-Kierkegaardian master of the Free School of the Cultural Sciences was neither a *naif* nor a bungler. Regarding questions of the political ramifications of theoretical and ideological matters in particular, Lukács had a keen practical sense. Aware that his views had already aroused controversy, he knew that when *History and Class Consciousness* appeared in 1923, it would not be met by approval from the main ideologues of Central European and Soviet communism. Yet it is probably also true that he did not anticipate the extent and quality of their hostility. Sensing by the close of 1922 that criticism would follow, he sought to deflect it in the preface he wrote to the work in December of that year. He indicated, for example, that while speaking more about Rosa Luxemburg (and "Luxemburgism" was on its way to becoming a heresy in the Communist movement) than about Lenin, he did not thereby mean to underestimate the decisive theoretical genius of the Bolshevik leader. Similarly, he stressed that, while critical of certain of Engels's positions as a theorist (which in fact drew heavy fire from the critics), he spoke in the spirit and from the standpoint of Marx—a disclaimer that only made matters worse. Lukács even included a word on the modest character of his enterprise, terming it simply an attempt to "clarify for myself and readers certain theoretical questions of the revolutionary movement."[2]

In fact, *History and Class Consciousness* offered some immodest proposals, among them the claim that the question of proletarian revolution is, at root, a question of proletarian class consciousness and that this decisive question could no longer be discussed in the terms customarily employed by Marxists. Yet the originality and power of his arguments were not in themselves the source of the difficulties that emerged. Rather, it was a matter of their colliding with novel and forceful developments of a different sort. Astute as he may have been, Lukács could not have foreseen fully that his book would get ground nearly to bits in the gears of the extensive ideological and organizational rigidification of the Communist movement between 1923 and 1926: the "Bolshevization" or "Russification" of the Third International.

The story is hardly simple. It includes, for example, the fact that, as Part Two delineates, *History and Class Consciousness* in its own manner offers elements contributing to the dogmatic Marxism of which it is simultaneously a blistering critique. Moreover, Lukács gradually opted for adherence to Bolshevized Marxism, variously muting and disavowing the critical edge of his own ideas. But the ideas themselves then set out on an independent journey, receiving sustenance and reinterpretation from other intellectuals on the Left. In the process, a "Western Marxism," a theoretical perspective without a social movement, began its career on the margins of the organized Left. We want to show, then, that not only *History and Class Consciousness* but the drama of responses to it, including its author's own, went further than Lukács could have imagined in clarifying "certain theoretical questions of the revolutionary movement."

A final prefatory note: the whole question of *History and Class Consciousness* and its reception during the period up to the triumph of Nazism in Germany belongs first and obviously to the history of Marxism in thought and action. But just as Lukács came to Marxism from immersion in the crisis of bourgeois culture at the turn of the century, bringing into his new Marxism materials from that culture, so the Lukács debate in Marxist circles in the post–World War I decade emphatically belonged to the larger, ongoing cultural crisis of the period. Far from having been a sectarian matter, the Lukács debate was part of the story of a generation of European intellectuals who, lacking the more comfortable certainty of their *belle époque* parents and the desperate cynicism of their roaring twenties successors, sought to discover and nurture new fundamental human values from a soil that was—and remains—at once fertile and unyielding: war and revolution.

Berlin: Malik Verlag, 1923

Lukács had put the finishing touches on *History and Class Consciousness* by Christmas 1922. This was during the second of what proved to be a nine-year exile in Vienna where, at the time, as Victor Serge reports, Lukács and others in the anti–Béla Kun faction of the Communist Party of Hungary—Kun having taken up residence in Moscow—were living in impoverished circumstances.[3] It was also the eve of a pivotal year in the history of the young Communist movement in Europe. For when *History and Class Consciousness* appeared in print in the spring of 1923, the Third International was about to complete its turn, in Helmut Gruber's phrase, "from a revolutionary international of Communist parties into a centralized and bureaucratic organization firmly tied to the developments in and policies of the Soviet Union."[4] This would seal a number of fates, among them that of *History and Class Consciousness*.

We shall return to the specifics of the vital political context of the book's publication, but first we want to indicate several related aspects, for example, the fact that 1923 was a notable year in other ways. While hardly new, Europe's preoccupation with the whole problem of consciousness and society, as well as with the interplay of hope and despair in an increasingly fractured world, was intensifying dramatically in the early 1920s. The shock and calamity of world war had placed these and virtually all other matters onto an emergency basis. Lukács's was only one of several key works to have appeared in 1923, seeking in diverse, even conflicting, ways to develop dialectical accounts of human consciousness in its social nexus: *Marxism and Philosophy* by Lukács's fellow Communist, Karl Korsch; Martin Buber's *I and Thou;* and Sigmund Freud's *The Ego and The Id.* Preceded by a year by T. S. Eliot's cultural grimace *The Wasteland* and followed by a year by the ecstatic visions of the first *Manifesto of Surrealism,* these were among the great theoretical expressions of a not so great year for most Europeans.

The issues of consciousness and society, hope and despair, were, moreover, closely bound to that of the intellectual in society and politics, concern with which had likewise been considerably sharpened by the war and the immediate postwar upheavals. While *History and Class Consciousness* did not explicitly address this question, the book cannot be separated from the "emergency situation of intellectual workers," to borrow the title of the book published by Alfred Weber in 1923.[5] Multifaceted, the issue itself ranged from employment and wage problems across the spectrum of questions concerning the responsibility of intellectuals (to science or politics) to the entire matter of the destiny of high culture and its bearers in the modern world. Lukács's book addressed itself to all of these problems, and one of the subterranean (if unintended) sources of its influence among Central European intellectuals was that *History and Class Consciousness*'s analysis of "reification" pertained as much to the situation of intellectuals as to that of the proletariat.

Written in Vienna, *History and Class Consciousness* was published in Berlin by the Malik Verlag, a house with a story of its own, one not unconnected to the matter of the intellectuals and politics in the postwar period. Malik's founder and guiding spirit was Wieland Herzfelde, poet and energetic cultural-political impresario who had traveled from young Dadaist and antimilitarist circles during World War I to affiliation with the Communist Party of Germany (*KPD*) in the early 1920s. Along with his brother, Helmut, a photographer and brilliant montagist who had adopted the name John Heartfield in response to German military designs on England, Wieland Herzfelde established the Malik Verlag in 1917, initially with simply a journal by that title. The name itself, which corresponds to the Hebrew *Melech,* meaning king, was taken from the title and hero of a novel by Else Lasker-Schuler and was meant to be sufficiently nondescript to pass through the wartime censorship. It was not, and the little venture was closed by the authorities in the last year of the war. Joined by Georg Grosz and other sympathizers from the left wing of Dada and Expressionism, the Herzfeldes, with financial support from a well-to-do young socialist intellectual, Felix Weil, reorganized Malik in 1919, soon thereafter establishing ties with the *KPD.*[6]

In broad terms, then, the early career of the Verlag and its associates paralleled Lukács's own: antibourgeois cultural rebels from the bourgeoisie politicized by the war and moving into contact with the revolutionary Left. By the early 1920s, Malik was turning out an expanding range of handsome but inexpensive works, many bearing John Heartfield's expert cover designs, as did *History and Class Consciousness.* Lukács's book appeared as the ninth volume of the "Little Revolutionary Library," whose advertised goal was to "contribute to and develop revolutionary knowledge" and which, along with the "Red Novel Series" and the "Revolutionary Drama Collection," were the house's main series.

Especially in light of Lukács's remark nearly a half-century later that, for all its flaws, *History and Class Consciousness* exerted a positive influence in its day insofar as it helped to draw intellectuals toward Marxism, it is notable that recruitment of intellectuals to the revolutionary cause was precisely the purpose of the Little Revolutionary Library.[7] With such works as Grosz's haunting volume of drawings, *The Face of the Ruling Class,* translations of Zinoviev's little book *Lenin,* and Aleksander Blok's *Downfall of Humanity* making indirect appeals, Wieland Herzfelde's own booklet, *Society, Artist, Communism,* and the translation of Henri Barbusse's *Le couteau entre les dents* (*With a Knife Between the Teeth,* 1921) presented impassioned pleas to intellectuals to recognize that militant communism offered the only way out of the crisis of bourgeois society and culture. Karl August Wittfogel's *Science of Bourgeois Society* (1924), while more scholarly, nevertheless had the same intent.[8]

If communist publishers then used such parlance, Herzfelde and his comrades must have said that *History and Class Consciousness* fit well into their program of publication. Yet this could not have been the sole consideration, for in this instance they had before them a demanding work, as lengthy as it was dense, and one that was sure to unleash controversy in the Communist camp. In view of the barrage of criticism by German and Soviet Communists with which the book was, after all, met and the fact that its first printing was the only printing authorized by Lukács (until 1968), it is tempting to inquire whether there may have been hesitation about or opposition to its publication in the first place.

The hardening of the Communist movement's intellectual arteries was, in fact, underway—and *History and Class Consciousness* was a critique of this process—but it had not yet reached the point it would attain by the close of 1923, with the official Communist attacks on Lukács's book being a significant stage in the process. As one participant recalled the situation, "already around 1922, the International was unintentionally modeling factotum officials who were prepared to give passive obedience."[9] And as Lukács himself noted that year, in the course of his polemic with the Béla Kun leadership of the Hungarian party, a bureaucratic and dogmatic mentality oriented toward narrow, rote thinking, was on the rise within the movement.[10] Nevertheless, debate and controversy, stifled shortly thereafter, were still evident in the Communist International. Had *History and Class Consciousness* been completed in 1924 or 1925—and it could not have been—one might seriously envision its repression.

The issue of bureaucratism in the International brings back into focus the political context in which Lukács's book appeared. It also suggests parallel and related developments in the Soviet Union, where the ailing Lenin had belatedly glimpsed the rising Medusa head of bureaucracy and where Trotsky, in December 1923, would publish his passionate if impotent denunciations of its paralytic effects. The fact is that in the "year of crucial importance"—1923—events in Central Europe brought to a head tendencies that had been underway in the Communist movement from its outset, and in so doing "put a period to the postwar revolutionary thrust from which all the Bolsheviks hoped and expected salvation."[11] While bureaucratization was key among these tendencies, it was itself in large measure a product of deeper forces, above all the dissolution of revolutionary impulses and energies in Europe and Russia. Yet this enervation of the revolution impressed itself upon many revolutionaries only gradually and unevenly, so fervent were their hopes and so deep their illusions. Indeed, *History and Class Consciousness* itself mirrored this complex political-psychological state of affairs: it was at once a sort of philosophical and sociological last rite spoken over the fading soul of the postwar revolutionary movement, and a reveille to its reawakening.

Following a year and a half of relative calm in the postwar storm, 1923 witnessed the apparent return of revolutionary possibilities, above all in Germany, where the year opened with the French occupation of the Ruhr, calamitous intensification of inflation, and budding fascist movements, all of which aroused the working class and seemed to put preparation for insurrection back onto the agenda. This, in any case, was the conclusion drawn by the Russian Executive of the International, which in the fall of 1923 corralled the hesitant leadership of the KPD—the so-called right-wing under Heinrich Brandler, long an opponent of what he deemed sectarian insurrectionary tactics—into what proved a disastrous course of action. Termed the "United Front From Above," it entailed Communist representatives entering the Left-socialist state governments of Saxony and Thuringia, especially volatile areas, with an eye toward immediately arming the proletariat for the seizure of power. Having overestimated the workers' will to revolution while underestimating the relative solidity of the national government, the "German October" moved rapidly from confusion through retreat to rout. A similarly ignominious defeat of Communist forces had occurred the previous month in Bulgaria, and the two episodes left the Central European Communist movement demoralized and in disarray.[12]

The Russian leadership's manipulative control of the International, already a key ingredient in the German and Bulgarian events, was greatly extended and deepened in their aftermath, that is, during 1924 and the succeeding years. In the German case, always central in this period, the chief effect of 1923, although not immediately apparent, was in E. H. Carr's words "to destroy the large measure of independence hitherto enjoyed by the KPD and turn it into a sparring ground for Russian factional disputes," namely, the battle between the Zinoviev-Stalin-Kamenev and the Radek-Trotsky factions over succession to Lenin, who had died in January 1924.[13] With differences in particulars and degrees, the effect was the same on the Communist International as a whole, a fact which offered grim vindication of the fear voiced by many European militants, among them Rosa Luxemburg, at the time of the founding of the Communist International in 1919: that it contained the spectre of eventual subjugation of the various national parties to the power and model of the International's Moscow-based Executive. Yet these Cassandra-like apprehensions, and the additional fact that many European Communists who had once shared them would turn and actively assist in carrying out the Russification or Bolshevization of the International in 1924 and afterward, only reflected the profound weaknesses of the revolutionary movement in Europe.[14] *History and Class Consciousness* presented a perspective on Marxism and a vision of emancipatory Communist revolution which contrasted sharply with the emergent *Verapparatisierung,* to use the vivid German expression (apparatusization), of the Communist movement.

"This 'New Current' in Marxism": The Role of Karl Korsch

Soon beleaguered and later prematurely confined to the historical rare bookshelf, *History and Class Consciousness* did not lack its supporters. From the standpoint of its critics among Communist (and socialist) ideologues, precisely this was part of the problem posed by the book: its potential impact had to be curtailed. As to its allies, however, participants in and observers of the political-philosophical debate that unfolded around *History and Class Consciousness* were quick to notice that Lukács's book bore especially close ties to another work that had also made its appearance in 1923: *Marxism and Philosophy* by the German Communist theoretician and militant, Karl Korsch.[15] For example, one reviewer of *History and Class Consciousness* writing from outside the Communist movement noted in 1924 that its author stood alongside Karl Korsch as one of the "new Communists" whose common theoretical standpoints showed an affinity for the work of the "young Marx";[16] another suggested in the same year that Lukács's and Korsch's books should be taken together as the major efforts to provide the Communist movement with adequate philosophical foundations.[17] Similarly, early in 1924—that is, still prior to the official Bolshevik denunciations at the Fifth World Congress of the International—the Communist intellectual Karl Wittfogel stressed in the introductory chapter of his *History of Bourgeois Society* that "recently and from diverse standpoints a number of Marxist theoreticians—Bukharin, Korsch, Lukács—have systematically demonstrated the 'reality' of the [ideological] superstructure and this author fully endorses the common tendency among these analyses."[18]

The connection was not lost on the orthodox Communist critics. "Lukács already has his disciples," wrote Abram Deborin, the influential Soviet philosopher, in his 1924 review of *History and Class Consciousness,* "and is in a sense the leading thinker of a whole tendency to which, among others, Comrades Korsch, [Béla] Fogarasi, and [Josef] Révai belong. This cannot be ignored; we must at least subject this 'new current' in Marxism to criticism."[19] The links between Lukács's and Korsch's works would, of course, have been visible to even the half-alert reader, since all that was required was a perusal of the brief afterword Korsch himself appended to the first edition of *Marxism and Philosophy:* "While this was being written," Korsch noted, "the book by Georg Lukács . . . appeared. As far as I can see at the moment, I am pleased to say that I am in basic accord with that author's analysis which, while based on broader philosophical foundations, touches at many points on the questions raised in my own essay. With regard to matters of method and substance on which we differ, I prefer to postpone a thorough confrontation to a later date."[20]

Before giving these remarks their requisite amplification—they belong to the opening phase of the Lukács debate—something should be said of Korsch himself.[21] Born in Germany in 1886, Korsch's intellectual and political formation paralleled Lukács's in broad terms while differing in numerous important particulars. A convinced but organizationally independent socialist during his student years at Berlin and Jena, where he pursued his degree in jurisprudence, Korsch, in contrast to Lukács's neo-Romantic outlook, moved in what could be called neo-Enlightenment or democratic-utilitarian currents of thought and sensibility. Active in the small progressive wing of the German student movement, the Free Students (*Freie Studenten*), Korsch joined the Fabian Society during his two-year sojourn in London prior to World War I, at the close of which he plunged into revolutionary movements, going from the left-socialist USPD (the Independent Social Democratic Party of Germany) into the KPD in 1920.

A professor of law and an intellectual with real philosophical impulses, Korsch focussed on the practical issues of socialism—the politically instrumental implications of theory, whether they were the reform socialist theory of his early years or the revolutionary Marxist theory he had adopted in 1920. Emerging as a leading functionary in the KPD in 1922, Korsch was minister of justice in the aborted United Front government in Thuringia in 1923, editor of the party's theoretical organ, *Die Internationale* in 1924, and expelled from the KPD as a Left-oppositionist in 1926. After his break with the Communist movement and the political isolation that followed, Korsch became the representative figure of the alternative path open to those who shared the ideas presented in *History and Class Consciousness*.

From divergent sources, then, Korsch and Lukács reached some common conclusions in 1923. Chief among them was the conviction that, in the final analysis, proletarian revolution hinged upon the subjective factor, proletarian class consciousness, and that understanding this factor required recognition of the Hegelian component of Marx's thought. The two theorists, working independently and making brief contact in 1922, further agreed that the outlook of the Second International and Marxist thought virtually as a whole during the latter part of the nineteenth century had been dominated by what Korsch called a "Hegel amnesia" and what Lukács called a "vulgar Marxism." By these terms they meant to characterize a standpoint in which dialectical and revolutionary understanding was displaced by a narrowly materialist and positivist approach that had reduced consciousness to an epiphenomenal reflection of economic structures and laws. As seen by Lukács and Korsch, such a Marxism was not and could not have been revolutionary; its constitutive premises could not comprehend, and thus not participate in, the process through which the proletariat could become the active and self-conscious maker of history.

It was no accident, as Marxists like to say, that *History and Class Consciousness* and *Marxism and Philosophy* should have appeared at nearly the same moment. As already noted the early 1920s in general and 1923 in particular amounted to a vintage season for intensive reflection on relations between consciousness and society. But more specifically, the common source of Lukács's and Korsch's efforts was a crisis in the Communist movement, one which had begun to emerge with initial clarity in the course of 1921 and 1922. Its main symptom, as indicated in *History and Class Consciousness* and *Marxism and Philosophy,* was a recrudescent positivism and mechanistic materialism within communism itself. Neither book explicitly stated this argument; both directed their critical shafts at the Marxism of the Second International and its sustained presence within postwar Social Democracy which, in turn, continued to exert great influence upon the European working class movements at large. Nevertheless, the specific and immediate occasion for Lukács's and Korsch's critiques was the reappearance of the older standpoints inside the new Communist movement. The common purpose of their works was to provide the internal provocation and self-criticism that would aid communism's progress toward a genuinely dialectical and revolutionary outlook.

Indirect substantiation for reading *History and Class Consciousness* and *Marxism and Philosophy* as confrontations with an emergent crisis of communism lies in the vehement denunciations of the books by Communists throughout 1924. In short, if social democracy and the whole legacy of the Second International were the sole culprit, why the furor among Communist ideologues? Because they recognized quite correctly that they, too, were under the critical lens. More direct evidence can be found in the active role Korsch played in drawing out the implications for communism contained in his own and Lukács's works. While Abram Deborin was correct when he termed Lukács the "leading thinker" of a new oppositional current within communism, Korsch was certainly its leading progenitor and was not—as Deborin mistakenly claimed—Lukács's disciple. The positions Korsch adopted between 1923 and

1926, and the ways in which they illuminate Lukács's evolution, are thus central to our theme, in particular because one recent commentator, attempting and partially succeeding in setting the record straight, has also generated some new difficulties.[22]

A sign of both the crisis unfolding within communism and the links between Lukács and Korsch appeared in a small episode in mid–1922. Earlier in the year, Korsch, in connection with his involvement in party educational work, had published two pamphlets, *The Quintessence of Marxism* and *Fundamentals of the Materialist Conception of History.*[23] The former, subtitled "A Common Sense Presentation," was a clear and, in most respects, schematic effort aimed at ground-level introduction to Marxist ideas; the latter, a more sophisticated essay anticipating the themes Korsch would soon develop in *Marxism and Philosophy,* also contained a collection of supporting quotations mostly from Marx and Engels but including material taken from the Bible, Shakespeare, Lenin, and a range of other sources. The main thrust of *Fundamentals* was to demonstrate what Korsch considered a dialectical, and thus revolutionary, approach to relations between economic and ideological factors.

The pamphlets elicited prompt disapproval from Hermann Duncker, a leading KPD functionary in educational work in the party's Thuringian section, where Korsch himself was located.[24] In Duncker's eyes, Korsch's rendition of Marxism's principles revealed definite idealist traces, typified by its penchant for bourgeois thinkers since Marx. Specifically, Korsch was taken to task for having included, without criticism, quotations from Wilhelm Dilthey's 1883 book, *Introduction to the Cultural Sciences,* which, Duncker insisted, could only becloud the difficult work of introducing proletarians to the materialist, and thus revolutionary, content of Marxism. Selections from Goethe, Schiller, and Herder evidently posed no problems, as these writers preceded Marx and presumably helped anchor Communist ideas in German tradition. Significantly, Duncker also left untouched the quotation from Auguste Comte, the grand master of positivism, that Korsch included in his documentary section. Only Dilthey, the turn-of-the-century idealist philosopher of history and culture, posed a problem and gave it focus.

Korsch promptly responded with a brief "Anti-critique" in the pages of *Die Internationale,* arguing that Duncker's position amounted to a drastic narrowing of Marxism to a strictly economic view of history and social life.[25] Further, he explicitly defended his inclusion of passages from Dilthey, one of which consisted of the statement that "man as a fact preceding history and society is a fiction of the genetic mode of explanation; that man which the healthy analytic science has as its object is the individual as a component of society."[26] While Dilthey's work has definite limits from a revolutionary standpoint, it nevertheless contributes much, Korsch insisted, to a real grasp of the materialist conception of history. In this connection, he encouraged Communist readers to examine the recent "exemplary" review of Dilthey's *The History of Hegel's Early Period* (published 1921) that had just appeared in the KPD daily, *Die Rote Fahne.* The author of the review was Georg Lukács.[27]

It is fitting that Korsch's first mention of Lukács in print should have been occasioned by their mutual interest in Wilhelm Dilthey, a giant of idealist-dialectical thought, against an emergent current of orthodox Marxist materialism. Obscure in itself, this 1922 exchange involving pamphlets and short reviews nonetheless foreshadowed in substance and style the more ample confrontation that was to follow. That Hermann Duncker would publish the first of the critical reviews of *History and Class Consciousness* (in May 1923) is also symptomatic here. More pertinent for the moment, however, is Korsch's role in the 1922 philosophical-methodological scuffle, for in addition to evoking Lukács as an ally, he was quick to draw what amounted to battle lines between two opposing conceptions of Marxist theory within the Communist camp.

While Lukács and Korsch may well have corresponded earlier, they actually met for the first and, perhaps, the only time in May 1922, at roughly the moment Duncker's criticism of Korsch had appeared and shortly prior to the latter's reply.[28] The occasion was a small gathering of left-wing intellectuals, mostly from the German and Hungarian Communist parties, in the Thuringian Forest. Called together by Korsch, by his wife, Hedda Korsch, also a KPD militant active in educational affairs, and by their friend, Felix Weil, not a Communist himself, the meeting was to have been the first in a projected series of "Marxist Work Weeks" but was affectionately called the "Summer Academy" by its participants. Among the dozen or so others present were Lukács's close comrade, Béla Fogarasi; Richard Sorge, later a top-level Soviet agent in the Far East; Boris Roninger, a young friend of Korsch who would play a role in the 1924 disputes with Zinoviev and Bukharin; and Karl Wittfogel and Friedrich Pollock, both of whom would a decade later be associates, along with Felix Weil, of the Institute for Social Research in Frankfurt. The Summer Academy did not reconvene.

We can venture the thought that at this brief gathering, Lukács and Korsch discussed some of the differences in "matters of method and substance" to which Korsch would refer less than a year later. We can also assume that Korsch would then prefer to "postpone . . . to a later date" any substantial reckoning over these differences because a sharper confrontation had begun to take shape between the perspective presented by Lukács and himself, on the one side, and a very different, increasingly dominant Communist standpoint, on the other. Late in May 1923, *Die Rote Fahne* carried Hermann Duncker's compact assault on *History and Class Consciousness*. Echoing his earlier criticisms of Korsch, he described "this new book on Marxism" as "dangerous." Then, focusing on the analysis of Engels as the *éminence grise* of vulgar Marxism, Duncker rejected Lukács's entire investigation into class consciousness as a thinly veiled idealism which could only dilute genuine Marxism.[29] If Lukács and Korsch exchanged notes over Duncker's review—a reasonable assumption, though there is no documentation—they probably touched upon a shared sense that it might well be followed by more of the same. Anticipated or not, that is what happened. The debacle of Central European Communism in the fall of 1923, the concurrent rigidification of the Russian Revolution, and the Bolshevization of the Third International that ensued, constituted the terrain on which the Lukács debate proceeded.

"We Cannot Tolerate Such Theoretical Revisionism": The Lukács Debate, 1923–24

What has come to be called the "Lukács debate" was a short-lived affair. Between the appearance of *History and Class Consciousness* in the spring of 1923 and the close of 1924, the key issues raised by the book were resolved within the Communist movement—unhesitatingly and decisively against Lukács. Within and even outside the Central European Left as a whole, discussion of the book continued throughout the decade, but intensive as the exchange was, it amounted to little more than aftermath. The significance of the Lukács debate's brevity and outcome is not difficult to establish; and, as the following delineates, contemporaries, too, were not slow in recognizing it. *History and Class Consciousness* and a few kindred works, such as Karl Korsch's, represented theoretical expressions of a European Marxist alternative to the emergent Soviet ideology. As such, they stood as obstacles to the Bolshevization or Russification of the Communist International.

The ease with which these obstacles were removed showed clearly that *History and Class Consciousness* had sunk few roots in the Communist movement, which was in any case in no mood for a searching discussion of its own philosophical foundations—a mood Lukács's critics encouraged and utilized. While the official Communist style of handling theoretical debate did not begin here, there is no doubt that in 1923–24 it was solidified into a standard procedure that has endured to this day. As to Lukács himself, he certainly had not intended to articulate a dissenter's doctrine. Thrust into the heretic's role, he responded cautiously. In retrospect, one can see that, with Rosa Luxemburg gone, Lukács could have emerged as the Trotsky of Europe, a role he quietly but firmly refused. Of course, Europe lacked more than its Trotsky; it lacked its revolution.

Hermann Duncker's initial review was soon followed by one similar to it from the pen of Béla Kun, who by 1923 was residing in Moscow where, as Zinoviev's close associate, he was vigorously and successfully opposing Lukács's faction within the splintered, émigré Communist Party of Hungary.[30] Not surprisingly, Kun dismissed *History and Class Consciousness* as a work alien to Marxism. If Kun's remarks lacked length, this brevity was counterbalanced by another Hungarian participant, Laszlo Rudas, who had been in the anti-Kun faction from 1920 to 1922 but had shifted sides in 1923. In a three-part essay begun early in 1924, Rudas subjected Lukács's book to extensive theoretical and political criticism.[31]

His critique centered around Lukács's refusal to see the Marxist dialectic as an objective science whose validity was not contingent upon human consciousness, intentions, or will. In *History and Class*

Consciousness, Rudas proclaimed, "The dialectic is not an objective theory of the laws of development of society and nature that is independent of man, but a theory of the subjective laws [*Gesetzmässigkeit*] of man."[32] Throughout his review, Rudas returned to the theme of Lukács's alleged idealism—his supposed claim that revolutionary theory "makes" the revolution.[33] A virtually identical charge was leveled from the opposite end of the leftist spectrum, namely, from Karl Kautsky, in his 1924 review of Korsch's *Marxism and Philosophy.*[34]

Rudas, meanwhile, wasted little time in raising the political implications of Lukács's theoretical errors: their "ultra-Leftism." In the context of his attempted refutation of Lukács's account of Engels, Rudas pointed out that "many (particularly bourgeois) assailants see Engels as the first vulgar Marxist." In particular, Rudas mentioned Arturo Labriola, the leading theoretician of Italian syndicalism who, after World War I, had entered the Giolitti cabinet as Labor Minister and thus "ended his 'revolutionary' career." "And I mention Arturo Labriola," he continued, "precisely because he *too* was a Left radical (in the sense of Lenin's 'infantile disorder') and because Labriola's political course is typical in this regard."[35]

Here a theme Lenin and Trotsky had presented in 1920–21 in their criticisms of ultra-Left tendencies within the revolutionary movement was raised to the level of a formula: political ultra-Leftism finds its theoretical foundations in subjective idealism, and, conversely, subjective idealism in Marxist theory expresses itself politically in ultra-Leftism. Moreover, and more simply, Rudas echoed the predissident Trotsky in particular in identifying the very focus on problems of class consciousness, that is, on the cultural and psychological preconditions of Communist revolution, as a lapse into ultra-Left errors.[36] The inevitable result, according to Rudas, was collaboration with the bourgeoisie and anticommunism. He closed the first installment of his serialized review, written in Moscow and dated June 1, 1924—that is, on the eve of the decisive Fifth World Congress of the International—by remarking that it would be worth Lukács's effort to subject his philosophical world view to stringent materialist self-criticism and revision "for philosophical opinions, as Lenin never tired of showing, have *objective social roots*" (italics in original).[37]

Further criticism emanated from Moscow when, in July 1924,

Pravda cited the quartet of Lukács, Fogarasi, Révai, and Korsch as theorists still in need of education in the fundamentals of Marxist philosophy, whose definition of truth lies in the "agreement of the theoretical representation with the objects outside it."[38] In addition, Abram Deborin, one of the leading Russian Marxist philosophers, who within a decade was himself condemned by Stalin as a Hegelian, brought this charge against Lukács in his own 1924 review. "In general," he noted at the outset, "Lukács's views are a colorful mishmash of ideas of orthodox Hegelianism made tasty by doses of Lask, Bergson, Weber, Rickert . . . Marx and Lenin. In the person of Comrade Lukács, we are without doubt dealing with an innovator."[39] The fact that the label "innovator" served as a term of abuse is typical of the official Communist approach to *History and Class Consciousness*.

Deborin compared Lukács's conception of the dialectic of subject and object within Marxism to the "pure idealism" of the Russian philosopher Bogdanov, whose writings had come under heavy attack in Lenin's 1908 work, *Materialism and Empirio-criticism*. Building on Lenin's interpretation of Marxian materialism, Deborin took Lukács to task for having failed to see that the objects of knowledge are forms of an objective reality which exist independently of human consciousness and which possess laws of their own, likewise independent of human contingencies.[40] As in the reviews by Duncker, Kun, Rudas, and *Pravda,* so in Deborin's: an inseparable body of truths formulated by the trinity of Marx, Engels, and Lenin was evoked against the innovators, diluters, and apostates.

It is significant that Lukács's Bolshevik critics left untouched that segment of *History and Class Consciousness* in which he presented the most direct challenge to any version of Marxism claiming to be a science outside and above historical-social determinations. This was the essay "Functional Change of Historical Materialism," which was originally composed in 1919 during the period of the Hungarian Soviet Republic. In the essay, Lukács addressed himself to the two-sided question of whether, as a method of historical understanding, Marxism could be applied directly to precapitalist societies and, on the other side, whether, following the proletarian revolution, Marxism would remain an instrument of class struggle. The very questions suggested a sharp critique of suprahistorical versions of Marxism. Lukács made his case explicit by answering both queries in the negative. Ignoring this radically historicist or historically relativist argument, the published criticisms of the book simply reasserted the thesis that Marxism is an objective science of the objective laws of social development valid throughout history.

All these critical commentaries, however, only prepared the groundwork for the decisive blow against *History and Class Consciousness,* which was delivered in June 1924 by Grigory Zinoviev in the course of his opening address to the Third International's Fifth World Congress. The relevant section of his remarks was entitled "The Struggle against the 'Ultra-Lefts' and Theoretical Revisionism," a further echo of the political-philosophical equation mentioned earlier.[41] Noting that, happily, the German party and the Executive of the International were successfully combatting those who would transform the Communist movement from a mass party into a sect by opposing work within the trade unions, Zinoviev proceeded to assault "theoretical revisionism . . . an international phenomenon." The key passage warrants full presentation:

> Comrade Graziadei in Italy published a book containing a reprint of articles attacking Marxism which he wrote when he was a Social Democratic revisionist. This theoretical revisionism cannot be allowed to pass with impunity. Neither will we tolerate our Hungarian Comrade Lukács doing the same thing in the domain of philosophy and sociology. I have received a letter from Comrade Rudas, one of the leaders of this faction. He explains that he intended to oppose Lukács, but the faction forbade him to do so; thereupon he left the faction because he could not see Marxism watered down. Well done, Rudas! We have a similar tendency in the German party. Comrade Graziadei is a professor. Korsch is also a professor—(Interruption from the floor: "Lukács is a professor, too!"). If we get a few more of these professors spinning out their Marxist theories we shall be lost. We cannot tolerate such theoretical revisionism in our Communist International.[42]

This was the voice of the party bureaucrat performing at demagogic full throttle. The central political import of Zinoviev's speech was readily visible to observers as well as to the parties to the dispute. In October 1924, for example, Karl Bloch, reviewing Zinoviev's *History of the Communist Party of Russia* (1923) in the pages of the prestigious "Weber *Archiv,*" commented that "the . . . revolutionary party (i.e., the Communist International) maintains a rigid right to authority and the leadership is enveloped in nothing less than an aura of infallibility. The canonization of Lenin and the condemnation of the heresies of Lukács and Korsch at the recent party congress reveal the tendencies of this development at their clearest."[43]

That Karl Bloch clearly had little sympathy for the Communist cause does not alter the accuracy of his observation. The condemnation of Lukács and, with him, Korsch, was from any standpoint an integral component of the "ideological Bolshevization" of the International.[44] The canonization of Lenin to which Bloch referred entailed the elevation of Lenin's texts and persona to virtually sacred status, replete with litany and icons, as Isaac Deutscher and other historians have shown.[45] In this process, Lenin's thesis regarding Marxism as an objective, scientific account of the laws of nature and society became absolute dogma, disagreement with which amounted to sacrilege. As a result, Marxism was transformed from a theory of society into what one recent analyst has termed a "legitimating science" of the politics of a particular party (the Communist International) and a particular state (the Soviet Union).[46]

This transformation still must be explained. Once the embryo of proletarian revolution in Europe (and Russia) had dissolved, Marxism as a theory of praxis was rendered impotent as a practical force. The activity which the theory was to raise to a critical, self-conscious, and self-directing plane was not there to be raised. Rather than fulfill the historic mission ascribed to it by the Marxian theory, Europe's proletariat returned, both by choice and by force, to obedience to the "laws" of capitalist development. This turn of events was the historical truth which the emergent Marxist-Leninist orthodoxy grasped; the objectivistic and scientistic standpoint, not Lukács's philosophy of praxis, expressed the immediate state of affairs.

Yet, as the French philosopher Maurice Merleau-Ponty stressed in his brilliant analysis three decades later, the ideologues of the new Marxist-Leninist orthodoxy took an historical truth and "translated it into a philosophical experience," freezing or, in Lukács's language, reifying a temporal fact into a natural one.[47] If the appeals to the objective and scientific character of both Marxism and history mirrored a decisive development in the postwar revolutions, they also played a key role within that development. For as Merleau-Ponty further pointed out, in condemning Lukács's and Korsch's perspectives, the "new dogmatism" of official Communist theory "placed the knowing subject (ultimately the Party itself) outside the tissue of history and accorded it access to absolute being, freed from the duty of autocritique, dispensed Marxism from applying its own principles to itself, and installed dialectical thought in a massive positivity which dialectical thought itself is unable to accept."[48] In place of the alleged subjective idealism of *History and Class Consciousness,* the Communist International had asserted the secret subjective "idealism" of the party.

"While Every Idea Shoots Beyond Reality": Friends on the Left, 1923–24

Karl Korsch was *History and Class Consciousness*'s most active defender, and more will be said regarding his continued role. But he was not its only defender. We have already referred, as did contemporaries, to Lukács's comrades in the Hungarian party, Béla Fogarasi and Josef Révai. If the phenomenon of "Lukácsism" can be said to have existed in the early 1920s, they were its most adept exponents.[49] Their interventions in the 1923–24 debate lent credence to the view that *History and Class Consciousness* had inspired a philosophical tendency within the Communist movement. In June 1924, while the International's congress was in session, Fogarasi's review of Korsch's *Marxism and Philosophy* appeared; it was an enthusiastic appraisal confirming the links between Korsch's and Lukács's works.[50] Starting with the orthodox assumption that removing bourgeois philosophical residues from Marxist theory was a necessity, Fogarasi went on to stress the unorthodox idea that chief among these residues are "naive realism and mechanistic materialism," rather than idealism. Korsch, he claimed, contributed much to this end by way of sophisticated "historical materialist account of historical materialism itself."[51] Precisely these elements—the critique of materialism and the effort critically to apply Marxism to itself—had raised the hackles of the orthodox ideologues.

Josef Révai's essay on *History and Class Consciousness* had come out some months earlier.[52] Lauding the book as the most important work in the history of Marxian thought since Marx himself, Révai emphasized that it contained the "first systematic attempt to make the Hegelian moment in Marxism—the dialectic—philosophically conscious."[53] As Lukács had surpassed Korsch, so Révai's analysis was more extensive than Fogarasi's in highlighting the opposition between Lukács's standpoint and that represented by the "older Marxists, above all Plekhanov and even Engels," who, he argued, had reduced the revolutionary dialectic of consciousness and being to a "materialistic metaphysics."[54] Considering that Zinoviev, Rudas, and others were at the time engaged in giving shape to precisely such a materialist ideology, they were not wrong in insisting that views such as Révai's and Fogarasi's could not be allowed to parade before them with impunity.

While in the context of the 1923–24 debate, the two Hungarians stood in the second rank behind both Lukács and Korsch—Deborin was not entirely mistaken in referring to them as Lukács's disciples—Révai, in particular, raised two highly suggestive and germane issues. In the course of his review, he pointed out that there had actually been *two* Hegels, both of whom had found their respective ways into Marxism. One was the Hegel who had erected the great pan-logical system, extending it beyond human history to the philosophy of nature. This Hegel, Révai argued, had been appropriated for Marxism by Engels and Plekhanov in their development of a sort of Marxist pan-logism and nature-dialectic, a theory of history lacking a human subject. The other Hegel (often spoken of in present-day terms as the Hegel of the *Phenomenology*) had, according to Révai, articulated a dialectic of the world-historical formation of consciousness, a dialectic of the historical subject. This was the Hegel, he concluded, that Marx had critically grasped and Lukács had retrieved.[55] Révai's insight radically shifted the terms of the debate that was unfolding—or would have, had he or Lukács had something to say about its terms.

Beyond this, Révai also contributed an original and fecund appraisal of Lukács's own theory of the formation of the proletariat as simultaneous subject and object of history. Within Lukács's theory, he emphasized, the proletariat emerges as history's subject only with and through the development of capitalism which, by reducing labor to the raw objectivity of a commodity, lays the basis for its coming to consciousness. But this, contended Révai, leaves unanswered the question of the subject of history *tout court*. In a phrase, who constituted history's subject prior to the formation of capitalism and the proletariat? "The modern proletariat, struggling for communism, is not the subject of ancient or feudal society. It comprehends these epochs as its own past, as stages leading to its own formation, but it is not their subject."[56]

In his remarkable response, Révai proposed that, in order to comprehend itself fully as the identical subject and object of a specific historical epoch (that of capitalism), the proletariat must "project itself into the past" as the subject and object of history as a whole. In this way, the proletariat understands its own inhumanity as part of the dehumanization of all class societies, against which it upholds the idea of man ("*Mensch*") as that which its own struggles will finally realize. Yet, Révai indicated, "the idea of 'man', even if the proletarian concept differs from the bourgeois version presented by Feuerbach, is nevertheless a conceptual mythology. But an unavoidable conceptual mythology."[57] With these remarks, Révai unintentionally broached a theme others would later pursue: the extent to which Lukács's interpretation of the proletariat itself was a "conceptual mythology."

Reflections such as Révai's, as well as the whole discussion of both *History and Class Consciousness* and Marxian theory generally, were all shaped, according to Lukács's intimate friend Ernst Bloch, by the immediate historical-political situation. "The West stands still," Bloch noted in his 1924 essay, "Actuality and Utopia: On Lukács's *History and Class Consciousness*"; "the German proletarian movement, languishing in the same swampy morass the entire land is in, bears its endless crises without the strength to transform them. Every putsch in Germany goes under, while every idea shoots beyond reality, without influence, almost without meaning."[58] Nevertheless, Bloch considered Lukács's ideas titanic, having a force that had sent human consciousness crashing through the long-standing walls of its bourgeois impasses. With his critique of reification, Lukács had, in Bloch's view, rediscovered Marx's key to the mysteries of the world and to the revolutionary resolution of its philosophical, theological, cultural, and practical contradictions.

Lukács, wrote Bloch, had "liberated thought, brought it into the historical-social process of becoming where it is no longer mere observation, but the most deeply informed expression of that very process itself." Moreover, this process of becoming was no longer Hegel's "pan-logism," but a "continuous human production and reproduction of those relations which, when ripped from their context, appear in bourgeois thought as isolated, quantified concepts of reflection, as things, as reified, self-contained systems." Finally, and for Bloch most essential, Lukács unveiled the "human 'We'" that unfolds and constitutes itself in history, preparing for its full realization in proletarian revolution.[59] Near the close of his extensive discussion, Bloch raised an idea which indeed underlay Lukács's whole project. It was contained, he suggested, in Marx's early statement that "mankind has long possessed the dream of that which it must only become conscious in order to possess in reality."[60] This dream, he implied, united philosopher and proletarian in a great "human 'We'" beyond the capitalist division of labor.

Yet, Bloch insisted characteristically, Lukács had not permitted himself to dream deeply or wildly enough. At the close of his pregnant review, Bloch drew a summary picture of both the deep affinities and final tensions between his own *Spirit of Utopia,* which had appeared in 1919 but which he had republished in an expanded edition in 1923, and *History and Class Consciousness.* In his own book, Lukács had taken Bloch to task for having called for a deepening of Marxism by way of a union of religious and social-economic revolutions. This, Lukács had argued, was based upon a misunderstanding of the real depths of the Marxian standpoint.[61] Bloch held his ground: while a towering achievement, *History and Class Consciousness* had failed to pass beyond a "limitation of homogenization" of Being "at the purely social dimension." The claims of religion, he insisted, "cannot be fulfilled through social reality." Nevertheless, Bloch concluded, in spite of his refusal to embrace it fully, Lukács finally shared in the deepest meaning of the dream of which Marx had spoken; he, too, was linked to the "metaphysics of cosmic dream-interpretation, of the conjuring up of the divine."[62]

Ernst Bloch was also a clever man. Not only was the revolutionary process, he noted, advancing with "crippled strides" at best.

For this reason and more, Lukács's book would have a difficult time finding sympathetic readers, "especially among the Russians [that is, the Bolsheviks], who act philosophically after a fashion, but since they think in the manner of uneducated dogs, will probably smell garbage in the book."[63] This remark, obviously polemical, proved to be prescient. It also pointed toward one of the central issues in the whole Lukács debate.

The Problem of the Professors: Anti-Intellectualism in the Lukács Debate

In certain crucial respects the gap between ideas and reality to which Bloch had referred had its social-political correlate in the tension between intellectuals and proletariat within the Communist movement. But not in all respects. On the one hand, for example, it is impossible to ignore the extent to which the attack on Lukács and *History and Class Consciousness* embodied an attack on intellectuals as congenital troublemakers in the revolutionary brigade. Thus, Zinoviev condemned Lukács, Korsch, and others not only as representatives of a calamitous idealism, but as professors, while Rudas, in the course of his dissection of Lukács's book, spoke several times of its author as "comrade philosopher" (*Genosse Philosoph*). Neither Zinoviev nor Rudas expanded on the meanings and implications of such references. They did not need to. For with them, they were invoking a time-tested theme within the working class movement. On the other hand, Zinoviev and Rudas were themselves intellectuals. Hostility to intellectuals, a powerful and readily manipulable bias in proletarian organizations, has not only been compatible with continued domination of such organizations by intellectuals; it has often served as a vital component of such domination.[64]

In the context of the Bolshevization of the Third International, this complex theme played a substantial role. The assault on Lukács as professor and philosopher was part of a broader movement against internal opposition as such. As Hermann Weber, author of a comprehensive study of the "Stalinization of the KPD," notes in this connection, when workers themselves opposed the party line, party leaders such as Bukharin, an intellectual, did not hesitate to proclaim that "the worker, even when his hands are completely black, is not always right."[65] Nevertheless, Weber adds, the long-standing working class mistrust of intellectuals was successfully mobilized by the International's leadership in its battle with the Left opposition between 1924 and 1926, remarking further that "intellectual-baiting was carried out with particular severity in 1925–26 by the Russian leaders of the Comintern, who themselves were almost all academics."[66]

What Weber terms "intellectual-baiting" was based upon a sort of theory that had had currency within the Marxist Second International and was in the early 1920s being recapitulated by its Communist successor. According to this "theory," philosophical idealism is the natural and spontaneous form of thought among intellectuals, while materialism is the equivalent thought form among the working class, immersed as its members are in the world of material production. Moreover, the implicit argument runs, professors or intellectuals are, by their class nature, revisionists, iconoclasts, dissidents, who, as Zinoviev made clear in his comments on Lukács, Korsch, and Graziadei, will invariably obstruct the smooth operation of the proletarian party and ideology. There is a double irony to all of this. For one thing, to the extent to which Zinoviev presupposed this informal theory, his position was at once unflattering to the capacity for critical, independent thought among workers and, as his own case would seem to indicate, inaccurate regarding intellectuals' in-born tendency toward dissidence. For another thing, it was not only Karl Kautsky, but Lenin, who had emphasized so strongly the decisive role to be played by intellectuals in the proletarian revolution.

Within this whole framework, which remains to the present day one of the deepest and most problematic dimensions in all of Marxism, Lukács's case contains some special features. While during his conversion he quickly proved himself to be a militant of great courage and readiness to embrace party discipline, Lukács nevertheless remained a very intellectual Communist intellectual. This was true, first of all, in the sense recently stressed by Michael Löwy, namely, that Lukács had been perhaps the outstanding "traditional intellectual" to have entered the Communist camp in the early part of this century.[67] In this connection, one thinks of his pre–World War I reputation—the high regard in which he had been held by Max Weber, Thomas Mann, Georg Simmel, and other contemporaries—and the fact that he had come to communism only after an arduous journey along some of the major paths of bourgeois thought. Beyond this, however, Lukács cut a singular figure in the Communist movement not only because he brought with him into that movement deep traces of his bourgeois philosophical past, but because he continued to be a man who lived by ideas, following to their outer limits what he understood to be their imperatives, acting in the belief that, in the words of the young Marx, ideas are "demons we can overcome only by submitting to them."

The impact Lukács's unique intellectual persona exerted on some of his comrades has already been noted in the partially amused, partially outraged response to the ethical philosopher from Heidelberg by the Hungarian Communist, Josef Lengyel.[68] By the time Zinoviev, Rudas, and others delivered their criticisms, the element of amusement had disappeared. But Lukács, the Communist intellectual, left an imprint on a decade; in the very radicalism of his being, he stood as *the* representative figure of the problematic intellectual in a proletarian movement. This is suggested in an intriguing and polemical little book by the then-socialist intellectual, Hendrik deMan, published in 1926: *The Intellectuals and Socialism.*[69]

Although he did not mention Lukács, deMan's reference was clear when he spoke of the "inferiority complex of intellectuals" which finds its "sharpest form among radical Marxists of bourgeois origin." While this is in fact not an accurate account of the sources of Lukács-as-type, deMan's description of the type was close to the mark. With these radical Marxists of bourgeois origin, he argued, "the idealization of the proletariat reaches its most extreme expression. The masses become a mystical substance possessing immanent qualities one never finds in flesh and blood workers. In the 'revolutionary mission' the 'burden borne by the oppressed' is forgotten. This view proceeds *ad absurdum:* for the proletarian . . . situation is contradictory to the concept of cultural renewal, indeed, to any autonomous culture, and any such notion can be devised only by bringing into play the most alien Hegelisms (*weltfremdesten Hegelei*)." The "worst dogmatists of 'proletarian' socialism of the strictest Marxian type," deMan continued, "have always been academics. The greater their distance from the real proletariat, the more easily these intellectuals viewed it as a piece on the chess-board of their theoretical, revolutionary-dialectical combinations."[70]

Beyond noting that, without exception, every comment by an intellectual on the problem of intellectuals is itself part of the history of the problem it addresses, there is no need to evaluate de-Man's remarks. They were inspired by Lukács and, as such, suggest some of the force with which Lukács, the intellectual, affected his contemporaries in the 1920s. There is, however, a certain irony in the fact that, while his presentation was more sophisticated than the demagogic strictures delivered by Zinoviev and even Rudas, and while he wrote from a standpoint sharply critical of communism as a whole, deMan's position in this context nevertheless resembled theirs in an obvious respect: they all shared the idea that, in relation to some purportedly real needs of the proletariat, theories such as Lukács's were dangerous fantasms. Dangerous or not, Lukács's ideas "shot beyond reality," in Ernst Bloch's phrase, finding no ground in the proletariat. It was a weighty fact.

CHAPTER

11

The Origins of "Western Marxism"

Strategic Retreat: Lukács's Response, 1924–26

BETWEEN 1924 AND 1926 Lukács's perspective underwent a complex but substantial shift. By the close of this two-year period, which saw the initial phase of Stalin's consolidation of his authority in the Soviet Union, Lukács completed his departure from the messianic revolutionary hopes that had still resonated through the pages of *History and Class Consciousness*. And he did this, moreover, in connection with an unambiguous affirmation of Soviet society and its ruling party, rejecting the various oppositional routes taken by, for example, Trotsky and Karl Korsch. If, between 1919 and 1923, Lukács can be said to have been Europe's philosopher of the Russian Revolution, by 1926 he would emerge as its philosopher of Leninist orthodoxy. But this strategic retreat was accompanied by both subtle and direct rear-guard skirmishes against the expanding power of ideological dogmatism and organizational rigidification within the Communist movement.

There is more than one way to approach the question of Lukács's responses to the attacks on *History and Class Consciousness*. One could argue, not unreasonably, that for all its original and heterodox features, the book stood firmly within the frame of Leninism and was denounced by the Leninists partly for sectarian reasons and partly because Lukács had insisted on retaining his inflammatory critique of Engels. In response to the attacks on him, then, Lukács in this view proceeded to set the record straight between 1924 and 1926 by revealing himself to be an increasingly orthodox Leninist. Conversely, the opposite but equally reasonable argument could be offered: that *History and Class Consciousness* had been an explosive critique of Leninist or Soviet Marxism and an embryo of a Western Marxism, from which Lukács beat a hasty retreat between 1924 and 1926, by which time he had about-faced fully into the arms of Stalinism. Neither of these approaches, the one suggesting a straight line, the other a reversal of direction, is unfounded; neither is sufficient. They suggest a third.

The gap, as he understood it, between the ideal and the real, between the ethical "ought" and the historical-present "is," had constituted the fundamental problem and the driving force of Lukács's thought since the first years of the century. While this can hardly be said to have been peculiar to Lukács, his development was nevertheless distinguished by both the self-conscious rigor with which he contended with the problem, and—an expression of that self-consciousness—the fact that he placed his own efforts precisely within an historical tradition of contending with it, a tradition reaching back essentially to the German Romantics and extending across Hegel, Kierkegaard, and Dostoevski down to his own day. His conversion to Marxism and communism following World War I was in this connection a decisive step; with it Lukács believed that he (and history) had entered the epoch in which ideal and real would be unified, not in aesthetic experience or mystical transcendence, but in the social world. Yet we have already seen how from the outset Lukács's early Marxism was structured by the sustained gap—now perceived through altered and altering lenses—between the "ought" and the "is."

The idea or feeling—or, possibly, illusion—of immanent and imminent reconciliation of ideal and real appeared in Lukács's early Marxism in the form of the messianic expectation that proletarian revolution would usher in a totally transformed and rejuvenated age. This, in turn, had found political expression in the ultra-Leftism that characterized his positions initially, but which he had begun to mute by the end of 1921. Yet, this "creeping moderation" involved more than merely the political dimension of Lukács's early Marxism: it reached toward the basic composition of his whole evolving outlook. For infused as it was with extreme historical and metaphysical expectations, Lukács's turn to Marxism also unveiled a new and quite different element in the trajectory of his work: on the level of philosophical emotion, a sense of arrival and resolution, of having reached the long-sought goal, if not in reality then in Marxian theory—at the proper philosophical level—historical rationalism in its Hegelian-Marxian variant. Turbulently novel by comparison to contemporary Marxisms, then, the very onset of Lukács's new Marxism was, in relation to the preceding stages of his journey, the calm after the storm. The element of theoretical flux, adventure, and search had been left behind, replaced by a new *esprit de système*.

But in fact they had been neither fully left behind, nor fully replaced. The two elements—messianism, and Romantic rejection of reality on one side, and a rationalistic systematizing spirit pointing toward reconciliation with reality on the other—intersected and did battle within Lukács's work from 1919 through the mid-1920s, with the latter side progressively gaining the upper hand. As we have stressed, *History and Class Consciousness* represented the great battle in this larger internal war. Labile, original, and dissentient in relation to the emergent Marxist-Leninist orthodoxy, the book also embodied Lukács's ongoing course away from intractable radicalism and toward acceptance of what the German revolutionary dramatist Georg Büchner a century earlier had decried as the terrible "fatalism of history." In retracing Lukács's road to Soviet Marxism, then, one should be prepared to follow both straight and veering lines which, moreover, had been initially plotted prior to his reactions to the attacks on his book.

It is worth noting at the start that strategic retreat from the imperatives of cultural-political radicalism was a generalized phenomenon of the period. While the picture is complex and the characters within it highly diverse, it is nevertheless the case that between 1922 and 1927 a number of important currents within the cultural avant-garde that had blossomed in Europe in the pre–World War I years experienced disillusionment and were forced toward reconsideration, reorientation, and often dissolution. Thus, for example, German Expressionism, for which Lukács, in spite of many common impulses, had little sympathy, discarded some of its wilder visions and techniques in favor of a "new objectivity" (*Neue Sachlichkeit*) precisely in 1924–25. This new direction in Expressionism was in large measure a response to the series of setbacks in the proletarian-revolutionary movement, in which the Expressionists, too, had placed great hopes.

Italian Futurism, which had begun prior to the war with ties to anarchism but had quickly migrated to the Fascist-nationalist wing, also faced a parallel crisis in 1922–23 when some of its leading practitioners took high positions in Mussolini's regime, thus capitulating, in the eyes of some of the militants, to the status quo. Futurism's "great days" were over, as were those of Dada and, for that matter, of the modernist schools (Constructivism and Futurism) in Russia. There were important exceptions: 1924 saw the French Surrealists burst onto the scene, while at roughly the same moment Trotskyism, with which André Breton and some compatriots would soon enter into alliance, was taking shape. A generation's mood is hard to specify since what may be a source of disillusionment or chastened wisdom for some can serve others as inspiration to new hope or rejuvenated extremism. Our point, then, is not to establish a rule regarding the mood among the cultural and political avant-gardes in Europe in the mid-1920s. It is instead to suggest that Lukács's own situation and choices in that period must be seen within the context of both parallel and divergent developments centering around a shared problem: the collapse of revolutionary expectations.

But the lens needs to be focused somewhat since Lukács's moves as a theorist were made under the impress of immediate political events: the defeats of the German and Bulgarian Communist parties in the fall of 1923; the quagmire in which the anti–Béla Kun faction in the exiled Hungarian party found itself; the death of Lenin in January 1924; and, of course, the denunciations of *History and Class Consciousness,* culminating in Zinoviev's address in June of that year. It will not be stretching matters unduly to propose that Lukács's frame of mind in 1924 resembled that of Victor Serge, who, in the chapter of his memoirs entitled "Europe at the Dark Crossroads: 1922–1926," recalled his own thoughts early in the year:

> Events continued to overwhelm us. Even where they took place at a distance I find it hard to separate them from my personal memories. All we lived for was activity integrated into history; we were interchangeable; we could immediately see the repercussions of affairs in Russia upon affairs in Germany and the Balkans; we felt linked with our comrades who, in pursuit of the same ends as we, perished or else scored some success at the other end of Europe. None of us had, in the bourgeois sense of the word, any personal existence: we

> changed our names, our posting and our work at the Party's need; we had just enough to live on without real material discomfort, and we were not interested in making money, or following a career, or producing a literary heritage, or leaving a name behind us; we were interested solely in the difficult business of reaching socialism.[1]

Serge, as was noted, had in fact met Lukács in Vienna in the early 1920s. His recollection of the encounter is apposite: in the Hungarian-born philosopher, Serge wrote, "I saw a first-class brain which could have endowed Communism with a true intellectual greatness if it had developed as a social movement instead of degenerating into a movement in solidarity with an authoritarian Power. Lukács's thinking led him to a totalitarian vision of Marxism within which he united all aspects of human life; his theory of the Party could be taken as either superb or disastrous, depending on the circumstances."[2] This is not only an excellent capsule appraisal of Lukács; it is specifically helpful in understanding both Lukács's response to the attacks on *History and Class Consciousness* and his development between 1924 and 1926.

Lukács's theory of the party and the quality of his personal "wager" on it in 1919 are close to the heart of the story. Neither the first nor the last revolutionary to place great store in "the party," Lukács was nevertheless singular in that he attributed to the party the very highest philosophical, and, therefore personal, meaning. We have already seen that he understood the Communist Party as far more than a mere political instrument, perceiving it instead as the living vessel of the proletariat's (and thus humanity's) "moral mission." Within the larger trajectory of his thought, moreover, the party had come to replace those earlier and always transitory moments of transcendence of the reified world—certain moments of aesthetic creativity and receptivity; mystical contact with a world beyond interests and ethics; and so forth. But the party, as Lukács fully understood, was a political institution and instrument. In this crucial respect it differed fundamentally from the previous images of transcendence. Nevertheless, he attributed to it what amounted to an only partially secular equivalent of divine sanction.

In addition, his wager on the party had been undertaken at great personal sacrifice. Again, this in itself was not peculiar to Lukács, although in view of his social past and its prospects, his decision was hardly ordinary. The point is simply—or not so simply—that Lukács placed the idea of individual self-sacrifice at the very core of both his own conversion to communism, and his theory of the party. In this basic Lukácsian sense, then, life within and for the party was the equivalent, and more, of what Serge called "activity integrated into history." It is not easy to envision events that would have caused him to revoke his decision.

Yet if his theory of the party played a decisive role in shaping the direction in which he would move between 1924 and 1926, it did not prevent him from developing criticisms, no matter how futile or self-defeating they may in retrospect seem to have been. The fact that he published no ripostes to the criticisms of *History and Class Consciousness* is symptomatic of his position, as is the fact that he either initiated or agreed to the decision not to let the book go into a second printing. More revealing of the complexity of that position, however, was the book he published—in a sense—instead. The small volume, *Lenin: A Study of the Unity of His Thought,* was written in February 1924, on the occasion of Lenin's death, and was published by the Malik Verlag in the summer of that year.[3]

Lukács's *Lenin* represents *Lukács*'s Lenin. The book was intended to contribute to the so-called "Leninism discussion" that unfolded within the Communist International following the master's death. In fact, what took place was not so much a discussion as part of the process of ideological Bolshevization of the International and, accompanying it, a ritualization of Lenin's thought, one of the victims of which was *History and Class Consciousness*. Not unwittingly, the new book contributed to the very tide it sought to stem. Calling Lenin "the greatest thinker to have been produced by the revolutionary working class movement since Marx," Lukács also insisted, against the anti-Communist critics, that "the Russian Communist Party's policy, Lenin's policy, is only contradictory insofar as it seeks and finds the dialectically correct solutions to the objective contradictions of its own social existence."[4] In such formulations, it is difficult to avoid noticing not only a note of dogmatism uncharacteristic of Lukács's previous Marxist writings, but also a note of resignation. Moreover, Lenin emerges here as the first and only among Lukács's contemporaries regarding whom he has not a single critical word to utter.

Lenin's genius, as seen by Lukács, consisted essentially in the fact that he was the great practitioner of the philosophy of Marxism presented in *History and Class Consciousness.* This is not the stated argument, although throughout the book Lukács comes close to it, defining Lenin as the actualizer of the "subject-object" dialectic. In this respect, his hymn to Lenin is a response to the published and anticipated critiques of *History and Class Consciousness.* On the other hand, it is also a criticism of the earlier book and of Lukács's first five years as a Marxist as well. For Lenin's achievement, he argued, lay equally in his role as head of the new Soviet state and as inventor of the revolutionary tactics of the Communist International. Lenin's "revolutionary *Realpolitik*" appeared, if not in the first place, as a criticism of Lukács's own earlier ultra-Leftism and messianism.[5] As we have noted, Lukács had begun to depart from these dimensions of his initial Marxism, although Rudas and Zinoviev were not mistaken when they detected them in *History and Class consciousness*.

The crucial element here is that the emergent reorientation (or de-messianization) of Lukács's outlook, combined with the events of late 1923 and 1924, prepared him to see a great deal in Lenin, even to the point of constructing a virtual Lenin mythology of his own. In the late Bolshevik leader he glimpsed the one Marxist who, in practice and in theory, had exerted a monumental impact upon his (and Lukács's) age. By comparison, Lukács's own political record and the reception of *History and Class Consciousness* appeared quite forlorn.

Yet Lukács's Lenin—a virtual *Weltgeist* in a sealed train—also amounted to a countermyth: a critique of the official Leninist Lenin. The danger, Lukács insisted, lay in viewing Lenin's "truths" as "recipes, prescriptions for correct practice." Rather than finding certain "general rules" and "applying them to specific cases," the true Leninist must follow Lenin by "proceeding from a concrete analysis of the concrete situation with the aid of the dialectical concept of history." Otherwise, the result is "a caricature, a *vulgar-Leninism*" (emphasis added).[6] In this hardly insignificant respect, the book on Lenin amounted to a reply to Lukács's critics. The shortcomings he was coming to perceive in his own position nevertheless did not appear to Lukács to have been as problematic as those centering around a mechanistic and abstract Leninism—at least not in 1924.

The fact was not lost on the orthodox Leninists. In the late summer 1924, for example, the German Communist theorist August Thalheimer greeted Lukács's latest effort as "a superfluous book."[7] Brief and hostile, the review is revealing. On the basis of Lukács's "highly praised dialectical thinking—of course, it is praised only by Lukács himself and his disciples—he has produced not only a bad work, but one that stands in direct contradiction to Lenin himself." Moreover, Thalheimer suggested, there is a "political background" to Lukács's effort, namely, that of posing "as the *representative dialectician*" (emphasis in original). This was, as far as Thalheimer was concerned, mere pose, since "in the Leninist plan of organization it is not a matter of an open or veiled 'return to Hegel', in the manner of Lukács and his friends, but a matter of grasping Marx's materialist standpoint."[8]

In the course of his review, August Thalheimer referred to a recent article by one of Lukács's "disciples" which attempted to further the idea of the Hungarian philosopher as the representative figure of "materialist dialectics."[9] The author of the article, not mentioned by name, was Karl Korsch, who, on the eve of the June 1924 Moscow congress, had published in *Die Internationale* a review article ("On Materialist Dialectics") dealing with the new (1923) edition of Hegel's *Logic;* Lukács's *History and Class Consciousness;* Nicolai Bukharin's *Theory of Historical Materialism;* and Korsch's own *Marxism and Philosophy.*[10] At issue in the review, as in the Communist International as a whole at this juncture, was the nature of the program for inculcating Leninist ideas at all levels of organization.

The article indicates that Korsch was initiating the counteroffensive from which Lukács himself was retreating. Citing Béla Kun's attack on *History and Class Consciousness* and an article by Thalheimer warning Communist readers of the dangers in picking up Hegel's *Logic* without a firm grasp on Marx's materialist critique of idealist dialectics, Korsch mockingly compared their anxieties with Lenin's call for the formation by Communist philosophers of a "sort of society of materialist friends of the Hegelian dialectic."[11] The attacks on Lukács, Hegel, and himself, Korsch polemicized further, only revealed the proximity between the so-called Marxist conception and the bourgeois conception of science.[12] At about the same time, Korsch also released a review of Lukács's book on Lenin, which not only endorsed it in general, but emphasized the idea that Lenin's own Leninism could not be identified with the more mechanistic and dogmatic Leninism of his followers.[13]

In context, these were heady and risky arguments, from which Korsch would briefly and tactically retreat in 1925, only to return in the following year to a reinvigorated oppositional stance.[14] The year 1926, as we will see, brought Lukács's completed accommodation with the given realities of the Soviet Union and the Communist International, tacitly granting, to paraphrase August Thalheimer's remark, that Stalin was the representative dialectician. At precisely that time, Korsch was taking the last steps in the opposite direction, culminating in his expulsion from the party as a Left-oppositionist in whose eyes the Soviet Union and the International had become counterrevolutionary obstacles in the proletariat's path to liberation.[15] Once a kindred spirit though never a disciple, Korsch became Lukács's political alter ego in 1926, with the isolation in which he subsequently found himself confirming for Lukács his own decision to tie his fate to the party.

Again, however, Lukács's road to accommodation with orthodoxy had its detours. The critical remarks on "vulgar Leninism" with which he had closed his *Lenin,* for example, were amplified in Lukács's 1925 review of Bukharin's *Theory of Historical Materialism.*[16] First published in 1922, the book had become a fundamental source of the Bolshevik conception of Marxism. While careful not to extend his comments toward a critique of the dominant Bolshevik outlook as a whole, Lukács nevertheless argued that Bukharin's position bordered on "bourgeois-natural-scientific materialism" which, in its concrete application to society and history, "occasionally blots out the decisive element of the Marxian method: tracing the roots of the ensemble of economic and 'sociological' phenomena to the social relations among men. [Bukharin's] theory retains the account of a false objectivity; it becomes fetishistic."[17]

If this were not sufficient proof that the Lukács of the critique of reification and of the subject-object dialectic was still vigorous in 1925, added confirmation was provided in the following year by two long essays dealing respectively with Ferdinand Lassalle and Moses Hess.[18] The central problem in both essays, which should be counted among the most powerful in Lukács's *oeuvre,* is what he termed "idealist dialectics." In developing his critique of the two main nineteenth-century socialist idealist dialecticians, Lukács was tacitly criticizing *History and Class Consciousness* only in small measure, if at all; his conception of idealist dialectics was not Thalheimer's or Rudas's. His intention appears to have been precisely and polemically the opposite: namely, to vindicate the standpoint articulated in *History and Class Consciousness* as a real contribution to revolutionary dialectical thought.

Yet, as Michael Löwy has recently emphasized, Lukács's 1926 essay on Moses Hess in particular also introduces a dimension to his understanding of dialectics that is not to be found in *History and Class Consciousness:* a *positive* account of the concept of "reconciliation" (*Versöhnung*) in Hegel's thought.[19] Prior to his conversion to Marxism, as Löwy perceptively indicates, the moment of reconciliation with reality was precisely what Lukács had found most repellent in Hegel. By 1926 he had come to see it not merely as one of the chief accomplishment's of Hegel's system—a sign of the philosopher's growing realism—but as a model for his own development. The political implications of the essay on Moses Hess, Löwy concludes, are profound: "They provide the methodological foundation of Lukács's adhesion to the Soviet 'Thermidor'."[20]

This is a suggestive and interesting reading of Lukács with which, however, we take issue in at least one respect: while it is true that Lukács introduced the systematic philosophical basis of his accommodation with Soviet orthodoxy only in 1926, the accommodation cannot be located in that year alone. Its *gestation* predates the essay on Moses Hess, reaching back, as we have argued, at least into *History and Class Consciousness* itself and making a more distinct appearance in *Lenin: A Study of the Unity of His Thought*. Lukács's view of Lenin, the revolutionary realist, and his picture of Hegel, the realist, are not identical, but neither can they be separated entirely from one another. That is, *Lenin* ought to be seen as the political embryo of the philosophical position presented in the essay on Hess.

But 1926 was a central year. The direction in which the Soviet state and the Communist International were moving had become unambiguously clear. If Lukács had had hopes—and he did—that something other than a "vulgar Leninism" might have succeeded, then by 1926 he had either to dispense with them or break with the party, as Karl Korsch did in that year. Lukács summarized his own option in a short and seemingly esoteric essay in 1926, "*L'art pour l'art* and Proletarian Poetry."[21] Following a capsule analysis of the crisis of bourgeois art, he turned to the fundamental question of the article and of his situation at the time: the question of "what proletarian revolution can offer to the development of art." The quiet simplicity of his reply—"Initially, very little"—is a fitting expression of the striking changes in outlook to which it actually referred. With his own earlier thoughts in mind, Lukács adds that revolutionary Marxists ought not to engage in utopian overestimations of the real prospects of proletarian revolution. For, he argues, not only has capitalism not been globally abolished, but in the Soviet Union capitalist structures and forms continue to exist in the revolution's first phase:

> The immense transformation we are experiencing [that is, developments in the Soviet Union], the transformation being carried out by the revolutionary proletariat, finds expression in the immediate, sensuous reality far less rapidly than a superficial glance would have led one to expect. This explains the "disillusionment" with the Russian Revolution on the part of many of those intellectuals who expected it to provide an immediate solution to their own special problems.[22]

Needless to say, at no point in "*L'art pour l'art* and Proletarian Poetry" did Lukács question either the doctrine or reality of "socialism in one country." Indeed, the article was written with the clear intention of defending it. As such, it marks the conclusive end of a phase in Lukács's journey. Yet, in at least one respect, it is a thoroughly typical Lukácsian statement. Precisely in his renunciation of the critical-utopian standpoint, which he calmly disposed of as a "superficial glance" and a misguided attempt by intellectuals to find quick solutions to their private problems, Lukács was being true to one of the basic and astonishing features of his entire career up to that point and beyond it: that of never looking back.

Mobilization on the Margins: "Western Marxism" as Intellectual Subculture in The 1920s

With the expulsion of Karl Korsch from the Communist Party, and with Lukács's final integration into it, what Korsch himself had called the philosophical struggle within the revolution was brought to an end. The revolution, too, had ended—in spite of Lukács's 1926 assertions. Yet if he had by that juncture forsaken certain of the critical implications of many of his own earlier Marxian ideas, the ideas themselves did not vanish from sight. Rather, while expunged from the mainstreams of the organized Left movements in Central Europe, many of Lukács's key ideas were nurtured (and reinterpreted) on the independent intellectual fringes. In the process, a "Western Marxism" took on loose but definable shape. A critical, humanistic Marxism, it spoke in the name of the interests of a distinterested audience: the European proletariat. It tended, moreover, to be a Marxism of professors and students. And in this respect, the initial formation of Western Marxism in the late 1920s anticipated the social-institutional site from which such ideas would be rediscovered and expanded three decades later. With the Nazi triumphs in the early 1930s, the discussion was interrupted, the discussants forced to scatter and continue their work in still more painful isolation.

Among *History and Class Consciousness*'s numerous remarkable features is this one: in the entire history of Marxism, there is no book that compares with it in the extent and intensity of its impact in its own day. That it was so vehemently and prominently denounced by orthodox Bolshevik ideologues doubtless contributed to awakening interest in a broader audience, but only in part. So did the drama of Lukács's own retreat from some of its central implications. Indeed, in attempting to reconstruct the discussion of *History and Class Consciousness* in the 1920s, one is struck by a recurrent and latent expectation among the participating intellectuals that, before too long, the man who formulated the critique of reification would surely part ways with the reified Soviet state and party to which he had tied his fate. But beyond and through these extrinsic factors ran another which stemmed from the book itself. Sympathizers and opponents alike appear to have agreed that, with the forceful originality of his fusion of Marxian and Leninist ideas with those of the most advanced currents of (German) bourgeois social and cultural theory, presented in the throes of a profound crisis of society, Lukács had produced a charismatic book.

In more prosaic terms, *History and Class Consciousness* was unique in that it was so widely discussed outside of Marxist circles.

In this connection, there is some truth to the cynical claim made years later by Franz Borkenau to the effect that the book could *only* have been discussed outside the labor movement since its themes were "proclaimed in a vocabulary unintelligible not only to workingmen, but to any mortals who had not enjoyed a Heidelberg education." Yet, Borkenau himself, a young Communist intellectual in the late 1920s, and in the next decade a brilliant historian and associate of the Frankfurt Institute for Social Research, was precisely one of those on whom *History and Class Consciousness* exerted deep and fruitful influence. Borkenau's 1939 summary statement on the book was most likely shared by many intellectuals who read it between the wars: he spoke of its "strange merging of the highest type of philosophical analysis and critical analysis—especially of the history of dialectics—with the crudest adoration of the changing orders of the central committee."[23]

However, *History and Class Consciousness* did not find many friends outside of Marxist circles either. No less a figure than Werner Sombart addressed himself to it in 1924, in the course of an essay on "The Concept of Historical and Social Laws in Marx." Sombart's remarks, a blend of begrudging admiration for Lukács's intelligence with thorough rejection of his ideas, can be taken as representative of a type of response to *History and Class Consciousness*. Describing Lukács as "doubtless the most talented of the younger Marxists, but also really not an *un*talented thinker at all," and speaking of the high level of his book, Sombart quickly emphasized that it only demonstrated the uselessness of Marx's dialectical method. The book, he asserted, "contains not a *single* fruitful idea, nor does it expand our horizon, although such texts may serve as keystones for the community of believing Communists" (emphasis in original).[24]

Later in the decade and in the hands of a younger generation of non-Marxist or anti-Marxist scholars, however, *History and Class Consciousness* appeared to contain much of value. In an interesting essay, "Intellectual History and Party History" (1930), the historian Hans Rothfels, for example, highlighted the importance of Lukács's book for an understanding of developments within Marxist parties in Germany. Focusing on relations between ideas and party policies, Rothfels noted that he found in Lukács's "protest" against "vulgar Marxism" a decisive clue to the process by which "the emphasis on the law-like character of economic development, by excluding action shaped by ideas, had opened the door to un-Marxist opportunism." Lukács and Marx, Rothfels concluded, but not the dominant Marxist traditions, recognized the "relative autonomy of 'ideology'," specifically, the vital role of "supra-economic forces" in the final transition to "the realm of freedom."[25]

Hans Mayer, the leftist sociologist of culture and another of the associates of the Frankfurt Institute for Social Research, has recalled that, during the latter part of the 1920s, the "indirect, underground impact" of *History and Class Consciousness* was "amazing." The book was studied by many professors and students, he notes, adding that "around 1930 it was stylish to speak of 'reification', and to apply Lukács's interpretation of the Marxian concept of 'commodity fetishism' to the problem of culture."[26] Mayer's remarks point to an interesting turn of intellectual events in Germany. For, as we have indicated in Part I, one of the seminal moments in Lukács's career was his immersion during the pre–World War I years in a university-based sociological critique of the reified world. But that critique was in large measure the Marxian critique stripped of its revolutionary impulses. What late nineteenth-century Marxists had ignored, Max Weber, Georg Simmel, Ferdinand Tönnies, and others had preserved—under a new sign: that of the fundamental insurmountability of reification. In 1918 and after, Lukács reconstructed this critique, restoring to it its lost revolutionary dimension. But by the late 1920s, then, if we follow Hans Mayer's suggestion, the critique of reification had returned to its academic habitat.

In connection with the theme of the migration of these ideas within German culture and the question of their academic domestication, two works of major importance appeared in the late 1920s and pertained directly to the unfolding discussion of Lukács: Martin Heidegger's *Being and Time* (1927) and Karl Mannheim's *Ideology and Utopia* (1929). The late Lucien Goldmann, one of the foremost commentators on Lukács's work, called attention thirty years ago to the possibility that Heidegger's book had been conceived as a reply to *History and Class Consciousness*.[27] Part of Goldmann's argument, more recently pursued by others, is that Heidegger had sought to retranslate Lukács's historically specific concepts of "class consciousness" and "reification" into ontological categories referring to features of the human condition itself—"authenticity" and "*Dasein.*"

Among the merits of Goldmann's thesis, whose other strengths and problems need not concern us here, is, first of all, that Lukacs's work highlights what has since become a somewhat more familiar connection: namely, that between Existentialist and Marxian thought. While the trajectory of Jean-Paul Sartre's career through and following World War II is the model in this regard, Lukács's own development toward Marxism is in many respects the first model. In Goldmann's terms, then, Martin Heidegger, though never a Marxist, would exemplify the Existentialist-Marxist nexus in reverse: from (Lukács's) Marxism to Existentialism. In addition, and to look momentarily ahead, it is notable that one of the younger intellectuals who in the late 1920s and early 1930s would contribute substantially to developing "Western Marxism" was one of Heidegger's students: Herbert Marcuse.[28]

The second major work, Mannheim's *Ideology and Utopia,* was even more clearly a response to *History and Class Consciousness.*[29] Karl Mannheim's early career in Budapest prior to World War I was deeply influenced by Lukács's work. A participant in the Sunday Circle and the Free School of the Cultural Sciences and a critical fellow traveller during the Hungarian Soviet Republic, the younger sociologist did not, however, follow his philosopher-teacher into the Marxist camp. And it is probably not stretching matters unduly to suggest that Mannheim's initial reservations regarding Marxism and Communism were strengthened by the course of Lukács's career in the 1920s.

In virtually direct reply to Lukács, Mannheim sought to liquidate Marxism's pretentions to historical truth by appropriating its theoretical elements for use in a sociology of knowledge which he turned against Marxism as a whole. His claim that Marxism is simply one among numerous "utopias" which get transformed into "ideologies" (partial social-historical truths which the groups or classes that uphold them have inflated into *the* truth), was especially potent in view of the actual transformations Marxism had undergone in the 1920s. Moreover, Mannheim's call for the formation of a new "free-floating intelligentsia" equipped with the insights of the sociology of knowledge offered an alternative to both Marxism and despair.

By 1930 a lively and fascinating discussion unfolded around *Being and Time* and *Ideology and Utopia,* although the participants recognized *History and Class Consciousness* as the real and proper starting point. Significantly, Lukács himself did not take part; the reasons for his abstention, while not precisely clear, may be surmised.[30] In 1928, for example, the Communist International took its "turn to the Left" according to which Social Democracy and virtually everything outside the Communist movement was defined as part of fascism. The policy introduced an official sectarianism that in no way exactly encouraged philosophical debate with non-Communist thinkers. For Lukács to have entered into the discussion at this juncture would have necessitated an explicit disavowal of *History and Class Consciousness*—a necessity which could be best avoided by silence.

With Lukács in the immediate but shadowy background, then, a discussion proceeded, with the themes and personalities involved giving further if still embryonic shape to a "Western Marxism." Two of the main independent Marxist critiques of Mannheim's *Ideology and Utopia* came from the pens of Max Horkheimer and Herbert Marcuse in 1929.[31] Rejecting both Mannheim's relativizing of all truth and, implicitly, Lukács's identification of Marxian truth with the policies of the Communist Party, Horkheimer and Marcuse both sought to uphold Marxism's validity even in the absence of clear links to the proletariat. Their essays stand among the seeds of what in the 1930s would emerge as the main theoretical current to have emanated from *History and Class Consciousness:* the "critical theory of society" of the so-called Frankfurt School.[32]

Much of the discussion revolved around the seemingly rarefied issue of epistemology or the theory of knowledge which, however, assumed an intensely political character, thanks to the ever-present phenomenon of Soviet Marxism and its positions on these issues. The conflict between Leninism and what amounted to "Lukácsism" indeed stood at the core of the debate. An extensive contribution by the sociologist Paul Eppstein, for example, makes this clear. In his 1928 essay "The Question of Reality in Historical Materialism," Eppstein investigated the fact that "within Marxism itself concepts of reality differ." These differences, he continued, "center around two major poles from which the problem of reality and the nature of comprehending it are articulated: a reflex theory and a philosophy of identity. As representatives of these polar conceptions, we shall examine the work of Lenin and Lukács."[33]

In the same year, Siegfried Marck, philosopher and Social Democrat who had reviewed *History and Class Consciousness* in 1924, published his *Dialectic in Contemporary Philosophy*. In a chapter on the Marxian dialectic, Lukács's book is sympathetically introduced in its opposition to Lenin's philosophical materialism and the official Marxism-Leninism of the Communist International.[34] Marck's book was in turn reviewed by Marcuse who noted with regard to the discussion of Lukács:

> Here a long and unfortunate error is at least corrected: Lukács's book is viewed and evaluated in terms of its essential and inestimable meaning for the development of Marxism. Marck finally puts an end to that primitive "critique" which sought to dispense with Lukács's investigations merely by labelling them "metaphysics"—a critique propagated in its worst form by the Communists. Marck's own critique, however, also touches on the basic flaw in the Lukácsian dialectic: namely, the concept of "correct" class consciousness. This concept and Lukács's overall conception of class consciousness shoot beyond the borders of historicity; they amount to a fixation "outside" the course of events and can be linked to history only in an artificial and abstract manner.[35]

Marcuse went on to defend Lukács's "polemic with Engels" and, against Marck's criticism, to insist that, ultimately, *History and Class Consciousness* had not sought to formulate a philosophical basis for transcendent values, but to generate a "concrete dialectic."[36]

It is not surprising that the sympathetic discussion of Lukács took place not only outside the frame of the Communist Party but also in the looser frame of German social democracy. This is, to be sure, mildly ironic since *History and Class Consciousness* contains so unrelenting a critique of the "vulgar Marxism" of social democracy. On the other hand, the party itself and its theoretical journal, *Die Gesellschaft* (*Society*), tolerated more wide-ranging discussion. Marck's and Marcuse's interventions indicate this, as does another contribution that appeared in the pages of *Die Gesellschaft* in 1930. Hannah Arendt's essay "Philosophy and Sociology" attempted to plot a course between Mannheim's reduction of philosophy to the social location of the philosopher and Lukács's position, which in her own view destroys itself in its very pretention to absoluteness (*Absolutheitsanspruch*).[37] The central issue for Arendt was that of grasping the difference between philosophy and sociology, finding her guides for this move in the work of Martin Heidegger and of Karl Jaspers who, we should recall, had been an associate of the Heidelberg seminar around Max Weber prior to World War I.

That *Die Gesellschaft* opened its pages to such discussion was one thing; the nature of "the old Marx-orthodoxy of Kautsky" and prewar social democracy was yet another. This was the implicit claim of the most important contribution to the philosophical debate at the close of the 1920s: Karl Korsch's essay "The Present Situation of 'Marxism and Philosophy'," which appeared in 1930 as the introduction to the second publication of his *Marxism and Philosophy*.[38] The main thrust of this new essay paralleled *Ideology and Utopia* inasmuch as Korsch himself raised the problem of Marxism as ideology, that is, false consciousness. But Korsch did not employ the term as Mannheim did. In his account, "the old Marx-orthodoxy of Kautsky and the new Marx-orthodoxy of Russian or 'Leninist' Marxism" amount to essentially *identical* Marxist ideologies, that is, standpoints *superimposed* upon the proletariat from without by bourgeois intellectuals, be they Leninist professional revolutionaries or Kautskyan professional reformers.[39]

Common to both orthodoxies, Korsch argued, is a predialectical, bourgeois-materialist outlook incapable of comprehending the dialectical interplay of consciousness and society. As a vivid example of his thesis Korsch cited the virtually identical responses on the part of Social Democratic and Communist ideologues to his own and Lukács's 1923 books. His succinct survey of the Communists' response is of primary interest to us because it provides the most explicit formulation of the idea of "Western Marxism." In the wake of the defeat of German Communists in the fall of 1923, the leading figures in the Soviet Union, in connection with their own battles to succeed Lenin, launched the Bolshevization of the International. They gave birth in this connection to a "strictly philosophical ideology which proclaimed itself the true and unfalsified reconstruction of Marxist philosophy, and on this basis took up a struggle against all other philosophical tendencies within the modern workers' movement."[40] But, Korsch went on, as this "Leninist-Marxist philosophy *moved westward,*" it met an opposing philosophical tendency "within the Communist International itself"—namely, in *History and Class Consciousness* and *Marxism and Philosophy* (emphasis added).[41]

Korsch also used the occasion to clarify relations between his own and Lukács's books. Noting that his original 1923 statement of solidarity with *History and Class Consciousness* had been mistakenly read as a statement of total agreement, Korsch indicated that, from his vantage point at the end of the decade, he was aware of more substantial differences between himself and Lukács. Yet with the exception of the undeveloped remark that, on the issue of Engels and the "dialectics of nature," he agreed neither with Lukács nor with the Leninists, Korsch elucidated little in this regard.[42] In fact, when all was said and done, he reiterated his basic kinship with *History and Class Consciousness,* almost by way of an appeal to its author to come to his "Western Marxist" senses: "in the main issue, the critical view of the old and the new, the Social Democratic and Communist Marx-orthodoxy, I believe that even today [1929] my work [*Marxism and Philosophy,* 1923] stands in a front with Lukács's."[43]

Severed from a social movement or political formation composed of scattered central European intellectuals, the "Western Marxist" front was hardly a power. That Lukács's collaboration would have provided a missing center and aura is undoubtedly true, as is the fact that this would have required a fundamentally different set of political choices from the ones he actually made. Yet pursuing history's "what if's" is not always a fruitless task. Thus we may at least speculate on the impact Lukács might have had on the history of twentieth-century European Marxist thought if he had followed the critical rather than the dogmatic currents of *History and Class Consciousness*.

As events actually developed, though, by 1930 Lukács was taking up residence in Moscow, having been expelled from Austria. Two years earlier, he had in fact taken a politically heretical step within the exiled Hungarian party with the intraparty publication of his "Blum-Theses" (named after his party pseudonym) which called for a coalition of republican and antifascist forces in Hungary just at the moment the Communist International was veering to the Left. The "Blum-Theses," Lukács's last major intervention in immediate political affairs until 1956, were thus denounced as a "Right-deviation," with their author promptly recanting.[44] On arriving in Moscow in 1930, Lukács was ready for scholarly work—in the midst of the forced collectivization of Soviet agriculture. It was also the year that saw the great Bolshevik poet Vladimir Mayakovsky, spurned by the revolution he had loved, take his own life.

What better time to read, as Lukács was able to do in the library of the Marx-Engels-Lenin Institute in Moscow, the handwritten pages of Karl Marx's "Economic and Philosophic Manuscripts" of 1844? There is no way of knowing the impact this may have had on him at the time.[45] The "Manuscripts" were published first in Germany in 1932, with the author of *History and Class Consciousness,* who had intuitively reconstructed some of the main themes of the unknown Marx text, again refraining from comment. Greeted by Herbert Marcuse as a "decisive event in the history of Marxist studies," the new manuscripts seemed almost to speak for Lukács. As Karl Löwith, one of the first reviewers, noted, they provided among other things documentary confirmation of the primacy Lukács had given to the Hegelian-dialectical core of Marx's thought, and to the critique of reification.[46]

Marcuse's own review provided a fitting summation: the 1844 "Manuscripts," he emphasized, made it clear that "all efforts to push aside or bashfully conceal the philosophical content of Marxian theory proceed on the basis of a total misunderstanding of the theory's original historical foundation. That is, they begin with that very separation of philosophy, economy, and revolutionary *Praxis* that Marx had struggled against as a product of reification."[47] However, this served more as a benediction than as an opening of a new round of theoretical debate. For within a year of the publication of the Marx "Manuscripts," the whole discussion was brought to an abrupt halt by the Nazi seizure of power. With its representatives forced to scatter and its founder-in-spite-of-himself now a renegade, "Western Marxism" did not have a great deal to show for itself after a decade of existence. But it did exist. And although from the vantage point of 1933 in Germany, one might well have hesitated to make optimistic predictions, "Western Marxism" would have a future, and a not uninteresting one.

CONCLUSION

Cycles, Ruptures and Lines: From the Young Lukács's Day to Ours

If there is a message in the preceding pages, it may be the following: Marxism, like any rationalistic and totalizing theory, contains built-in tendencies toward formalization and dogmatism. It also contains, of course, countertendencies. The formalistic and dogmatic tendencies are intensified as the theory attaches itself to social-political institutions (working class organizations, parties, and, in this century, states), which entail an even greater propensity toward rigidity in the form of separation of leaders and led, bureaucratization, routinization of functions, and so forth. From such a standpoint, the history of Marxism as a theory and practice is marked by rather long periods in which formalism and/or dogmatism predominate (the rise of the German Social Democratic Party, 1880s–1914; Stalinism), punctuated by rather brief ruptures (the new Marxism expressed by the young Lukács and some others in the early 1920s; the New Left in the 1960s).

These ruptures are linked to breaks in the continuum of formalized history itself, moments when masses of people cease to bear history as a weight, choosing instead, in the words of the poet Harvey Blume to "catch at a new life" (Marx and Engels, 1847–49; the young Lukács and the upheavals of the post–World War I period; the New Left and the student and civil rights revolts). The experience of the ruptures includes recollection of their predecessors, which are invariably repressed and forgotten at other times: thus, the young Lukács retrieved and reinterpreted the young Marx; the New Left rejuvenated the young Lukács. The history of Marxism, then, is not linear and progressive, but cyclical. If this scheme amounts to an adequate interpretation of reality, one question we shall finally need to respond to is, In what direction is

Marxism headed today, now that the rupture of the 1960s has been leveled?

To get to that point, however, some of the particulars of the young Lukács's thought and its fate require brief review. Two components examined in depth in Part One of this book stand out: the neo-Romantic anticapitalism and the philosophical idealism of the young Lukács. By the former term we mean his critique of modernity itself, the world of industrial progress and efficiency, utilitarian-positivistic thought, urbanization, bureaucratization, and the like. His perspective, as we have tried to show, was well developed before he became a Marxist, growing out of a largely German tradition of cultural criticism centering around defense of *Gemeinschaft* and *Kultur* (organic community and qualitative cultural values) against *Gesellschaft* and *Zivilization* (atomized society). With some exceptions, the leading voices of this tradition of response to the industrial capitalist world of the *fin de siècle* were antisocialist, anti-Marxist, and generally on the right-wing nationalist segment of the political spectrum. One of the young Lukács's signal and most infamous contributions is that he brought this current of social and cultural theory into Marxism.

In doing so, he revived part of what Merleau-Ponty called the youth of Marxism. One of the most compelling aspects of Marx's early work (1843–44) is its fusion of the Enlightenment and Romantic standpoints into a single vision, grasping modern scientific culture and industrial technique as both liberating and imprisoning forces. With some important exceptions (for example, Diderot), Enlightenment thinkers and their early nineteenth-century Utilitarian heirs stressed the former view, Romantics the latter. In Marx's early writings the belief in the emancipatory power of industrialization is contained within a radical critique of the alienation of labor in capitalist-industrial production, a critique linked to his great, eschatological vision of a redemption of the alienated through their own revolutionary action.

Marx's unifying transformation of the Enlightenment and Romantic poles, however, proved short-lived. In the subsequent development of his own work, but above all in the course of Marxist thought during the last several decades of the nineteenth century, the Enlightenment root (faith in science and technology) blossomed while its Romantic half was snuffed out. The growth of this

Marxist version of the idea of progress, according to which development in science, technology, and industrial forms under capitalism leads society closer to socialism, was noted by critical contemporaries, above all those inspired by romanticism. In the early years of the twentieth century, for example, Gustav Landauer, the German communitarian-anarchist, surveyed the Marxism of the day and posed the question of its origins. Rejecting the standard replies—Hegelian philosophy, British political economy, French revolutionary and utopian socialist thought—Landauer replied: the origin of Marxism is steam. The industrial machine and factory, he insisted, are the gods to which Marxism pays homage. It was a penetrating exaggeration.

Marxism's increasingly unreflective belief in the redeeming powers of industrialization was one of the factors that kept the young Lukács at a distance prior to 1919. Conversely, when he converted to Marxism in the vortex of postwar revolutionary upheavals, it was to a Marxism he himself was beginning to recast with the handtools of neo-Romantic criticism. For the moment, only two aspects of this effort need emphasis. First, the young Lukács's neo-Romantic Marxism was soon shunted aside by the bigger and better productivist ideology fashioned in the Soviet Union, which was the order of the day in the Marxist movement for decades. Second, this vital dimension of the young Lukács's work was a major source of its revival in the 1960s, since the New Left was precisely an attempt to break with the religion of industrial progress that had again come to prevail within Marxism, not to mention Western society as a whole.

The neo-Romanticism of the young Lukács's work was accompanied by philosophical idealism, the second level on which he returned to the young Marx. One does not proceed very far into the young Lukács's Marxist writings before being struck by the parallels with Marx's texts prior to 1845. Today, interest in the young Marx is hardly an earth-shattering matter, but this is only because we are, in a sense, the young Lukács's disciples. As we have seen, prior to his efforts, beginning in 1919, virtually no one, least of all the Marxists, was deeply interested in Marx's youthful work. The prevalent view was that such texts as "The Critique of Hegel's Philosophy of Right" (1843), *The Poverty of Philosophy* (1844), and the "Theses on Feuerbach" (1844), were part of Marx's pre-

Marxist phase. They were, in other words, still anchored in Hegelian-idealist premises, awaiting Marx's discovery of the materialist and scientific dialectic. The idea that these early writings might constitute the revolutionary core of Marx's whole work had been foreign to Marxists—and others—for decades.

The young Lukács's intervention consisted of his restoration of the young Marx, not in the sense of retrieving texts, but in the sense of reliving and recreating a historical-philosophical experience. The young Marx had come to Marxism through a radical critique of Hegelian philosophy but, simultaneously, through an equally radical critique of materialism. In the first of his "Theses on Feuerbach" he presented a compressed version of this often overlooked process:

> The chief defect of all previous materialism including Feuerbach's is that the object, actuality, sensuousness is conceived only in the form of *object* or *perception,* but not as *sensuous human activity, practice,* not *subjectively.* Hence in opposition to materialism the *active* side was developed by idealism—but only abstractly since idealism naturally does not know actual, sensuous activity as such. Feuerbach wants sensuous objects actually different from thought objects: but he does not comprehend human activity itself as *objective.* Hence . . . he regards only the theoretical attitude as the truly human attitude, while practice is understood and fixed only in its dirtily Jewish form of appearance. Consequently he does not comprehend the significance of "revolutionary," of "practical-critical" activity (emphasis in original).

In the young Marx's view, then, philosophical materialism is a necessary but insufficient condition for revolutionary theory; its defect—the "theoretical attitude," the failure to grasp the subjectivity of "actuality"—must be overcome. And he seeks to overcome the defect through the mechanism of a critically transformed idealism which, while abstract by itself, nevertheless contains the "active" and subjective side.

As Marx's thinking developed, his initial critique of materialism was muted. Moreover, in Friedrich Engels's work during the 1880s and 1890s and in the writings of Karl Kautsky, the dean of Marxist theory in the following decades, the idea that Marxism is a philosophical materialism took over. As the young Lukács would discover, the history of Marxism had tended toward precisely the sort of materialist thinking Marx had initially found defective: passive, contemplative, focusing exclusively on the supposedly primary world of external matter. Without too drastic an oversimplification, by substituting Engels and Karl Kautsky for Feuerbach, we get a capsule picture of the Marxism the young Lukács would criticize before, during, and after he became a Marxist.

The parallel in the history of nineteenth-century Marxism between the dissolution of Marx's critique of materialism and the dissolution of his critique of industrialization is not fortuitous. They are two sides of one process which can be clarified by looking briefly at another parallel: that between the young Marx's and the young Lukács's routes to Marxism. There are sharp differences, yet like the young (pre-Marxist) Marx, the young (pre-Marxist) Lukács was immersed in an idealist intellectual culture with socially critical impulses, though still lacking a developed theory of revolution. Central here is the idealist conviction regarding the world-constituting power of consciousness, or mind. From his starting point in the young Left-Hegelian circles of the early 1840s, Marx brought this conviction into the Marxism he was beginning to construct. The young Lukács was able to decipher and reconstruct this idealist moment in Marxism because he had already adopted its foundations from the neo-Kantian and neo-Hegelian circles in which he was moving during the decade prior to 1919. He was, in other words, already well-equipped theoretically to recapitulate Marx's transformation of idealism into a theory of revolutionary class consciousness and proletarian "practical-critical" activity.

He did not have to do so; theoretical preparedness for a new theoretical act often remains just that. Two additional components entered the picture. One was the young Lukács's deep (neo-Romantic) ethical rejection of the capitalist world. But this, significantly, did not propel him toward Marxism prior to 1919—that Marxism whose materialism and enthusiasm for industrialism only mirrored capitalism. The second component through which Lukács took his leap into Marxism and communism was, to borrow another of Merleau-Ponty's phrases, the "youth of revolution." That is, the young Lukács, like the young Marx, became a Marxist by way of a broadly shared philosophical trajectory within the maelstrom of emergent, collective revolutionary movements. It is not enough, Marx had written in 1843, for theory to press toward reality; reality itself must also press toward theory. This is what we mean by the youth of revolution: the upsurge of efforts by broad numbers and groups of dominated or oppressed peoples to break with the old forms of life and give new shape to their destiny. This is what Marx perceived in the spread of artisans' rebellion across Europe in the mid-1840s and it is what Lukács found himself in the midst of at the close of World War I. Among the unique elements of the phenomenon of revolution's youth is its capacity to generate a deep faith in the power of collective human will or desire radically to transform the world. It is a moment in which history itself appears to become idealistic.

As it happened, the revolutions of the young Marx's and the young Lukács's times never got very far beyond their youthful phases. It appears that the "youth of Marxism" they respectively articulated underestimated the "opacity of history," its obdurate materialism. The consequences of the defeat of revolution in both instances were complex and far-reaching, but what is interesting is their bearing on the problem of the cycle in the history of Marxism. Marx's attempt to account for the defeat of the revolutions of 1848 and the subsequent period of capitalist growth yielded impressive results: for example, the *Eighteenth Brumaire of Louis Napoleon* and *Das Kapital* and the founding, in 1864, of the First International Workingmen's Association. Yet neither Marx's theoretical gifts nor the formation of proletarian organizations could revitalize "practical-critical" activity in revolutionary form. Moreover, history's own conservatism (or materialism) can also press toward theory—and did so in the latter half of the nineteenth century by deepening those currents in Marx's thought and that of his disciples toward the idea of the objective, law-like character of history which, independent of human will, generates the conditions for socialism.

Before retracing the young Lukács's response to the dissolution of the postwar revolutions, more must be said regarding what he brought to revolution in the first place. We have seen that what the young Marx had called the "active side" of the revolutionary equation, missing from Feuerbach's materialism, was preserved by (Kantian and Hegelian) idealism in abstract form. If, as we have also indicated, this active side had departed from the mainstream of Marxism itself by 1900, the question arises, Where had it gone? In part, it was nurtured by the minority leftist currents within the Marxist movement: in the writings of Rosa Luxemburg, for example, and the group around Anton Pannekoek in Holland, for whom the idea of the mass strike, exemplified in the 1905 Revolution in Russia, offered a radical, voluntaristic corrective to the more staid, evolutionary stance of the influential German Social Democratic Party. In part it was preserved by independent Marxist intellectuals, scattered non-Marxist socialists, and anarchists who shared roots in idealist traditions, among them, Gustav Landauer, Rodolfo Mondolfo and his associates in Italy, Max Adler and several other "Austro-Marxists," and the otherwise not like-minded Frenchmen, Jean Jaurès and Georges Sorel.

Beyond them, the philosophical "active side" was developed outside the Marxist and working class movements by idealist philosophers and social theorists, foremost among whom were some of the young Lukács's direct and indirect mentors: Wilhelm Dilthey, Henri Bergson, Edmund Husserl, Wilhelm Windelband, Georg Simmel, Emil Lask, and Max Weber. They undertook, beginning around 1890, a "neo-idealist defense of subjectivity" against the materialism and positivism which prevailed in both bourgeois and Marxist circles. Moreover, although these theorists were hostile to socialism, revolutionary or otherwise, their diverse emphases on the roles of subjectivity, will, imagination, intuition, and consciousness in history contained important socially critical impulses. Specifically, these neo-idealists preserved and developed traces of the young Marx's critique of alienation and industrialization, which had also tended to disappear from the Marxism of the period. They were, however, inverted traces of Marx's critique. As we have stressed, Max Weber's analysis of the bureaucratic rationalization of society, or Georg Simmel's theory of the tragedy of culture, for example, turned Marx's critique of the social processes of capitalism into processes constitutive of the "modern world" or the "human condition." Beginning in 1919, the young Lukács would invert the inversion, transforming the neo-idealist and neo-Romantic perspectives on subjectivity and alienation into a rejuvenated Marxian theory of revolutionary proletarian praxis.

But the revolution that nurtured the young Lukács's Marxism was short-lived. Its most advanced manifestations, the workers' and soldiers' councils which sprouted in Berlin, Munich, Budapest,

Turin, Vienna, and other cities, proved to be hopelessly fragile shoots of new life. Momentarily shaken, the ruling groups of Europe, often aided by Social Democratic leaders, reconsolidated their power. Where the radical sections of the revolution were not battered by armed or judicial repression, they were isolated from broad constituencies. In Russia, where to everyone's surprise the revolutionary victory sustained itself, the radical, anticentralist currents were by 1921 faring little better than in Europe. Communism, in power in Russia and institutionalized in Europe (and elsewhere) in the form of the Third International, was showing early signs of authoritarian bureaucratization.

The young Lukács's Marxism is the clearest, critical expression and internalization of this web of contradictions. Even as he began to reconcile himself to a state of affairs that had not gone according to expectations, he nevertheless continued to judge events in the critical light of the revolution's wilder hopes: an end to the "reified" world of commodity production and the realization of a truly human community. We have seen the consequences of his efforts, his denunciation by the Communist International, and his road to self-censorship. At the end of the 1920s, Karl Korsch first suggested that there was something cyclical to this entire story. As previously noted, in his 1923 *Marxism and Philosophy* Korsch had spoken of a "Hegel-amnesia" in the Marxist movement of the latter half of the nineteenth century, arguing that it signified a forgetting of the revolutionary-dialectical core of Marx's work. In its place, a mechanical and deterministic materialism had developed. But this, Korsch believed, was overcome by the revival of revolutionary activity and a renewed critical-dialectical Marxism with conscious roots in Hegel—Korsch's own work and Lukács's. With the collapse of the revolutionary moment of the early 1920s and the rise of bureaucratism and dogmatism in the Communist movement, Korsch left the movement in 1926. Three years later, in his new introduction to the republication of *Marxism and Philosophy,* Korsch stressed that the Marxist-Leninist ideology that had become the order of the day in communism was in essence a reproduction of the old, mechanistic materialism of the prewar Social Democratic Party, that is, "Kautskyism."

In age and thinking, Lukács himself was by 1930 no longer the young Lukács. He would remain engaged for the rest of his long life in a complex debate with his own youthful work. As an émigré in the Soviet Union from 1930 to the end of the World War II (when he returned to Hungary), his position was never secure, although unlike the majority of foreign Communists there, he survived the "great terror." Turning away from directly political themes, he devoted himself to studies in the history, sociology, and philosophy of literature, preserving elements of a critical Marxist humanism, but equally capable of swamping them in bursts of Stalinist dogmatism. Yet he never managed to satisfy the official keepers of orthodoxy, who continued to view him as a troublesome intellectual. The suspicions were not unfounded, although among communism's heretics, Lukács had unquestionably been the most loyal. He emerged as an active figure in the anti-Stalinist Petöfi Circle, one of the intellectual progenitors of the 1956 revolution in Budapest, in which he participated without enthusiasm as Deputy Commissar of Public Education in the short-lived government under Imre Nagy, the same post he had occupied in the 133-day revolutionary regime in Hungary under Béla Kun in 1919.

The most resonant echoes of the young Lukács's work were not, however, to be heard in the mature Lukács. As he announced his Marxist-Leninist shift away from his apprenticeship, the intellectuals gathered around the Institute for Social Research in Frankfurt, Germany, began to build upon *History and Class Consciousness*'s Hegelian-Marxist critique of reification in bourgeois society and thought, making it the basis for the "critical theory" they elaborated in the 1930s and 1940s. Moreover, the "Frankfurt School" theorists (Max Horkheimer, T. W. Adorno, Herbert Marcuse, and others) deepened those elements of the young Lukács's Marxism which pointed toward a critique of Stalinism in particular and dogmatic Marxist orthodoxy in general.

An outstanding feature of the Frankfurt School's work, however, was that while many of its associates revived, deepened, and carried in new directions many of the young Lukács's themes, they did so not in the midst of revived revolution, but in connection with the rise of Fascism and Stalinism. The social-historical underpinning of their work was the uninterrupted defeat of revolutionary hopes. Not surprisingly, some of their number glimpsed a tragic element not only in Marxism, but in the impulse to social liberation throughout history. In *Dialectic of Enlightenment* (1947) Max Horkheimer and Theodor Adorno spoke of the early phases of both religious and social revolutionary movements in which the "theoretical and practical systems of these outsiders of history are . . . not very rigid and centralized; they differ from the successful systems by the element of anarchy." Yet, they argued, the initial, libertarian experience of such movements is no grounds for optimism since "the history of the old religions and schools like that of the modern parties and revolutions teaches us that the price for survival is practical involvement, the transformation of ideas into domination," that is, into hierarchy and the manipulation of people, language, and thought.[1]

As this withering pessimism was being presented, its authors were returning home to Frankfurt following their American emigration. At the same time, Lukács had returned to the new, postwar Communist Hungary. These, however, were not the only options; a new generation of potential heirs to the young Lukács's ideas was able to take some new steps. The rise of a critical Marxian phoenix from the ashes of World War II was not on the agenda; instead, it was a matter of "outsiders of history" nurturing certain themes and visions. Appropriately, the initial step in this process was obscure: the work of a young Rumanian Jew, Lucien Goldmann, who had emigrated to Zurich during the war, where in 1945 he wrote a dissertation inspired by both Heidegger and the young Lukács on the theme of "Man and Community in Kant's Philosophy." In the foreword he referred to the young Lukács, none of whose works were any longer in print, as the greatest philosopher of the century. Goldmann then rewrote his German-language thesis for publication (1948) in France, to which he had further emigrated. Isolated, crossing borders, acquiring new tongues, addressing invisible audiences, Lucien Goldmann's journey symbolized the situation of critical Marxism at mid-century.

Goldmann's arrival in France coincided with the turn toward Marxism of some of France's leading existentialist philosophers, among them Maurice Merleau-Ponty and Jean-Paul Sartre. The parallels between their intellectual-political trajectory and that of the young Lukács are striking. In both instances there was a conversion to Marxism by idealist philosophers whose work had preserved what the young Marx called the (philosophical) "active side" of the concept of revolutionary-practical activity. As the young Lukács had come to Marxism from pre–World War I German neo-idealism, so Merleau-Ponty's and Sartre's route passed through the teachings of Martin Heidegger and Edmund Husserl; moreover, their efforts to work out a new phenomenology of consciousness were deeply influenced by the French "Hegel renaissance" of the pre–World War II period. Again like the young Lukács, Sartre and Merleau-Ponty elaborated a new Marxism outside and against the mainstream, which in their case was the official dialectical materialism of the Soviet Union and the European Communist parties. A final parallel: as in the young Lukács's experience (but in contrast to that of the Frankfurt School intellectuals), the turning point for the French existentialists was direct contact with a form of the youth of revolution—the anti-Fascist Resistance and the working-class radicalism of the immediate postwar years. Their links to collective experience and social struggle propelled them away from fixation on the subjectivity of the isolated individual toward envisioning a "We-subject," the proletariat as communal existentialist.

Merleau-Ponty's *Humanism and Terror* (1947) exemplifies the prospects and problems of this new course; it is actually two books, whose paradoxical relationship is a summary of the dilemmas of independent Marxists in the immediate postwar years. In the first part Merleau-Ponty sought to show that the Marxian conception of history as displayed by Arthur Koestler in his *Darkness at Noon* is a travesty, substituting as it does an iron determinism for a dialectical grasp of the relations between human consciousness, activity, institutions, and time. Merleau-Ponty drew upon both his own existential-phenomenological roots and his study of *History and Class Consciousness*. In the book's second part, refusing to make any concessions to the emerging cold-war liberal anticommunism, he tried to show that the Stalin purge trials, specifically the trial and confession of Bukharin, which had served as the basis for Koestler's novel, were not travesties but grim necessities of the revolution's progress.

Merleau-Ponty soon broke with this latter view and with every attempt to defend the Soviet Union, including those of his former friend, Sartre. In *Adventures of the Dialectic* (1955) he presented what remains the most lucid brief commentary on *History and Class Consciousness*. He took up this book again, he noted, "in order to measure today's communism, to realize what it has renounced, and to what it has resigned itself." Not satisfied with nostalgia for a better Marxian theory, however, he pursued the question of why Lukács's work of the early 1920s was so "poorly received by the orthodoxy, particularly the Marxist-Leninists." The fate of the young Lukács's (and the young Marx's) work, according to Merleau-Ponty, reveals an "internal difficulty of Marxist thought." In its youthful phases, Marxism is dialectical, a "paradoxical mode of thought, the discoverer of an entangling relationship between the dialectician and his object, the surprise of a spirit which finds itself outdistanced by things and anticipated in them." Conversely, it lacks the capacity to express the "inertia of the infrastructures, the resistance of economic and even natural conditions." In the wake of defeated revolutions, the attempts to resolve this dilemma have invariably led Marxists to a bad materialist rationalism and determinism—Hegelianism without dialectic. He glimpsed the outlines of a cycle: the conflict between the young Lukács and Marxism-Leninism, Merleau-Ponty concluded, "is already found in Marx as a conflict between dialectical thought and naturalism, and the Leninist orthodoxy eliminated Lukács's attempt just as Marx himself had eliminated his own first 'philosophical' period."[2]

The mature Lukács did what he could to forestall the development of "existential Marxism." His *Existentialism or Marxism* (1947; 1961) took Sartre, Merleau-Ponty, and Simone de Beauvoir to task not only for their original phenomenological positions (a "carnival of festishized interiority") but also for their postwar turn to the Left. What the French philosophers saw as a potential third way between liberalism and Stalinism, Lukács saw as petit-bourgeois thought in thin disguise.[3] Then, when in 1956 the French Communist Party published its denunciation of Merleau-Ponty's *Adventures of the Dialectic*, which had appeared the previous year, Lukács contributed a note distancing himself from his youthful errors and advising others to do the same.[4]

A decisive year in the history of Marxism and communism, 1956 witnessed Khruschev's secret speech exposing Stalin's tyranny and the crushing of the Hungarian revolution by Soviet armed force under Khruschev's direction. In that year, a German Marx scholar, Iring Fetscher, published an important interpretation of the situation of critical, humanistic Marxism in the light of both recent events and past history. Influenced by the young Lukács, Karl Korsch, the Frankfurt School theorists, and the existential Marxists, Fetscher surveyed Marxism in terms of its movement from a "philosophy of the proletariat into a proletarian ideology." In the history of the reception of Marx's thought, he argued,

> the vision of a free proletariat, self-consciously acting to transform itself and reality, is always put forward by intellectuals who stand more or less outside political action. . . . Revolutionary humanism remains an episode confined to small cliques of intellectuals. It is pointless to defend the young Marx against orthodox dialectical materialism, because his vision has shown itself to be manifestly unreal. As deep as his revolutionary activism (and mysticism) may be, it was not in touch with political reality. The humanistic imperatives get lost on the road to realization, while the exponents of the ideologization of Marxism only fulfill the judgment of history. The yearning of West European intellectuals for a "pure" Marxian revolution is an illusion; the ideological rigidification of Marxism into dialectical materialism is an "irony of destiny"—or a "cunning of reason."[5]

Fetscher's view echoes Horkheimer's and Adorno's "transformation of ideas into domination" and Merleau-Ponty's "internal difficulty of Marxist thought." Like the latter's thesis, Fetscher's conception had behind it the weight of historical evidence. Yet to speak as he did in the name of the irony of destiny is always a difficult matter for the simple reason that destiny *is* ironic. We have no intention of dispensing with Fetscher's pessimism, which informs our own analysis. Nevertheless, just as he was pronouncing his eulogy at the graveside of ideas associated with the young Lukács and the young Marx, a new process was at play which would rejuvenate those ideas. Arising from the tremors unleashed by the events of 1956 and emergent changes in postwar capitalist societies, the incipient New Left was initially confined to the sorts of small cliques of intellectuals of which Fetscher had spoken. By the mid-1960s, however, the New Left burgeoned into an extensive social movement, carrying with it an unprecedented renaissance of young Lukácsian themes.

East and West, between the mid-1950s and early 1960s, numerous small groups formed and located vital elements in the prehistory of a potentially new Marxism in the work of the young Lukács and other related heterodox thinkers whose ideas and programs had been suppressed by the dominant Marxist currents. Among the bearers of these efforts were such journals as *Socialisme ou Barbarie, Internationale Situationiste,* and *Arguments* in Paris; *Praxis* (which carried articles by some of Lukács's students, later known as the Budapest School) in Belgrade; *New Left Review* in London; *Studies on the Left* in Madison, Wisconsin; and *Das Argument* in Frankfurt, West Germany. Their pages reflect, along with other issues, the start of wide discussion of the young Lukács, one that had been short-circuited by the Communist International in the mid-1920s. Not surprisingly, this activity included the first translation of *History and Class Consciousness* (parts had been published in Japanese translation in 1927), although when the French *Arguments* circle released their edition in 1961, they did so over Lukács's own objections. Greater access to the infamous text would not have had any bearing on the history of Marxist movements, but in fact it was a rare book. To give an extreme but revealing example, prior to the appearance of the French edition, only a single copy of *History and Class Consciousness* was available to the associates of the Yugoslav journal *Praxis*.

Two sociological aspects of the appearance of these journals and intellectual groups indicate that this revival of the young Lukács—our short-hand term for New Left Marxism—was taking place on a new terrain and pointing in directions to which neither the classical Marxian nor many of the young Lukács's ideas fully applied. First, while numerically small and politically marginal, the journals and groups of the late 1950s and early 1960s contained the embryo of international discussion, no longer confined to one place at a time—Central Europe in the early 1920s or Paris in the post–World War II years. Second, to an increasingly notable degree the intellectuals involved in these developments were connected to universities and university milieux. This in itself was not a new phenomenon. The novelty lay in the fact that the audiences for the ideas being developed were based in and around universities, not in and around working class organizations, and, above all, in the fact that the social character and roles of universities were undergoing major changes. They were becoming mass institutions, knowledge industries, and, as such, bearers of volatile social antagonisms.

With universities and students at or close to the center, a New Left social movement spread across the Western world and parts of the rest of the globe in the late 1960s. This was one of the ruptures in history of which we spoke earlier, and in it the young Lukács's ideas found their first extensive audience. It was not the audience which he, let alone the great majority of Marxists, had in mind. Yet, the intended audience, the industrial proletariat, had rarely been receptive. Viewed as a whole, the New Left insurgency of the late 1960s was a multiclass phenomenon, which is to say, a diversified, internally contradictory human phenomenon of revolt, consisting of students, youth, national minorities, women as women, radical religious groups, and so forth. Moreover, the movement(s) emanated from the cultural and political contradictions of contemporary capitalist (and socialist) society, rather than from immediate economic contradictions.

Within the framework of this complex movement, only segments of its student and intellectual currents revived the young Lukács's ideas. Yet the underlying source of this revival was not that his ideas provided a long-lost clue to the puzzle of how the proletariat becomes revolutionary. On the contrary, the young Lukács's heirs in the 1960s reinterpreted his work as a critique of their own experience in capitalist (and socialist) society—as a contribution to their own radicalization. For at its root, the rebellion of students and intellectuals was directed against the reification of everyday life, the process by which human life is transformed under modern conditions of production into things, marketable goods, numbers. A critique of reification lay at the heart of the young Lukács's work, pre-Marxist and post-Marxist. In that work, sections of the New Left grasped a vital theoretical anticipation of their own activity.

Yet if the links between the young Lukács's ideas and the New Left were real, they were also tenuous. Substantial portions of the movement retrieved young Lukácsian themes by intuition and in action, while smaller numbers were attentive to the theoretical issues. At the same time, the movement of students and intellectuals as a whole was compulsively resistant to critical, humanistic Marxist theory. On the one side there was a tendency to reject theoretical thought, even thought itself, as the enemy of revolution, even of life itself. In this view, only one idea counted: the idea of action. On the other side stood the tendency to embrace, in the form of revived Marxist and Marxist-Leninist orthodoxy, an arid intellectualism. Here, too, only one idea counted: the correct line derived from the science of dialectical materialism. These tendencies, which became pronounced in 1968 and after, were not contradictory. Numerous individuals moved from one to the other with relative ease. The unifying element is that in both instances critical thinking was eliminated. Between 1968 and 1972, in the face of increased governmental repression and harassment supported by the "silent majority" of the population, the American New Left tortured itself with the twin-blade of actionism and dogmatism.

Of these two self-destructive elements, only one has shown any staying power: rigid Marxism. Thus the past ten years has witnessed the growth of a bevy of Marxist-Leninist and openly Stalinist sects. Quite separate from this development in political-organizational terms, but related to it culturally, the recent period has also been characterized by the blossoming of a new, academically based Marxist scientism, for whose representatives the young Lukács and the young Marx appear to be some sort of fluffy humanism lacking any social-scientific status whatsoever. Moreover, in many segments of the American Left today, one notices a paradoxical, though not original, sense of relief that, thanks to inflation and recession, we are back to the basic economic problems of capitalism and thus need no longer trouble ourselves over cultural or ideological matters. On the surface—and probably beneath it—it appears that Marxism is once again passing through another turn of its cycle, with the phase of New Left vitality now replaced by one more long spell of ideological and practical rickets. Iring Fetscher's prognosis regarding the ineluctable triumph of the "rigidification of Marxism into dialectical materialism" appears to have been vindicated.

The present terrain offers other possibilities, thin as they may be. From the standpoint of the outline history of Marxism we have sketched, the most promising feature today is an ironic one: the Marxist movement internationally is in a state of disarray and fragmentation, showing no signs of consolidation. No organization capable of managing Marxism's destiny is on the horizon. In America there is a parallel picture. The neo-Stalinist sects control little more than their own memberships, and even those not for long. It is a time, as one of the sects put it not long ago, of splits and fusions. In contrast to past periods of ideological rigidification on the Left, there is now more space than ever for study, discussion, and dissemination of critical Marxian, neo-Marxian and post-Marxian ideas. Reappraising the young Lukács today, then, means sustaining a permanent rupture in Marxism, a goal of the present book.

Notes

PREFACE

1. Maurice Merleau-Ponty, *The Adventures of the Dialectic,* trans. Joseph Bien (Evanston, Ill: Northwestern University Press, 1973), pp. 30–58.

2. From among the growing number of works on "Western Marxism" see the following: Russell Jacoby, "Toward a Critique of Automatic Marxism: From Lukács to the Frankfurt School" *Telos* 10 (Winter 1971):119–46; Paul Piccone, "Phenomenological Marxism," *Telos* 9 (Fall 1971):3–31; Martin Jay, *The Dialectical Imagination: A History of the Frankfurt School and the Institute of Social Research, 1923–1950* (Boston: Little Brown, 1973); and Mark Poster, *Existential Marxism in Postwar France: From Sartre to Althusser* (Princeton, N.J.: Princeton University Press, 1975). More negative appraisals can be found in Neil McInnes, *The Western Marxists* (New York: Library Press, 1972), and Perry Anderson, *Considerations on Western Marxism* (London: New Left Books, 1976).

CHAPTER 1: REVOLUTIONARY WITHOUT A REVOLUTION

1. There exists no comprehensive biography of Lukács. Ferenc Fehér's work in preparation will doubtless place the relations between Lukács's thought and life on a new level. We have in the meantime relied on a number of sources: Erhard Bahr, *Georg Lukács* (Berlin: Colloquium, 1970); Fritz Raddatz, *Lukács* (Reinbeck: Rowohlt, 1972); Yvon Bourdet, *Figures de Lukács* (Paris: Anthropos, 1972); István Mészáros, *Lukács' Concept of Dialectic* (London: Merlin, 1972); Johanna Rosenberg, "Das Leben Georg Lukács'," in Werner Mittenzwei, ed., *Dialog und Kontroverse mit Georg Lukács* (East Berlin: Reclam, 1975), pp. 396–428; and the typed transcript of Lukács's autobiographical notes, "Gelebtes Denken," from the "Lukács Archive" in Budapest.

2. The "von" in the Lukács family name signifies the dominant feature of Hungarian social development at the time: the absorption of the financial and industrial bourgeoisie by the traditional landed nobility and the crown. The impact of this phenomenon upon the development of Hungarian politics, culture, and the socialist movement in particular during the period of Lukács's early years is thoroughly traced in Zoltan Horvath, *Die Jahrhundertwende in Ungarn: Geschichte der Zweiten Reformgeneration* (Neuwied and Berlin: Luchterhand, 1966). A perceptive sociologically oriented account can be found in Michael Löwy, *Pour une sociologie des intellectuels révolutionnaires: L'évolution politique de Lukács, 1909–1929* (Paris: P.U.F., 1976), pp. 78–105.

3. Was Lukács also a wandering Jew? Literally yes, although Jewishness appears to have played no explicit role in his life. His father, born Jakob Löwinger, and mother, Adél Wertheimer, were Jews, changing the family name to Lukács in 1883. When Georg Lukács

applied for habilitation to the Heidelberg University in 1918, he listed his religious affiliation as Evangelical, and it may be that the family had for practical purposes converted. When, during the pre–World War I years, he corresponded with Martin Buber, in whose *Legend of the Baal-Shem* Lukács was deeply interested, it was due more to his overriding interest in mystical currents than in things Jewish. The two faiths on which he was most focused in this period were in any case medieval and Russian Orthodox Christianity. In view of the religiosity of his thinking and sensibility, it would not be quite appropriate to place him among Isaac Deutscher's "Non-Jewish Jews," all of whom (Marx, Freud, Einstein, Trotsky, Luxemburg, and so on) were avidly secular and modernizing thinkers. After his "conversion" to Marxism in 1919, though, he would fit somewhat more smoothly into this category.

4. István Mészáros, "Die Philosophie des 'tertium datur' und des Koexistenzdialogs," in Frank Benseler, ed., *Festschrift zum achtzigsten Geburtstag von Georg Lukács* (Neuwied and Berlin: Luchterhand, 1965), p. 190.

5. *Die Seele und die Formen* (Berlin: Egon Fleischel, 1911), p. 26.

6. *Theorie des Romans: Ein geschichtsphilosophischer Versuch Über die Formen der grossen Epik* (Neuwied and Berlin: Luchterhand, 1965), pp. 20–22. Originally written in 1914–15, "Theorie des Romans" was first published as an essay in 1916 in the *Zeitschrift für Ästhetik und Allgemeine Kunstwissenschaft* and then in unrevised form as a book in 1920, by which time Lukács had become a Communist. This is one of a number of minor philological curiosities we have not been able to resolve.

7. Ibid., p. 90.

8. Review of Thomas Mann's *Royal Highness* in Georg Lukács, *Essays on Thomas Mann,* trans. Stanley Mitchell (London: Merlin, 1964), p. 137. The review was originally published in Hungary in 1909.

9. For analyses of "romantic anticapitalism" parallel to our own, see Ferenc Fehér, "Am Scheideweg des romantischen Antikapitalismus: Typologie und Beitrag zur deutschen Ideologiegeschichte gelegentlich des Briefwechsels zwischen Paul Ernst und Georg Lukács," in Agnes Heller et al., *Die Seele und das Leben: Studien zum frühen Lukács* (Frankfurt-am-Main: Suhrkamp, 1977), pp. 241–327; and Löwy, *Pour une sociologie des intellectuels révolutionnaires,* pp. 17–105.

10. Recent examples of what we consider reductionist approaches to Lukács's *oeuvre* are Ben Brewster, "Révai and Lukács," *Theoretical Practice* 1 (January 1971): 14–21; Gareth Stedman-Jones, "The Marxism of the Early Lukács," *New Left Review* 70 (November-December 1971): 27–64; and George Lichtheim, *Lukács* (New York: Random House, 1970).

11. Laszlo Rudas, "Orthodoxer Marxismus?" *Arbeiter-Literatur* 9 (1924): 493.

12. Need it be added that we do not intend to *separate* Lukács's development from the influences upon it?

13. *Die Seele und die Formen,* pp. 28–29.

14. This sentence from Marx's "Toward a Critique of Hegel's *Philosophy of Right:* Introduction" (1843) appears several times in Lukács's writings between 1919 and 1920.

15. In 1902–3, Lukács published theater reviews in *Magyar Szalon* ("Hungarian Salon") and *Jovendo* ("The Future").

16. Regarding Szabó's "sovereign influence" on critically minded Hungarian intellectuals between 1900 and 1918, see Horvath, *Die Jahrhundertwende in Ungarn,* pp. 354–59; Oskar Jászi, "Ervin Szabó und sein Werk," *Archiv für die Geschichte des Sozialismus und der Arbeiterbewegung,* 1922, pp. 22–37; and the more recent and extensive work, Tibor Süle, *Sozialdemokratie in Ungarn: Zur Rolle der Intelligenz in der Arbeiterbewegung, 1899–1910* (Köln: Reyersbach, 1967), passim.

17. Süle, *Sozialdemokratie in Ungarn,* pp. 52–59.

18. Ibid., pp. 59–60. Cf. Horvath, *Die Jahrhundertwende in Ungarn,* p. 323.

19. Süle, *Sozialdemokratie in Ungarn,* p. 92.

20. Ibid., pp. 101–9.

21. On the Thalia Theater project and Lukács's role in it, see: Mészáros, "Philosophie des 'tertium datur,'" pp. 190–92; Josef Czímer, "Theater Review," *New Hungarian Quarterly* 8, no. 28 (Winter 1967):208; and Jose Ignacio Lopez Soria, "L'expérience théâtrale de Lukács," *L'homme et la société* 43–44 (January–June 1977):117–31.

22. In a later recollection of this early period, Lukács noted that he was "one of those whose early years of development were overshadowed by the patriotic traditions which hardened into the rigid and obtuse academicism prevailing after 1867. At that time only the first faint indications of the ideological revolution were visible . . . [in a situation] . . . which stifled all genuine protest." Georg Lukács, "Béla Bartok," *New Hungarian Quarterly* 7, no. 41 (Spring 1971):43.

23. Lukács's interest in German culture antedates the failure of the Thalia project which, however, pushed him westward with new force.

24. The term "second reform generation" refers to the intellectual opposition in Hungary from the late 1890s to World War I, its forerunner, the first reform generation, having been that of the 1840s and 1850s. Horvath, *Die Jahrhundertwende in Ungarn* is the history of the second reform generation.

25. Our remarks on the outlooks, problems, and achievements of the journals and their circles rely on Horvath, *Die Jahrhundertwende in Ungarn,* pp. 134ff., 35ff.; David Kettler, "Culture and Revolution: Lukács in the Hungarian Revolutions of 1918/19," *Telos* 10 (Winter 1971):35–92, especially pp. 38–54; and Süle, *Sozialdemokratie in Ungarn,* pp. 19–24.

26. One of the main projects of the Social Scientific Society was the organization in 1904 of a Free School of the Social Sciences, an educational program for workers. The premise of its organizers, whose guiding light was Oskar Jászi, was that an educated working class is the precondition of modernization and socialism, as well as the only way to avoid violent revolution. Courses in natural sciences, hygiene, business law, history, Russian literature, and the "woman question" were among those presented to working class students. In 1905 the school listed an enrollment of 2,000 students. See, Horvath, *Die Jahrhundertwende in Ungarn,* pp. 134–35.

27. The crux of Lukács's differences with the *Huszadik Század* group was his opposition to the belief that modernization on the Western model was Hungary's dominant imperative. While at the time he saw no precise alternatives, Lukács devoted himself to exposing the calamitous consequences for life and culture that the West's modernization had already left in its wake.

28. Horvath, *Die Jahrhundertwende in Ungarn,* p. 353.

29. On Lukács and Endre Ady, see: Mészáros, *Lukács' Concept of Dialectic,* pp. 23–26; and Andrew Arato, "Lukács's Path to Marxism, 1910–1923," *Telos* 7 (Spring 1971):128–29.

30. Georg Lukács, "Ady Endre" (1909), in *Magyar Irodalom, Magyar Kultura* (Budapest: Gondolat, 1970), p. 45.

CHAPTER 2: IN THE "IRON CAGE"

1. This theme has been carefully developed in two essays by György Márkus in Agnes Heller et al., *Die Seele und das Leben* (Frankfurt-am-Main: Suhrkamp, 1977): "Die Seele und das Leben: Der junge Lukács und das Problem der 'Kultur,'" pp. 99–130; and "Lukács' 'erste' Ästhetik: Zur Entwicklungsgeschichte der Philosophie des jungen Lukács," pp. 192–240. An English translation of the first of these appears in *Telos* 32 (Summer 1977).

2. Paul Breines, "Introduction to Lukács," *Telos* 5 (Spring 1970):1–20.

3. Andrew Arato, "The Neo-Idealist Defense of Subjectivity," *Telos* 21 (Fall 1974):108–61.

4. György Lukács, *A modern dráma fejlödésének története*, 2 vols. (Budapest: Franklin, 1911). This work, hereafter referred to as *Dramahistory*, has not yet appeared in a Western European language.

5. The essay appeared in a volume by the same title: György Lukács, *Esztétikai kultura* (Budapest: Athenaum, 1913).

6. György Lukács, *A lélek és a formák* (Budapest: Franklin, 1910). The volume appeared in German as well: *Die Seele und die Formen* (Berlin: Egon Fleischel, 1911). It is now in English: *The Soul and the Forms*, trans. Anna Bostock (Cambridge, Mass: MIT Press, 1976). Our references are to the German edition, although when there are differences between it and the Hungarian original, we refer to the latter as well.

7. György Lukács, "A lelki szegénységröl," *Szellem* II (Budapest, 1911). Lukács published the essay in German: "Von der Armut am Geiste. Ein Gespräch und ein Brief," *Neue Blätter* 2 (1912):67–92. It is now in English: "On the Poverty of Spirit," trans. John T. Sanders, *The Philosophical Forum* 3, nos. 3–4 (Spring-Summer 1972):371–85. Our references are to the German edition.

8. We refer to the German translation, "Zur Theorie der Literaturgeschichte" in *Text und Kritik* 39/40 (October 1973):24–51.

9. Our references are to the original Hungarian edition and to the 1914 German translation of its important second chapter, "Zur Soziologie des modernen Dramas," *Archiv für Sozialwissenschaft und Sozialpolitik*, 1914, pp. 303–45, 662–706. It is difficult to fathom why at least the German essay is not mentioned by some of the most sensitive and knowledgeable analysts of Lukács's pre-Marxian work, among them, Lucien Goldmann and Alberto Asor-Rosa. The consequence of the lapse, particularly in Goldmann's important studies, is an ultimately onesided picture in which Lukács appears as an early Existentialist who lacked any socio-historical account of the crisis of modern man. See, for example, Lucien Goldmann, "The Early Writings of Georg Lukács," trans. Joy Humes, *Tri-Quarterly* 9 (Spring 1967):165–81; and his "Georg Lukács: L'Essayiste," *Recherches Dialectiques* (Paris: Gallimard, 1959), pp. 247–59; and Alberto Asor-Rosa, "Der junge Lukács: Theoretiker der bürgerlichen Kunst," *Alternative* 12 (October 1969):174–203. For further critical discussion of Goldmann and Asor-Rosa, which in the case of the latter goes beyond questions of philology, see Andrew Arato, "The Search for the Revolutionary Subject: The Young Lukács, 1910–1923" (Ph.D diss., University of Chicago, 1975), pp. 226–31.

10. *Die Seele und die Formen*, pp. 171ff.; 41ff.; and "Ariadne auf Naxos," in W. Marholz, ed., *Paul Ernst zu seinem 50. Geburtstag* (Munich: Krustenbrot, 1916), p. 15.

11. "Soziologie des modernen Dramas," p. 308.

12. Ibid., p. 327.

13. Ibid., p. 321.

14. Ibid., pp. 665–66.

15. Ibid., p. 666.

16. See Georg Simmel, *Philosophie des Geldes*, 4th ed. (Munich and Leipzig: Duncker & Humblot, 1922), part II, chap. 6.

17. See Andrew Arato, "Neo-Idealist Defense of Subjectivity," pp. 141–62.

18. Cited in Georg Lukács, *Die Zerstörung der Vernunft* (Neuwied and Berlin: Luchterhand, 1960), p. 397.

19. Lukács, *Esztétikai kultura*, p. 14.

20. Ibid., p. 12.

21. *Dramahistory*, vol. I, pp. 87–88.

22. "Soziologie des modernen Dramas," pp. 309–10.

23. Ibid., pp. 314–15.

24. Ibid., p. 666.
25. Ibid., p. 314.
26. *Esztétikai kultura,* p. 14.
27. Ibid., p. 19.
28. Ibid., p. 16.
29. ("The Ways Have Parted") in *Esztétikai kultura,* p. 33.
30. Ibid., pp. 37–38.
31. *Esztétikai kultura,* p. 19.
32. *Dramahistory,* vol. I, pp. 6–8. We discuss Lukács's early literary theory only symptomatically here, that is, in terms of its indications for his philosophy and social theory. For an indispensable corrective, see Ferenc Fehér, "Die Geschichtsphilosophie des Dramas, die Metaphysik der Tragödie und die Utopie des untragischen Dramas. Scheidewege der Dramatheorie des jungen Lukács," in Heller et al., *Die Seele und das Leben,* pp. 7–53.
33. *Dramahistory,* vol. I, pp. 11–14.
34. Ibid., p. 24ff.
35. Ibid., pp. 18–19.
36. Ibid., pp. xi–xii, 50, 71.
37. Ibid., p. 53.
38. Ibid., pp. 56–57.
39. Ibid., p. 67.
40. Ibid., p. 58.
41. Walter Benjamin and T. W. Adorno would later maintain that only the flanking action of the allegory—allegorical modernism—is able to represent (but not to symbolize) the tragedy of culture. Lukács, however, *always* rejected allegory as a principle of form. From the subsequent Benjamin-Adorno standpoint, then, the early Lukács was asking for the impossible: the symbolic representation of a situation that had reduced all symbolism to rubble and eclecticism. Nevertheless, the early Lukács's posing of the problem leads not only to his own rejection of modernism, but also to its sympathetic interpretation by others.
42. *Dramahistory,* vol. I, pp. 112–13.
43. Ibid., pp. 117–18.
44. Ibid., pp. 99–101.
45. In this connection, it would be a mistake to identify Lukács's concept of individuality with Simmel's, including the latter's concept of subjective culture. Lukács discusses the social and cultural problem of individuality within the same context, while Simmel insisted on two separate contexts.
46. *Dramahistory,* vol. I, p. 152.
47. Ibid., p. 144.
48. "Soziologie des modernen Dramas," pp. 662, 667. Lukács implicitly recognizes that individuality as a new value contains, in Fehér's phrase, an "increment of liberation," even when this individualism's first manifestations are crushed under the weight of history, objective spirit, and new institutions. But, unable clearly to distinguish alienated from nonalienated forms of objectification, Lukács ends by overemphasizing alienation. For further discussion of this whole problem, see Ferenc Fehér, "Is the Novel Problematic?" *Telos* 15 (Spring 1973):47–74.
49. "Soziologie des modernen Dramas," p. 668.
50. Ibid., p. 674.
51. Ibid., p. 677ff.
52. Ibid., p. 343. Lukács's view of the increasing passivity of the heroes of modern drama anticipates his argument in *History and Class Consciousness* that, in the reified world, individuals are reduced to spectators of their own activity.
53. Ibid., p. 665.

54. Ibid., pp. 665, 669.
55. Ibid., p. 666.
56. *Dramahistory,* vol. I, p. 75ff.
57. "Soziologie des modernen Dramas," p. 694.
58. Ibid., p. 684.
59. As Márkus has recently made clear, these two alternatives correspond to Lukács's two major substantive perspectives: a philosophical-existential line of analysis culminating in an individualist-ethical answer and an historical line of analysis culminating in a political-collectivist answer—without an excess of optimism. We would add an additional distinction within the second alternative between the sociological-historical (*Dramahistory*) and the philosophical-historical (*Theory of the Novel*). Only the former, with its social dimension and class analysis, culminates in a stress on political movements. See Márkus, "The Soul and Life," *Telos* 32 (Summer 1977), p. 98ff.
60. "Soziologie des modernen Dramas," p. 669.
61. *Die Seele und die Formen,* p. 10.
62. *Eszétikai kultura,* pp. 19–20.
63. *Dramahistory,* vol. II, p. 155.
64. Ibid., p. 156.
65. *Eszétikai kultura,* p. 25. This was also Max Weber's view. Given his thesis that socialism would solidify rather than destroy the "iron cage," a socialist world view represented in Weber's eyes a deterministic surrender to the tragedy of culture.
66. Ibid.
67. Again, the similarities to Max Weber's thought are striking. Regarding influences here, as we indicate in Chapter 4, they tended to move in *both* directions.
68. *Eszétikai kultura,* p. 26.
69. Ibid., pp. 29–30.

CHAPTER 3: THE PROBLEMATIC INDIVIDUAL

1. See, for example, the laudatory review by Carl Brinkmann, *Logos,* 1912, pp. 248–49.
2. *Die Seele und die Formen,* (Berlin: Egon Fleischel, 1911), p. 52.
3. See Agnes Heller, "Das Zerschellen des Lebens an der Form: György Lukács und Irma Seidler," in Agnes Heller et al., *Die Seele und das Leben* (Frankfurt-am-Main: Suhrkamp, 1977), pp. 54–98. Cf. György Márkus, "The Soul and Life," *Telos* 32 (Summer 1977), an essay on which we heavily rely in our presentation of Lukács's essayistic philosophy.
4. *Die Seele und die Formen,* p. 104. Lukács's view of Goethe, with whom he would always occupy himself, would pass through numerous changes. While we cannot examine them here and may risk oversimplification, we will nevertheless note that by the time of his *Goethe und seine Zeit* (1947; enlarged ed., 1950; English translation, 1968), Lukács's concept of the Novalis-Goethe relation had reversed itself: Goethe's more "realistic" acceptance of the contemporary order had taken on new meaning. As one commentator has pointed out in this regard: "the classicists (Hegel, Goethe, and implicitly Lukács) tried to live after the revolution (French and Russian) in the name of its traditions by making compromises with the present, whereas the Romantics (Hölderlin and Trotsky) could find only a purist and sectarian solution." L. Stern, "Georg Lukács: An Intellectual Portrait," *Dissent* 2 (Spring 1958):172.
5. *Die Seele und die Formen,* p. 104.
6. Ibid.
7. Ibid., pp. 105–6.

8. Ibid., p. 109.
9. Ibid., p. 107.
10. Ibid., pp. 107–8.
11. Ibid., p. 108ff.
12. Lukács and Rudolf Kassner, on whom *Die Seele und die Formen* contains an essay, were largely responsible for "rediscovering" Kierkegaard for Europe. As one contemporary has recalled, Lukács's Kierkegaard essay "was one of the first places in which Kierkegaard, who was almost completely forgotten, experienced a resurrection. . . . Lukács was one of the very few who brought the notions of Kierkegaard back into view before the war." Paul Honigsheim, "Memories of Max Weber," in his *On Max Weber,* trans. Joan Rytina (New York: Free Press, 1968), p. 27.
13. *Die Seele und die Formen,* pp. 72, 77. Throughout his essay, Lukács hints at Kierkegaard's critique of Hegel, about which he later planned to write a study, stressing the critique of the system, dialectical transitions, and collective subjectivity.
14. Lucien Goldmann, "Georg Lukács: l'Essayiste," *Recherches Dialectiques* (Paris: Gallimard, 1959), pp. 253–54.
15. *Die Seele und die Formen,* p. 69.
16. As we now know, Kierkegaard was also closest to having been Lukács's alter ego. See Heller, "Das Zerschellen des Lebens an der Form: György Lukács und Irma Seidler," in Heller et al., *Die Seele und das Leben,* pp. 54–98. Heller's essay is in fact partially modeled on Lukács's "Sören Kierkegaard und Regine Olsen."
17. *Die Seele und die Formen,* p. 88.
18. Ibid., pp. 69–71.
19. Ibid., p. 71.
20. Ibid., p. 89.
21. Ibid., pp. 89–90.
22. Max Weber, *The Protestant Ethic and the Spirit of Capitalism* (New York: Scribner's, 1958), pp. 55, 80, 154.
23. Ibid., pp. 181–82.
24. *Die Seele und die Formen,* pp. 184–85.
25. Ibid., p. 183.
26. Ibid., pp. 185–86.
27. Ibid., pp. 186–87.
28. Ibid., pp. 187–88.
29. Ibid., pp. 226–27.
30. Ibid., pp. 230–31.
31. There are several textual hints that Lukács prefers the Kantian posture in the dialogue, although the other side is certainly not dismissed. All three characters are, however, deliberately presented as being rather ridiculous.
32. *Die Seele und die Formen,* p. 331.
33. Ibid., p. 328.
34. Ibid., p. 335.
35. Ibid., p. 348.
36. Ibid., p. 332.
37. Ibid., pp. 335–37.
38. Ibid., pp. 343–44.
39. Ibid., pp. 333–34.
40. Cf. Ferenc Fehér, "Das Bündnis von Georg Lukács und Béla Balázs bis zur ungarischen Revolution 1918," in Heller et al., *Die Seele und das Leben,* pp. 131–76.
41. *Die Seele und die Formen,* pp. 345–46.

42. Cf. *Dramahistory,* vol. I, p. 99. Thus Lukács appears to have retained two separate positions on the possibility of modern tragedy. It is possible if it remains completely formal, *or* if it symbolizes the tragedy of culture itself. For further analysis of this issue, see Fehér, "Die Geschichtsphilosophie des Dramas. . . ," in Heller et al., *Die Seele und das Leben,* pp. 7–53.

43. "Von der Armut am Geiste: Ein Gespräch und ein Brief," *Neue Blätter,* 1912, pp. 67–92.

44. *Die Seele und die Formen,* p. 87.

45. Heller, "Das Zerschellen des Lebens an der Form," passim.

46. And the German edition of *Die Seele und die Formen* could then safely be dedicated to the deceased Irma Seidler. Lukács's unpublished diary in the "Lukács-Archive" in Budapest includes his consideration of suicide.

47. "Von der Armut am Geiste," p. 81.

48. Ibid., p. 83.

49. Ibid., pp. 71–72.

50. Lukács's position here foreshadows his later concept of the revolutionary party. See below, Chapter 7.

51. Cf. Fehér, "Das Bündnis von Georg Lukács und Béla Balázs. . . ," passim.

52. "Von der Armut am Geiste," p. 90.

53. Ibid., p. 73.

54. Ibid. Emphasis added.

55. Ibid., p. 78.

56. Ibid., p. 72.

57. Ibid., p. 74.

58. "Von der Armut am Geiste," pp. 85–86.

59. Ibid., p. 75.

60. Ibid., p. 74. Emphasis added.

61. Ibid., p. 85.

CHAPTER 4: BETWEEN HEIDELBERG TO MARX

1. See Lukács's preface to his *Magyar Irodalom, Magyar Kultura* (Budapest: Gondolat, 1970), p. 13.

2. Marianne Weber, *Max Weber: Ein Lebensbild* (Heidelberg: J. C. B. Mohr, 1950), p. 509.

3. See the fascinating recollections of the Weber circle in Paul Honigsheim, *On Max Weber,* trans. Joan Rytina (New York: Free Press, 1968).

4. Marianne Weber, *Max Weber,* p. 511.

5. Regarding Lukács's impact on Max Weber, see Arthur Mitzman, *The Iron Cage: An Historical Interpretation of Max Weber* (New York: Knopf, 1970), pp. 271–76; cf. Honigsheim, *On Max Weber,* p. 25ff.

6. Honigsheim, *On Max Weber,* p. 24.

7. Ibid., p. 26.

8. Ibid., p. 25.

9. "Zum Wesen und zur Methode der Kultursoziologie," *Archiv für Sozialwissenschaft und Sozialpolitik,* 1914–15, p. 220.

10. Ibid.

11. Ibid.

12. Ibid., p. 221.

13. Ibid., p. 220.

14. Review of Croce's *Zur Theorie und Geschichte der Historiography* (German trans., 1915), in *Archiv für Sozialwissenschaft und Sozialpolitik,* 1915, pp. 878–85.

15. Ibid., pp. 879–81.

16. Ibid., p. 884.

17. Ibid., pp. 884–85.

18. Ibid., pp. 883–84. Cf. Lukács review of Thomas Masaryk's, *Zur russischen Geschichts- und Religionsphilosophie* (1913), in *Archiv für Sozialwissenschaft und Sozialpolitik,* 1914, pp. 873–74.

19. See György Márkus, "Die Seele und das Leben," in Agnes Heller et al., *Die Seele und das Leben* (Frankfurt-am-Main: Suhrkamp, 1977), p. 99 (Eng. translation in *Telos* 32 [Summer 1977]).

20. *Heidelberger Philosophie der Kunst* (Neuwied and Berlin: Luchterhand, 1976), Chapter 3.

21. "Georg Simmel (Nachruf)," *Pester Lloyd,* October 1918. Reprinted in Kurt Gassen and Michael Landmann, eds., *Buch des Dankes an Georg Simmel* (Berlin: Kohlhammer, 1958), pp. 171–76.

22. See Chapter 2.

23. In the following discussion we rely heavily on György Márkus, "Lukács' 'erste' Ästhetik," in Heller et al., *Die Seele und das Leben,* pp. 192–240.

24. *Philosophie der Kunst,* p. 9.

25. "Elöadás a festészetröl" ("Lecture on Painting"), in *Ifjukori Müvek* (1902–1918) (Budapest: Magvetö, 1977), p. 809.

26. *Philosophie der Kunst,* p. 81.

27. Ibid., pp. 159–60.

28. "Lecture on Painting," pp. 809–10.

29. *Philosophie der Kunst,* p. 85.

30. Ibid., pp. 89–90.

31. "Lecture on Painting," p. 826.

32. *Philosophie der Kunst,* pp. 159–60.

33. Ibid. p. 161.

34. Márkus, "Lukács' 'erste' Ästhetik. . . ," p. 210.

35. *Philosophie der Kunst,* p. 203.

36. Ibid., pp. 14–15.

37. Béla Balázs, "Notes from a Diary," *New Hungarian Quarterly* 13 (August 1972): 124.

38. "Trisztán hajoján" ("On the Ship of Tristan"), in *Magyar Irodalom, Magyar Kultura,* p. 97.

39. *Paul Ernst und Georg Lukács: Dokumente einer Freundschaft,* ed. Karl August Kutzbach (Emsdetten: Lechte, 1974), pp. 66–67. Letter dated April 14, 1915.

CHAPTER 5: THE GERMAN WAR AND THE RUSSIAN IDEA

1. This confrontation of terms is derived from Ferenc Fehér, "Am Scheideweg des romantischen Antikapitalismus," in Agnes Heller et al., *Die Seele und das Leben* (Frankfurt-am-Main: Suhrkamp, 1977), pp. 241–327.

2. *Paul Ernst und Georg Lukács: Documente einer Freundschaft,* ed. Karl August Kutzbach (Emsdetten: Lechte, 1974), p. 151. Letter dated April 5, 1919.

3. For an excellent discussion and description, see Fehér, "Am Scheideweg des romantischen Antikapitalismus," p. 282.

4. *Dokumente einer Freundschaft,* p. 86. The authenticity of Ernst's reconstruction is supported by key passages in Lukács's unfinished and unpublished wartime (late 1915)

essay, "Die deutschen Intellektuellen und der Krieg," *Text und Kritik* 39/40 (October 1973): 65ff.

5. 1962 Preface, *Theorie des Romans* (Neuwied and Berlin: Luchterhand, 1965), p. 5.

6. See "Die deutschen Intellektuellen und der Krieg," passim, for what Lukács thought of their arguments favoring the war, particularly their view of the war as a new *Gemeinschaft*.

7. *Magyar Irodalom, Magyar Kultura* (Budapest: Gondolat, 1970), p. 136.

8. *Theorie des Romans,* p. 41.

9. Ibid., pp. 31–33. Here Lukács maintains that art is a visionary or utopian reality, but he rejects its Luciferian dimension: the aestheticization of alienated existence and the false identification of art with a totalizing metaphysics. Contrary to some commentaries, the problem of alienation, which Lukács recognizes does not originate in art, cannot in his view be overcome within art.

10. *Theorie des Romans,* pp. 42–45.

11. Ibid., p. 56.

12. Ibid., pp. 22–24.

13. Ibid., pp. 26, 64–65.

14. For a reexamination of this issue, see Ferenc Fehér, "Is the Novel Problematic?" *Telos* 15 (Spring 1973): 47–74.

15. *Theorie des Romans,* p. 27.

16. Ibid., pp. 68–69.

17. Ibid., pp. 60–62.

18. Ibid., pp. 64, 76.

19. Amplification of this theme can be found in Andrew Arato, "The Neo-Idealist Defense of Subjectivity," *Telos* 21 (Fall 1974): 108–61.

20. *Theorie des Romans,* p. 93.

21. Ibid.

22. Ibid.

23. Ibid.

24. György Márkus, "Die Seele und das Leben," in *Die Seele und das Leben,* p. 104.

25. "Halálos fiatalság" ("Deathly Youth," 1917–1918), in *Magyar Irodalom, Magyar Kultura,* p. 114.

26. *Theorie des Romans,* p. 135ff.

27. Ibid., p. 141

28. Ibid., pp. 145–48.

29. Ibid., p. 149.

30. *Dokumente einer Freundschaft,* pp. 65–74.

31. Lukács made this remark in a footnote to the original publication. It is not included in the republication of *Theorie des Romans*. See, however, "Theorie des Romans," *Zeitschrift für Ästhetik und Allgemeine Kunstwissenschaft* 2 (Summer 1916): p. 225.

32. *Theorie des Romans,* pp. 157–58.

33. Cf. Fehér, "Am Scheideweg des romantischen Antikapitalismus," p. 275ff.

34. "A vándor énekel" ("The Wanderer Sings," 1911), in *Magyar Irodalom, Magyar Kultura,* p. 79.

35. "On the Ship of Tristan," pp. 100–101; "Deathly Youth," p. 113.

36. "Deathly Youth," p. 116.

37. For a somewhat different statement of this alternative, see Fehér, "Am Scheideweg des romantischen Antikapitalismus," pp. 319–20.

38. Ibid., p. 317.

39. *Dokumente einer Freundschaft,* pp. 128–29.

40. György Márkus, "Lukács' 'erste' Ästhetik," in *Die Seele und das Leben*, p. 216ff.

41. Ibid., pp. 221–22.

42. For amplification, see Andrew Arato, "The Search for the Revolutionary Subject: The Young Lukács, 1910–1923" (Ph.D. diss., University of Chicago, 1975), pp. 333–35.

43. Republished in *Ifjukori Müvek*, pp. 837–45. The lecture treated the theme of "Conservative and Progressive Idealism." A French translation appears in Michael Löwy, *Pour une sociologie des intellectuels révolutionnaires* (Paris: P.U.F., 1976), pp. 301–7.

CHAPTER 6: WAGER ON COMMUNISM

1. We rely here on the fine survey of the Budapest group in David Kettler, "Culture and Revolution: Lukács in the Hungarian Revolutions of 1918/19," *Telos* 10 (Winter 1971):35–92, especially p. 54ff.

2. Ibid., p. 55.

3. Zoltan Horvath, *Die Jahrhundertwende in Ugarn* (Neuwied and Berlin: Luchterhand, 1966), pp. 505–6.

4. According to Kettler, the audience at Free School lectures never numbered more than fifty, although these, he notes, attended regularly.

5. "Georg Simmel (Nachruf)," in Kurt Gassen and Michael Landmann, eds. *Buch des Dankes an Georg Simmel* (Berlin: Kohlhammer, 1958), pp. 171–76.

6. Kettler, "Culture and Revolution," p. 67ff.

7. Ibid., p. 68.

8. Information on the organization and leadership of the Communist Party of Hungary can be found in Rudolf L. Tökés, *Béla Kun and the Hungarian Soviet Republic: The Origins and Role of the Communist Party of Hungary in the Revolutions of 1918–1919* (New York: Praeger, 1967), pp. 242–46.

9. *Paul Ernst und Georg Lukács: Dokumente einer Freundschaft* ed. Karl August Kutzbach (Emsdetten: Lechte, 1974), p. 151. Letter dated April 5, 1919.

10. On Lukács's friends' stunned reactions to his "conversion," see Kettler, "Culture and Revolution," p. 68ff.

11. See Max Weber, "Science as a Vocation" (1918), in Hans Gerth and C. Wright Mills, eds., *From Max Weber: Essays in Sociology* (New York: Oxford, 1958), p. 154; and Thomas Mann, *Betrachtungen eines Unpolitischen* (1918) (Frankfurt-am-Main: S. Fischer, 1968), pp. 76–77.

12. József Lengyel, *Visegráder Strasse* (East Berlin: Dietz, 1959), pp. 139–40.

13. István Mészáros, *Lukács's Concept of Dialectic* (London: Merlin, 1972), pp. 17–21.

14. "A bolsevizmus mint erklölcsi probléma," *Szabad Gondolat*, December 1918, pp. 228–32. The German translation appears in Jörg Kammler, ed., *Georg Lukács: Taktik und Ethik. Politische Aufsätze* I (Darmstadt and Neuwied, 1975), pp. 27–33. There is now an English translation, with a nice introduction by Judit Tar, in *Social Research* 44, no. 3 (Autumn 1977):416–24.

15. "Taktik und Ethik," *Georg Lukács Werke: Frühschriften* II (Neuwied and Berlin: Luchterhand, 1968), pp. 45–53.

16. Ferenc Fehér, "Am Scheideweg des romantischen Antikapitalismus," in Agnes Heller et al., *Die Seele und das Leben* (Frankfurt-am-Main: Suhrkamp, 1977), pp. 275ff.

17. "The Role of Morality in Communist Production," 1919, in *Georg Lukács Werke: Frühschriften* II, p. 90.

18. A number of the accusations against Lukács for allegedly having terrorized writers during the Soviet Republic are recounted in Tökés, *Béla Kun and the Hungarian Soviet Republic*, p. 179. While he presents no documentation of the charges, Tökés does indicate

that Lukács advocated moral reeducation rather than execution of bourgeois and counter-revolutionary prisoners (p. 153). Regarding Lukács's opposition to imposition of the party line in literature, see Kettler, "Culture and Revolution," p. 77ff.

19. Examples of this picture of Lukács can be found in Ypsilon (Pseudonym), *Pattern for World Revolution* (Chicago and New York: Ziff-Davis, 1947), pp. 152–59; and Victor Zitta, *Georg Lukács' Marxism: Alienation, Dialectics, Revolution* (The Hague: Martinus Nijhoff, 1964), p. 99ff.

20. *Georg Lukács Werke: Frühschriften* II, p. 61. The essay appears in revised form in *History and Class Consciousness*.

21. The critique of Engels's "dialectic of nature," which occupies a prominent place in the revised version, is not present in the original 1919 version.

22. "Das Problem geistiger Führung und die 'geistigen Arbeiter,'" in *Georg Lukács Werke: Frühschriften* II, pp. 54–60.

23. See the English translation in *Telos* 5 (Spring 1970):21–30; and the introduction to it, pp. 1–20.

24. This essay was revised and included in *History and Class Consciousness*. The German translation of the original Hungarian version can be found in *Georg Lukács: Taktik und Ethik. Politische Aufsätze* I, pp. 108–23.

25. Cited in Kettler, "Culture and Revolution," p. 35.

26. A composite picture can be derived from Tökés, *Béla Kun and the Hungarian Soviet Republic*, pp. 137–74; Kettler, "Marxism and Culture," p. 76ff; and Frank Eckelt, "The Internal Policies of the Hungarian Soviet Republic," in Iván Völgyes, ed., *Hungary in Revolution, 1918–1919: Nine Essays* (Lincoln: University of Nebraska Press, 1971), pp. 61–88.

27. In *Georg Lukács Werke: Frühschriften* II, pp. 90–94.

28. For recent critical discussions of the idea of a society beyond law and institutions in both Marx and Lukács, see Mihály Vajda, "Law, Ethics and Interest," *Telos* 34 (Winter 1978):173–79; and Cornelius Castoriadis, "From Marx to Aristotle, From Aristotle to Us," *Social Research*, Winter 1978.

29. In *Georg Lukács Werke: Frühschriften* II, pp. 70–78.

CHAPTER 7: WAGER ON THE PARTY

1. Among the signers were: Richard Beer-Hoffman, Richard Dehmel, Paul Ernst, Maximilian Harden, Alfred Kerr, Heinrich Mann, Thomas Mann, Bruno Frank, Franz Baumgarten, and Emil Praetorius. Indicating their distance from Bolshevism, their statement read in part: "Not the politician but the man and thinker, Georg v. Lukács, should be defended. He had earlier given up the seductions of the comfortable life that was his inheritance, in favor of a different post: that of responsible, solitary thought. When he turned to politics, he sacrificed what was dearest to him, his freedom of thought, in favor of the work of the reformer, which he intended to fulfill. . . . Saving Lukács is no party matter. It is the duty of all who have personally experienced his human purity, and the many who have admired the high spirituality of his philosophical-aesthetic works, to protest against the extradition" (*Berliner Tageblatt*, November 12, 1919; reprinted in *Paul Ernst und Georg Lukács: Documente einer Freundschaft*, ed. Karl August Kutzbach [Emsdetten: Lechte, 1974], pp. 155–56). According to Franz Ferdinand Baumgarten, who along with Paul Ernst organized the effort, Gerhart Hauptmann refused to sign. "I have," Baumgarten also wrote to Ernst in connection with attempts to solicit further signers, "gathered many new items for my little collection of *documents humains*. I am really agitated over Max Weber. Puritans are always the worst pharisees. So he didn't say no, but instead sent a declaration so

pointless that he won't have to worry about seeing it published" (ibid., p. 157; letter dated December 11, 1919).

2. Victor Serge, *Memoirs of a Revolutionary, 1901–1941,* trans. Peter Sedgwick (London: Oxford University Press, 1963), pp. 114–92. Antonio Gramsci was also in Vienna at this time, but there is no evidence of any contact with Lukács.

3. "Legalität und Illegalität" (1920), in *Georg Lukács Werke: Frühschriften* II (Neuwied and Berlin: Luchterhand, 1968), p. 439.

4. These were: "Legalität und Illegalität"; "Klassenbewusstsein"; and "Rosa Luxemburg als Marxist."

5. "Vorwort" (1967), *Georg Lukács Werke: Frühschriften* II, pp. 15–16.

6. In an article dated June 1920, Lenin referred to *Kommunismus* as an "excellent journal" which had nevertheless been infected with "indubitable symptoms of the 'infantile disorder of Left-wing Communism.' . . . One number of the journal," he continued, "contains an article by Comrade G.L. entitled 'On the Question of Parliamentarism,' which the editors designate as controversial . . . G.L.'s article is very Left-wing and very poor. Its Marxism is purely verbal; its distinction between 'defensive' and 'offensive' tactics is artificial; it gives no concrete analysis of precise and definite historical situation; it takes no account of what is most essential (the need to take over . . . all fields of work and all institutions in which the bourgeoisie exerts its influence, etc.)." V.I. Lenin, *Collected Works,* vol. 31 (London and Moscow: Lawrence & Wishart, 1966), p. 165.

7. Excellent though divergent accounts of *Kommunismus* can be found in two recent studies of the political dimensions of Lukács's early Marxism: Rudi Dutschke, *Versuch, Lenin auf die Füsse zu Stellen: Uber den halbasiatischen und den westeuropäischen Weg zum Sozialismus. Lenin, Lukács und die Dritte Internationale* (Berlin: Wagenbach, 1974); and Jörg Kammler, *Politische Theorie von Georg Lukács: Struktur und historischer Praxisbezug bis 1929* (Darmstadt and Neuwied: Luchterhand, 1974). Cf. Massimo Cacciari, "Sul Problema dell'Organizzazione Germania, 1917–1921," in Cacciari, ed., *György Lukács: Kommunismus, 1920–1921* (Padua: Marsilio, 1972), pp. 7–66.

8. See, for example, Lukács's "Organizationsfragen der dritten Internationale," *Kommunismus* 1, nos. 8/9 (March 15, 1920):238–50.

9. See, for example, the passionate and astute essays by Anton Pannekoek, "Die Entwicklung der Weltrevolution und die Taktik des Kommunismus," *Kommunismus* 1, nos. 28/29 (August 1, 1920):976–1018; and Henriette Roland-Holst, "Die Aufgabe der kommunistischen Partei in der proletarischen Revolution," *Kommunismus* 2, nos. 1/2 (January 15, 1921):20–33, with three additional installments in the three subsequent numbers of the journal; and Vladimir Sorin, "Die kommunistische Partei und Sowetinstitutionen," *Kommunismus* 1, nos. 8–9 (March 15, 1920):280–87.

10. See especially, Lukács's "Die moralische Sendung der kommunistischen Partei," *Kommunismus* 1, nos. 16/17 (May 1, 1920):482–88; his "Vor dem dritten Kongress," ibid. 2, nos. 17/18 (May 15, 1921):583–92; and the unsigned editorial statement, "Die Krise der Kommunistischen Internationale und der 3. Kongress," ibid., nos. 27/28 (August 1, 1921):881–90.

11. See in this connection, Béla Fogarasi, "Die Aufgaben der kommunistischen Presse," *Kommunismus* 2, nos. 25/26 (July 15, 1921):845–54. The article brings Lukács's theory of reification to bear on the format and internal organization (specialization) of the bourgeois press, stressing the not always obvious ways in which they are reproduced within the Communist press.

12. On the factional struggle within the Communist Party of Hungary and the end of the journal *Kommunismus,* see Dutschke, *Versuch, Lenin auf die Füsse zu Stellen,* p. 247ff; Kammler, *Politische Theorie von Georg Lukács,* p. 222ff. and footnotes; and Rudolf

L. Tökés, *Béla Kun and the Hungarian Soviet Republic* (New York: Praeger, 1967), p. 215ff. The view of Kun as an "incarnation of intellectual inadequacy" is presented in Serge, *Memoirs of a Revolutionary,* p. 187. In 1922 Lukács himself saw Kun as the representative of the tendency toward "soulless bureaucracy" in the Hungarian party and the International. Kun, he argued, based all decisions on the principle of pleasing Moscow and advocated greater centralization of the Hungarian party solely in order to retain his personal power. "The empty machine created in this way," Lukács argued, "can show results only by fabricating reports, inquests, statistics, newspaper clippings, and so on. Thereby its do-nothing impotence not only appears to be feverish activity, but it also creates the 'objective' basis for its own expansion. . . ." 'Noch einmal Illusionspolitik," in Laszlo Rudas, ed., *Abenteuer- und Liquidatorentum: Die Politik Béla Kuns und die Krise der KPU* (Vienna, 1922), pp. 254–61. This volume was not available to us; the article is reprinted in *Georg Lukács Werke: Frühschriften* II, pp. 155–60.

13. "Önkritika," *Proletár* 1, (August 1920): 13–14. Reprinted in Jörg Kammler, ed., *Georg Lukács: Revolution und Gegenrevolution. Politische Aufsätze* II (Darmstadt and Neuwied: Luchterhand, 1976), pp. 42–46.

14. "Zur Frage des Parlamentarismus" (1920), in *Georg Lukács Werke: Frühschriften* II, pp. 95–104. This is the essay which drew Lenin's ire.

15. "Klassenbewusstsein" (1920), in *Georg Lukács: Taktik und Ethik. Politische Aufsätze* I (Darmstadt and Neuwied, 1975), p. 217.

16. "Die kommunistische Partei und die politischen Arbeiterräte in Deutschland" (1920), in *Georg Lukács: Revolution und Gegenrevolution,* p. 103ff.

17. "Die Krise des Syndikalismus in Italien" (1920), in *Georg Lukács: Revolution und Gegenrevolution,* pp. 131–33. The quotation is actually from the theses of the 1920 Communist International Congress. While Lukács cited them with approval, his own views were more favorable to those of the Syndicalists. Cf. his words of praise for the factory occupations, pp. 133–34.

18. "Die Moralische Sendung der kommunistischen Partei" (1920), in *Georg Lukács Werke: Frühschriften* II, pp. 105–11.

19. "Klassenbewusstsein" (1920), in *Georg Lukács: Taktik und Ethik,* pp. 202–18. Lukács would include this essay in *History and Class Consciousness,* expanding it substantially for that purpose. In this case, the changes primarily involve more abundant demonstration of the original theses; indeed, the 1920 version is almost wholly incorporated into the revised 1922 text. The changes that did appear concern his deemphasis on the realm of culture and on the importance of the workers' councils. In contrast, the essay "What is orthodox Marxism?" was largely re-written for *History and Class Consciousness*.

20. See Vladimir Sorin, "Die kommunistische Partei und Sowetinstitutionen." Lukács was not alone in developing only a limited critique of bureaucracy, one that not only exempted the party from the critique, but expected remedies precisely and only from it. Although he became suspicious of the Comintern and even more so of the Hungarian party, he never approached the question of the bureaucratic nature of the Leninist party. His criticism of the Hungarian party, moreover, had to stop halfway as well, since he was unwilling (under the sway of the Russian Idea and the prestige of October) to confront the foundations of the problem in Moscow.

21. For guides through the dense underbrush of this story, see: Dutschke, *Versuch, Lenin auf die Füsse zu stellen,* p. 299ff.; Rudolf Tökés, "Béla Kun: The Man and the Revolutionary," in Iván Völgyes, ed., *Hungary in Revolution, 1918–19* (Lincoln, Neb.: University of Nebraska Press, 1971), pp. 188–98; and Andrew Arato, "The Search for the Revolutionary Subject: The Young Lukács, 1910–1923" (Ph.D. diss., University of Chicago, 1975), p. 23ff.

22. "Opportunismus und Putschismus" (1920), in *Georg Lukács Werke: Frühschriften* II, pp. 112–20.

23. See, for example, "Spontaneität der Massen, Aktivität der Partei" (1921), in *Georg Lukács Werke: Frühschriften* II, pp. 135–43; and "Organisatorische Fragen der revolutionären Initiative" (1921), ibid., pp. 144–54. The latter essay can now be seen as preparatory to the chapter on organization in *History and Class Consciousness*.

24. "Organizatorische Fragen der revolutionären Initiative," pp. 151–53.

CHAPTER 8: THEORY OF REIFICATION

1. The 1922 synthesis led to the more or less elaborate reconstruction of the earlier essays as well. For an analysis of the methodological and political gains and losses, see Andrew Arato, "The Search for the Revolutionary Subject: The Young Lukács, 1910–1923" (Ph.D. diss., University of Chicago, 1975). All references are to the original German edition, *Geschichte und Klassenbewusstein* (Berlin: Malik Verlag, 1923), with page numbers in the text itself in parentheses.

2. Lukács reminds us that *Kapital* uses a three-part conceptual distinction of Hegel's logic: illusion (*Schein*), appearance (*Erscheinung*) and essence (*Wesen*). This is lost in the English translation of *Kapital*.

3. For a brilliant critique of this conception, see Cornelius Castoriadis, "From Marx to Aristotle, from Aristotle to Us," *Social Research,* Winter 1978.

4. Cf. Max Weber, *The Theory of Social and Economic Organization,* trans. A. M. Henderson and T. Parsons (New York: Free Press, 1964), pp. 246–47.

5. Marx, *Das Kapital* I, in *Marx-Engels Werke,* vol. 23 (Berlin: Dietz, 1964), pp. 674–75. This text is Marx's own summary of the underlying theme of part IV of *Kapital,* dealing with the concept of "relative surplus value" by unfolding the development of "manufacture" and "machine industry."

6. Max Weber, *The Protestant Ethic and the Spirit of Capitalism* (New York: Scribner's, 1958), p. 16. No lines could better characterize the society that would emerge from the Bolshevik revolution, as Weber always predicted with respect to "socialism." On the other hand, Weber believed that an economic market and political democracy would inhibit this development. Lukács's attempt to derive the factory structure from the commodity form is intended as part of his critique of Weber. Yet his resistance (as we shall see) to the Bolshevik model of socialism—society as a single factory—indicates that he took Weber's warning seriously.

7. Weber, *The Theory of Social and Economic Organization,* p. 248. For two discussions of the material content of Weber's concept of formal rationality, see Herbert Marcuse, "Industrialization and Capitalism in the Work of Max Weber," in *Negations,* trans. Jeremy J. Shapiro (Boston: Beacon Press, 1968), pp. 201–26; and Jean L. Cohen, "Weber and the Dynamics of Rationalized Domination," *Telos* 14 (Winter 1972):63–86.

8. We have in mind the experience of the reconstruction of capital in the first phase of German fascism and in neo-capitalism. Cf. Mihaly Vajda, "The Rise of Fascism in Italy and Germany," *Telos* 12 (Summer 1972):3–22.

9. Lukács also decisively rejected philosophies that disregarded the results of the special sciences in favor of an irrationalist principle of life. He meant to use many of the results of the special sciences as aspects of the immediacy which must be the beginning of all dialectic. The argument that he meant to do away with the positive results of modern science and industry is groundless. Cf. Gareth Stedman-Jones, "Marxism of the Early Lukács," *New Left Review* 70 (November–December, 1971): 45–46.

10. Immanuel Kant, *Kritik der reinen Vernunft,* in *Werke* III and IV (Frankfurt-am-Main: Insel, 1964), A426, B454; A434, B462ff.; A444, B472ff.; A462, B490ff.

11. Lukács tends to disregard the Hegelian notion of the great individual (which reappears in a new form in Max Weber). This is not unjustified because in Hegel's *Philosophy of History* even the great individual is ultimately only an instrument.

12. To be sure, the young Marx came to the working class through his understanding of the concept of "needs," especially "radical needs." The proletariat could realize radical philosophy only because it had radical needs that transcended the order which philosophy negated only abstractly. Lukács did not, in 1923, rediscover the Marxian theory of needs. Thus, he thought of the proletariat as identical subject-object in terms of a notion of class consciousness that was tied only to a rather mythologizing category of unknown universal interest. For the young Marx (the old Marx and Marxism were far less clear on this point), the category of interest was tied to the notion of political revolution, that is, the creation of civil (*bürgerliche*) society by a class able to represent its interest as universal interest. But in the end, the interest guiding a merely political revolution remained particular. Proletarian revolution attained its universality (and the universality of its interest) only through the radical needs of *individual* proletarians. For a complete analysis of the problem of "needs" in Marx, see Agnes Heller, *Marx's Theory of Need* (London: Allison and Busby, 1977), and the review of this book by Jean Cohen in *Telos* 33 (Fall 1977):170–84.

13. Maurice Merleau-Ponty, in the Lukács chapter of *The Adventures of the Dialectic,* and Jürgen Habermas, in the new introduction to *Theory and Practice* (Boston: Beacon Press, 1974), indeed manage to contribute some important points toward an answer, but on the basis of (1) a seriously reduced notion of theory as the interrogation of its addressees, and (2) a reconceptualization and rehabilitation of the intersubjective domain within which the question and the answer would be uttered. In such a context, the validity of social theory would depend on its being recognized by its addressees as an advanced form of their own consciousness. Lukács's mix of a particular brand of Hegelianism in theory (stressing the absolute and denouncing the objective spirit) and Leninism in politics (based on the instrumentalization of the addressees of theory) was not open to this solution, which Merleau-Ponty, in his battle against the Communism of his day, nevertheless read into Lukács.

14. On this whole question, see Jean Cohen's Ph.D. dissertation. "The Crisis of Class Analysis in Late Capitalism," New School for Social Research (1979).

CHAPTER 9: THEORY OF REVOLUTION

1. On this whole question, see Jean Cohen, "The Crisis of Class Analysis in Late Capitalism," New School for Social Research (1979), and her "System and Class: The Subversion of Emancipation," *Social Research,* Winter 1978. We are examining the problem of class through Lukács's eyes in 1922, not from the viewpoint of more recent analyses.

2. V. I. Lenin, *Imperialism: the Highest Stage of Capitalism,* in *Selected Works,* vol. I (Moscow: Progress Publishers, 1970), pp. 686–88, 766–69. For an early (1921) Communist critique of socialism, see Alexandra Kollontai, *The Workers' Opposition* (Philadelphia: Solidarity Pamphlet no. 7, n.d.). For a recent general critique of this "traditional" concept of socialism, see Moishe Postone, "Necessity, Freedom, Time," *Social Research,* Winter 1978.

3. Cf. Lenin, *Selected Works,* vol. II, pp. 663, 700–3. Also see E. H. Carr, *The Bolshevik Revolution,* vol. II (London: Macmillan, 1952), pp. 95–99; and Lou Jean Fleron and Fred Fleron, "Administration Theory as Repressive Political Theory: The Communist Experi-

ence," *Telos* 12 (Summer 1972):76ff. and 80ff. on the content of Lenin's notion of state capitalism vis-à-vis labor and industrialization.

4. Cited in E. H. Carr, *The Bolshevik Revolution,* vol. I (Baltimore: Penguin, 1966), p. 251ff.

5. Any fair examination of Kollontai's *Workers' Opposition* must unfortunately come to this conclusion. Cf. R. V. Daniels, *The Conscience of the Revolution: Communist Opposition in Soviet Russia* (Cambridge, Mass.: Harvard University Press, 1960), pp. 128–29.

6. There are remarkable parallels all along the line between Burkharin and Lukács. In 1919, from the point of view of the group around Lenin, they were advocates of the immediate possibility of workers' self-management and were frightened by the thought of any institutional constraints against the working class. During the period of War Communism, Bukharin (accepting the militarization of labor) totally reversed himself on self-management, and both he and Lukács—quite independently, since there were never any organizational or personal relations between them—increasingly represented the party (in the case of Bukharin, the Soviet state) as the "general will" of the proletariat. Thus, they both argued that when the party imposes a rigid work discipline on the workers, this is only a self-imposed discipline. The remarkable thing is, of course, that on the level of philosophy, the two were polar opposites, and Lukács was to dedicate a famous essay of 1925 to the refutation of Bukharin's mechanistic conception of dialectics. But the two were bound together on the level of revolutionary theory by an increasingly unsuccessful rearguard action dedicated to the preservation of at least some of the socialist promises of 1917. The culmination of their parallel retreat was a "right"-wing evolutionist alternative within the movement, which must have seemed preferable to the "right"-wing authoritarian alternative of Stalin in the 1920s.

CHAPTER 10: THE "LUKÁCS-DEBATE"

1. Michael Löwy, *Pour une sociologie des intellectuels révolutionnaires: L'evolution politique de Lukács, 1909–1929* (Paris: P.U.F., 1976), pp. 255–81.

2. *Geschichte und Klassenbewusstsein,* (Berlin: Malik Verlag, 1923), pp. 5–12.

3. Victor Serge, *Memoirs of a Revolutionary, 1901–1941,* trans. Peter Sedgwick, (London: Oxford University Press, 1963), p. 187.

4. Helmut Gruber, ed., *International Communism in the Era of Lenin: A Documentary History* (New York: Fawcett, 1967), p. 409.

5. Alfred Weber, *Die Not der geistigen Arbeiter* (Munich: Duncker and Humblot, 1923).

6. We have relied for our information on *Der Malik-Verlag, 1916–1947: Ausstellungskatalog,* text by Wieland Herzfelde (East Berlin: Deutsche Akademie der Künste, n.d.).

7. Lukács, "Vorwort," *Georg Lukács Werke. Frühschriften* II (Neuwied and Berlin: Luchterhand, 1968), p. 23. See also the excellent brief discussion and recollection by Hans Mayer, "Widerruf des Widerrufs," *Der Spiegel* (August 31, 1970), pp. 126–28.

8. Toward this end, Malik regularly advertised its books in such non-Communist publications as Kurt Tucholsky's journal, *Die Weltbühne*.

9. Serge, *Memoirs of a Revolutionary,* p. 162.

10. Lukács, "Noch einmal Illusionspolitik" (1922), in *Georg Lukács Werke. Frühschriften* II, p. 185.

11. Max Eastman, "Introduction" to Leon Trotsky, *The New Course* (1923) (Ann Arbor: Universty of Michigan Press, 1965), p. 1.

12. In-depth analyses of the 1923 events and their impact can be found in Werner T.

Angress, *Stillborn Revolution: The Communist Bid for Power in Germany, 1921–1923* (Princeton, N.J.: Princeton University Press, 1963); Franz Borkenau, *World Communism: A History of the Communist International* (Ann Arbor: University of Michigan Press, 1962), pp. 243–56; E. H. Carr, *A History of of Soviet Russia: The Interregnum, 1923–1924* (Baltimore, Md.: Penguin, 1969), pp. 209–51; and Hermann Weber, *Die Wandlung des deutschen Kommunismus: Die Stalinisierung der KPD in der Weimarer Republik,* vol. I (Frankfurt-am-Main: Europäische Verlagsanstalt, 1969), pp. 23–119.

13. Carr, *The Interregnum,* p. 251.

14. For a similar view, see the discussion by Jane Degras, "United Front Tactics in the Comintern, 1921–1928," in Gruber, *International Communism in the Era of Lenin,* pp. 491–97.

15. Korsch's work first appeared as an essay, "Marxismus und Philosophie," in *Archiv für die Geschichte des Sozialismus und der Arbeiterbewegung* II (1923):74–121. It was published as a small book in the same year, although we have not been able to locate a copy. In 1929 Korsch, who by then had broken with organized Communism, wrote a new essay, "The Present Situation of the Problem 'Marxism and Philosophy,'" which was published, along with the 1923 essay and several of his shorter pieces from 1923–24, as a new, expanded edition: *Marxismus und Philosophie* (C. L. Hirschfeld, 1930). For that edition, Korsch revised his original statement of agreement with Lukács, but only slightly. Cf. Fred Halliday, trans., *Marxism and Philosophy* (New York: Monthly Review, 1970). For this edition Halliday replaced the three short essays Korsch had included in the 1930 edition with two other essays by Korsch from 1922 and 1924.

16. Siegfried Marck, "Neukritische und Neuhegelsche Auffassungen der marxistischen Dialektik," *Die Gesellschaft* 1(1924):573–78.

17. Carl Brinkmann, review of *History and Class Consciousness, Archiv für Sozialwissenschaft und Sozialpolitik* 3(1924):816–17. Brinkmann, whose identity we have not established, had in 1912 reviewed Lukács's *The Soul and the Forms* in *Logos,* the journal of Heidelberg neo-Kantian thought.

18. Karl August Wittfogel, *Geschichte der Bürgerlichen Gesellschaft: Von ihren Anfängen bis zur Schwelle der Grossen Revolution* (Berlin: Malik Verlag, 1924), p. 14. There is an interesting little history attached to Wittfogel's reference to Lukács, Korsch *and* Bukharin. In 1925 and 1926, Lukács would criticize both Wittfogel's and Bukharin's books as representative texts of a positivistic and mechanistic Marxism. See *Georg Lukács Werke: Frühschriften* II, pp. 598–608 (on Bukharin), and pp. 609–11 (on Wittfogel).

19. Abram Deborin, "Lukács und seine Kritik des Marxismus," *Arbeiter-Literatur* (1924):618.

20. Korsch, "Nachwort" to "Marxismus und Philosophie," p. 121.

21. For biographical and analytical material on Karl Korsch, see Claudio Pozzoli, ed., *Arbeiterbewegung: Theorie und Geschichte, Jahrbuch* I: *Über Karl Korsch* (Frankfurt-am-Main: Fischer, 1973), especially the two essays by Michael Buckmiller; *Telos* 26 (Winter 1975–76), especially the essays by Breines, Mattick, Kellner, Ceppa, and Cerutti; and Paul Mattick, "The Un-Dogmatic Marxism of Karl Korsch," *Survey* 53 (October 1964):86–97.

22. See the editor's long introduction to Douglas Kellner, ed., *Karl Korsch: Revolutionary Theory* (Austin and London: University of Texas Press, 1977). Kellner, who brings together much new material pertaining to Korsch in the early and mid-1920s, goes to great lengths to prove that the author of *Marxism and Philosophy* "was an unambiguous champion of the Soviet Union, Leninism and the Bolshevization of the KPD . . . until 1925" (pp. 32–33). This is not the place to present a thorough criticism of Kellner's odd and distorted argument. We note only that our comments on Korsch's role in the "Lukács debate" point

to a different interpretation, as do a number of Kellner's own comments. He claims, for example (pp. 37–38), that Korsch's views were "continuous with the positions of Leninism," but then adds that he was "operating with an idealized concept of Lenin which had little in common with either the historical Lenin or the Lenin who was being deified and retooled by the apologists for Soviet Marxism in Moscow." How this can be reconciled with the view of Korsch as an "unambiguous champion" of "Leninism" is not exactly clear.

23. Karl Korsch, *Quintessenz des Marxismus* (Leipzig: VIVA, 1922), and *Kernpunkte der materialistischen Geschichtsauffassung: Eine quellenmässige Darstellung* (Leipzig: VIVA, 1922).

24. Hermann Duncker, review of Korsch's *Quintessenz des Marxismus* and *Kernpunkte der materialistischen Geschichtsauffassung* in *Die Internationale* 4, no. 23 (May 28, 1922):537–40; and no. 24 (June 4, 1922):562–63.

25. Karl Korsch, "Eine Antikritik," *Die Internationale* 4, no. 25 (June 18, 1922):586–88.

26. Cited by Korsch in *Kernpunkte der materialistischen Geschichtsauffassung*, p. 28. The passage is from Dilthey's *Einleitung in die Geisteswissenschaften* (1883).

27. Korsch, "Eine Antikritik," p. 588. Lukács's review of Dilthey's *Die Jugendgeschichte Hegels* (1921) appeared in *Die Rote Fahne* (May 3, 1922). It is reprinted in Jörg Kammler, ed., *Georg Lukács: Organization und Illusion: Politische Aufsätze* III (Darmstadt and Neuwied: Luchterhand, 1977), pp. 118–22.

28. For information regarding the "Summer Academy" at which Korsch and Lukács met, the authors thank Mrs. Hedda Korsch. In 1922, Lukács, along with a number of comrades from the Communist Party of Hungary, were sent to Berlin, where they remained for the year. The occasion was the decision by the Executive of the Communist International to resolve the factional battle in the Hungarian party by temporarily disbanding the party as a whole and removing the anti-Kun faction from Vienna. Contact between Lukács and Korsch, then, took place at the time both men were at work on their respective books, *History and Class Consciousness* and *Marxism and Philosophy*. It has been suggested that the two had corresponded earlier (1921) and that Korsch tried to secure a position for Lukács at the Jena University. This is plausible, but we have no supporting evidence. See the interesting article by Yvon Bourdet, "Georg Lukács im Wiener Exil, 1919–1930," in Gerhard Botz et al., eds., *Geschichte und Gesellschaft: Festschrift für Karl R. Stadler zum 60. Geburtstag* (Vienna: Europaverlag, 1974), pps. 297–329.

29. Hermann Duncker, "Ein neues Buch über Marxismus," *Die Rote Fahne* (May 27, 1923), n.p.

30. See Chapter 7.

31. Laszlo Rudas, serialized review of *History and Class Consciousness, Arbeiter-Literatur* 9 (1924):493–517; 10 (1924):669–97; 12 (1924):1064–89. Rudas and Lukács had known one another for sometime. Both, for example, had been associates of the Socialist Students League in Budapest in 1902. A member of the original Central Committee of the Communist Party of Hungary, Rudas was part of the *Kommunismus* group in Vienna; his contributions to the journal indicate Lukács's influence. While initially a member of the anti-Kun faction, Rudas left Vienna in 1923 for Moscow, where he became Kun's secretary.

32. Ibid., p. 504.

33. Ibid.

34. Karl Kautsky, review of *Marxism and Philosophy, Die Gesellschaft* (1924):306–14.

35. Rudas, serialized review, p. 496. Emphasis added.

36. See, for example, Leon Trotsky, "On the Policy of the KAPD" (the ultra-Left Communist Workers' Party of Germany), in his *The First Five Years of the Communist International*, vol. I (New York: Pioneer, 1945), pp. 137–52.

37. Rudas, serialized review, p. 517.

38. *Pravda* (July 25, 1924). Cited in Merleau-Ponty, *Adventures of the Dialectic,* trans. Joseph Bien (Evanston, Ill.: Northwestern University Press, 1973), p. 59.

39. Deborin, "Lukács und seine Kritik des Marxismus," p. 618. On Deborin's role in the philosophical disputes of the mid- and late-1920s, see Rene Ahlberg, "The Forgotten Philosopher: Abram Deborin," in Leopold Labedz, ed., *Revisionism: Essays on the History of Marxist Ideas* (New York: Praeger, 1962), pp. 126–41; and Oskar Negt, ed., *Abram Deborin–Nikolai Bucharin: Kontroversen über dialektischen und mechanistischen Materialismus* (Frankfurt-am-Main: Suhrkamp, 1969), especially Negt's excellent introduction, "Marxismus als Legitimationswissenschaft: Zur Genese der stalinistischen Philosophie," pp. 7–48.

40. Deborin, "Lukács und seine Kritik des Marxismus," pp. 629–33.

41. The full text of this section of Zinoviev's speech appears in Peter Ludz, ed., *Georg Lukács: Schriften zur Ideologie und Politik* (Neuwied and Berlin: Luchterhand, 1967), pp. 719–26.

42. Ibid., pp. 720–21. The Italian ultra-Leftist, Amadeo Bordiga, was also attacked by Zinoviev.

43. Karl Bloch, review of Zinoviev, *Archiv für Sozialwissenschaft und Sozialpolitik,* 1924, p. 818.

44. For analysis of "ideological Bolshevization," see Weber, *Die Wandlung des deutschen Kommunismus,* vol. I, pp. 89–97.

45. See Isaac Deutscher, *Stalin: A Political Biography,* 2d ed. (New York: Oxford University Press, 1967), pp. 265–79.

46. Oskar Negt, "Marxismus als Legitimationswissenschaft," passim.

47. Maurice Merleau-Ponty, *The Adventures of the Dialectic,* p. 66.

48. Ibid., p. 60.

49. Like Lukács, they did not remain proponents of "Lukácsism" for very long. By the end of the 1920s, Fogarasi had become an orthodox (Soviet) Marxist, concerning himself with questions of dialectical logic, while Révai, a brilliant and clever figure, would emerge in post–1945 Hungary as the chief ideologue in cultural affairs, from which post he consistently denounced Lukács's various heresies.

50. Béla Fogarasi, "Karl Korsch: Marxismus und Philosophie," *Die Internationale* 7, no. 12 (June 15, 1924):414–16.

51. Ibid., p. 415.

52. Josef Révai, review of *History and Class Consciousness,* in *Archiv für die Geschichte des Sozialismus und der Arbeiterbewegung* II (1923):227–36. Cf. the discussion of the review in Merleau-Ponty, *Adventures of the Dialectic,* pp. 53–57.

53. Révai, review of *History and Class Consciousness,* p. 229.

54. Ibid., p. 228.

55. Ibid., pp. 235–36.

56. Ibid., p. 235.

57. Ibid., p. 236.

58. Ernst Bloch, "Aktualität und Utopie: Zu Lukács' *Geschichte und Klassenbewusstsein,*" *Der Neue Merkur,* October 1923–March 1924, pp. 457–77. Bloch's review is reprinted in his *Philosophische Aufsätze zur objektiven Phantasie* (Frankfurt-am-Main: Suhrkamp, 1969), pp. 598–621. Our references are to the latter edition. For further discussion of relations between Lukács and Bloch—one of the extraordinary intellectual dialogues of our century—see Paul Breines, "Bloch Magic," *Continuum* 7, no. 4 (Winter 1970):50–55; the incisive article by Sándor Radnoti, "Bloch und Lukács: Zwei radikale Kritiker in der 'gottverlassenen Welt,'" in Agnes Heller et al., *Die Seele und das Leben* (Frankfurt-am-

Main: Suhrkamp, 1977), pp. 177–91; and the discussions throughout Löwy, *Pour une sociologie des intellectuels révolutionnaires,* especially his 1974 interview with Bloch, pp. 292–300.

59. Bloch, "Aktualität und Utopie," p. 599.

60. Ibid., p. 601.

61. See *Geschichte und Klassenbewusstsein,* pp. 210–11.

62. Bloch, "Aktualität und Utopie," pp. 620–21.

63. Ibid., p. 601.

64. For recent analyses of the important problem of intellectuals within Marxism, see Alvin W. Gouldner, "Prologue to a Theory of Revolutionary Intellectuals," *Telos* 26 (Winter 1975–76):3–39; and George Konrad and Ivan Szeléni, *The Intellectuals' Road to Class Power* (forthcoming, Harcourt Brace and Jovanovich, 1979).

65. Cited in Weber, *Die Wandlung der deutschen Kommunismus,* vol. I, p. 326.

66. Ibid., p. 372. Weber also suggests that the hostility to intellectuals entailed elements of anti-Semitism.

67. Löwy, *Pour une sociologie des intellectuels révolutionnaires,* p. 107ff.

68. József Lengyel, *Visegráder Strasse* (East Berlin: Dietz, 1959), pp. 139–41.

69. Hendrik deMan, *Die Intellektuellen und der Sozialismus* (Jena: Diederichs, 1926).

70. Ibid., pp. 19–20.

CHAPTER 11: THE ORIGINS OF "WESTERN MARXISM"

1. Serge, *Memoirs of a Revolutionary,* p. 177.

2. Ibid., p. 187.

3. Lukács, *Lenin: Studie über den Zusammenhang seiner Gedanken* (Berlin: Malik-Verlag, 1924). It is reprinted in *Georg Lukács Werke: Frühschriften* II, (Neuwied and Berlin: Luchterhand, 1968), pp. 521–588. There is an English translation by Nicholas Jacobs, *Lenin: A Study on the Unity of his Thought* (London: New Left Books, 1970). Our references are to the German version in *Georg Lukács Werke: Frühschriften* II.

4. *Georg Lukács Werke: Frühschriften* II, pp. 522–23.

5. "Revolutionary *Realpolitik*" is the title of the important final chapter of Lukács's book.

6. *Georg Lukács Werke: Frühschriften* II, p. 583.

7. August Thalheimer, "Ein überflüssiges Buch," *Arbeiter-Literatur* 7/8 (July-August 1924):427–28.

8. Ibid., p. 428.

9. Ibid.

10. Korsch, "Über materialistiche Dialektik," *Die Internationale* (June 2, 1924):376–79. The article is signed "K." It is reprinted in the 1930 edition of *Marxismus und Philosophie* but is not included in the English edition. It is included in Douglas Kellner, ed., *Karl Korsch: Revolutionary Theory* (Austin and London: University of Texas Press, 1977).

11. Ibid., p. 377.

12. Ibid., pp. 378–79.

13. Korsch, review of Lukács's *Lenin, Die Internationale* (June 15, 1924):413–14.

14. See, for example, Korsch's enthusiastic short review of Stalin's *Fundamentals of Leninism* (1924), in *Die Internationale* (November 7, 1924):668–70.

15. In 1926 Korsch and Ernst Schwartz launched the Left-opposition journal, *Kommunistische Politik,* to which Korsch was the major contributor, outlining with great vigor his view of the Soviet Union and the Third International as roadblocks along the way to proletarian

revolution. Korsch and his group had no great affection for Trotsky, the key Left-oppositionist in the Soviet Union. The feelings were mutual. See, Korsch et al., "Auseinandersetzung mit Trotzki," *Kommunistische Politik* 2 (August 1927):7–9; and Trotsky's criticism of the "Korsch group," in his "La défense de l'URSS et l'opposition" (1929), in *Écrits* I (Paris: Marcel Rivière, 1955), pp. 213–75.

16. Lukács, review of Bukharin, in *Archiv für die Geschichte des Sozialismus und der Arbeiterbewegung,* 1925, pp. 224–27. The essay is reprinted in *Georg Lukács Werke: Frühschriften* II, pp. 598–608.

17. *Georg Lukács Werke: Frühschriften* II, p. 600.

18. Lukács, "Die neue Ausgabe von Lassalles Briefen," in *Archiv für die Geschichte des Sozialismus und der Arbeiterbewegung,* 1925, pp. 401–23; reprinted in *Georg Lukács Werke: Frühschriften* II, pp. 612–39. And "Moses Hess und die Problem der idealistischen Dialektik," in *Archiv für die Geschichte des Sozialismus und der Arbeiterbewegung,* 1926, pp. 105–55; reprinted in *Georg Lukács Werke: Frühschriften* II, pp. 643–86.

19. Michael Löwy, *Pour une sociologie des intellectuels révolutionnaires,* (Paris: P.U.F., 1976), pp. 227–42.

20. Ibid., p. 231.

21. Lukács, "L'art pour l'art und proletarische Dichtung," in *Die Tat,* 18 (June 1926):220–23. The article is reprinted in *Paul Ernst und Georg Lukács: Documente einer Freundschaft,* ed. Karl August Kutzbach (Emsdetten: Lechte, 1974), pp. 176–80. For amplified discussion, see Paul Breines, "Introduction to Lukács," *Telos* 5 (Spring 1970), pp. 16ff.

22. Lukács, "L'art pour l'art und proletarische Dichtung," in *Die Tat,* p. 223.

23. Franz Borkenau, *World Communism: A History of the Communist International* (1939) (Ann Arbor: University of Michigan, 1962), p. 174.

24. Werner Sombart, "Der Bergriff der Gesetzmässigkeit bei Marx," in *Schmollers Jahrbuch für Gesetzgebung, Verwaltung und Volkswirtschaft im deutschen Reiche* 47 (1924):30–31.

25. Hans Rothfels, "Ideengeschichte und Parteigeschichte," in *Deutsche Vierteljahrsschrift für Literaturwissenschaft und Geistesgeschichte* 8 (1930):768.

26. Hans Mayer, "Dank an Georg Lukács," in his *Literatur der Übergangszeit* (Wiesbaden: Limes, 1949), p. 219.

27. Goldmann originally presented this argument in his *Mensch, Gemeinschaft und Welt in der Philosophie Immanuel Kants: Studien zur Geschichte der Dialektik* (Zurich: Europa, 1945), pp. 241–47. He did not include the argument, first presented as an appendix, in the French editions (1948; 1967) of his book: *Introduction à la philosophie de Kant.* See, however, his expansion of the theme in William Q. Boelhower, trans., *Lukács and Heidegger: Towards a New Philosophy* (London and Boston: Routledge & Kegan Paul, 1977). Cf. the suggestive commentary by Rainer Rochlitz, "Lukács et Heidegger: Suits d'un débat," in *L'Homme et la société* nos. 43/44 (January-June 1977):87–94.

28. See, for example, Herbert Marcuse, "Beiträge zu einer Phänomenologie des historischen Materialismus," in *Philosophische Hefte* no. 1 (July 1928):45–68. An English translation appears in *Telos* 4 (Fall 1969):3–34. See also Marcuse's doctoral dissertation, completed under Heidegger's direction: *Hegels Ontologie und die Theorie der Geschichtlichkeit* (Frankfurt-am-Main: Klostermann, 1932). For discussions of the Marcuse-Heidegger-Lukács nexus, see Martin Jay, *The Dialectical Imagination* (Boston: Little Brown, 1973), pp. 71–76; and Paul Piccone and Alex Delfini, "Herbert Marcuse's Heideggerian Marxism," *Telos* 6 (Fall 1970):36–46. Lucien Goldmann has also addressed the question in his "La pensée de Herbert Marcuse," *La Nef* 36 (January–March 1969):35–57.

29. Karl Mannheim, *Ideology and Utopia: An Introduction to the Sociology of Knowledge,* trans. Louis Wirth and Edward Shils (New York: Harcourt Brace & World, 1961).

First published in 1929, Mannheim revised and expanded the work for the Wirth and Shils English translation, which was published in 1936. See also Mannheim's 1920 review of Lukács's *Theory of the Novel* in Kurt H. Wolff, ed., *From Karl Mannheim* (New York: Oxford University Press, 1971), pp. 3–7; and Lee Congdon, "Karl Mannheim as Philosopher," *Journal of European Studies* 7 (March 1977):1–18.

30. Lukács's major reckoning with Existentialism, in part Heidegger's (and Husserl's) but primarily that of their French heirs, Sartre and Merleau-Ponty, appeared in 1947, in a work whose dogmatic arguments are punctuated with numerous incisive observations: *Existentialisme ou Marxisme,* trans. E. Keleman (Paris: Nagel, 1961).

31. Max Horkheimer, "Ein neue Ideologiebegriff?" in *Archiv für die Geschichte des Sozialismus und der Arbeiterbewegung,* 1930, pp. 33–56; and Herbert Marcuse, "Zur Wahrheitsproblematik der soziologischen Methode," in *Die Gesellschaft* 6 (1929):356–69. For discussion of some of the issues involved, see: Gian Enrico Rusconi, *La Teoria Critica della Società* (Bologna: Mulino, 1968), pp. 161–72; Jay, *The Dialectical Imagination,* pp. 63–65; Jay, "The Frankfurt School's Critique of Karl Mannheim and the Sociology of Knowledge," *Telos* 20 (Summer 1974):72–89; and the exchange between Martin Jay and James Schmidt in *Telos* 21 and 22.

32. See Russel Jacoby, "Towards a Critique of Automatic Marxism," *Telos* 10 (Winter 1971); Jay, *The Dialectical Imagination,* passim; and "General Introduction," Andrew Arato and Eike Gebhardt, eds., *The Essential Frankfurt School Reader* (New York: Urizen, 1978), pp. xi–xxiii.

33. Paul Eppstein, "Die Fragestellung nach der Wirklichkeit im historischen Materialismus," *Archiv für Sozialwissenschaft und Sozialpolitik,* 1928, pp. 449–507.

34. Siegfried Marck, *Die Dialektik in der Philosophie der Gegenwart* I (Tübingen: Kohlhammer, 1929), pp. 119–35.

35. Herbert Marcuse, "Zum Problem der Dialektik," in *Die Gesellschaft* 7 (1930):29–30.

36. Ibid., p. 30.

37. Hannah Arendt, "Philosophie und Soziologie: Anlässlich Karl Mannheim, 'Ideologie und Utopie,'" in *Die Gesellschaft* 7 (1930):163–76.

38. Karl Korsch, *Marxismus und Philosophie* (1930). See note 15.

39. Ibid., pp. 31–48.

40. Ibid., pp. 49–50.

41. Ibid., p. 50.

42. Ibid., pp. 52–53, note 20.

43. Ibid., p. 34.

44. Lukács, "Thesen über die politische und wirtschaftliche Lage in Ungarn und über die Aufgaben der Kommunistischen Partei Ungarns" ("Blum-Thesen," 1928), in Peter Ludz, ed., *Georg Lukács: Schriften zur Ideologie und Politik* (Neuwied and Berlin: Luchterhand, 1967), pp. 290–322.

45. Beginning in 1930, Lukács's numerous intellectual-autobiographical accounts would characterize his work of the 1920s as his apprenticeship in Marxism. Whether, when he first read Marx's "1844 Manuscripts," he took some private satisfaction in the knowledge that the document confirmed many of the arguments in *History and Class Consciousness,* we do not know. It is likely, but not demonstrable, that he read it as a *corrective* to his own 1923 work rather than as either confirmation *or* as documentation of Marx's own "apprenticeship." For Lukács's later view, see his *Der junge Marx: Seine philosophische Entwicklung von 1840–1844* [1955] (Pfullingen: Neske, 1965).

46. Karl Löwith, "Max Weber und Karl Marx," in *Archiv für Sozialwissenschaft und Sozialpolitik,* 1932, pp. 53–99, 175–214.

47. Herbert Marcuse, "Neue Quellen zur Grundlegung des historischen Materialismus," in *Die Gesellschaft* 9 (1932):160.

CONCLUSION

1. Max Horkheimer and Theodor W. Adorno, *Dialectic of Enlightenment* (1944), trans. John Cumming (New York: Herder and Herder, 1972), pp. 214–15.

2. Maurice Merleau-Ponty, *The Adventures of the Dialectic,* trans. Joseph Bien (Evanston, Ill.: Northwestern University Press, 1973), pp. 63–64.

3. Lukács, *Marxisme ou Existentialisme,* trans. E. Keleman (Paris: Nagel, 1961), passim.

4. See Roger Garaudy, ed., *Mésaventures de l'anti-marxisme: Les malheurs de M. Merleau-Ponty* (Paris: Éditions Sociales, 1956), pp. 156–57.

5. Iring Fetscher, *Marx and Marxism,* trans. John Hargreaves (New York: Herder and Herder, 1971), p. 179.

Index